THE NORTHAMPTONSHIRE
REGIMENT, 1914·1918

THE
NORTHAMPTONSHIRE
REGIMENT, 1914-1918

COMPILED UNDER
THE DIRECTION OF
THE REGIMENTAL
HISTORY COMMITTEE

The Naval & Military Press Ltd

Reproduced by kind permission of the Central Library,
Royal Military Academy, Sandhurst

Published by
The Naval & Military Press Ltd
Unit 10, Ridgewood Industrial Park,
Uckfield, East Sussex,
TN22 5QE England
Tel: +44 (0) 1825 749494
Fax: +44 (0) 1825 765701
www.naval–military-press.com

*Jacket illustration, taken from 'Deeds That Thrilled The Empire',
shows Sergeant William Ewart Boulter, of the Northamptonshire
Regiment, winning the Victoria Cross.*

*In reprinting in facsimile from the original, any imperfections are inevitably reproduced
and the quality may fall short of modern type and cartographic standards.*

Printed and bound by Antony Rowe Ltd, Eastbourne

To the Memory of

THE SIX THOUSAND AND FORTY
SOLDIERS OF ALL RANKS WHO
GAVE THEIR LIVES FOR THEIR
KING AND COUNTRY WHILE
SERVING WITH THE REGIMENT
DURING . THE . GREAT . WAR
1914–1918

CONTENTS

CONTENTS—*Continued*.

CHAPTER XIV.

CHAPTER XV.

CHAPTER XVI.

———

APPENDICES.

———

MAP.

FOREWORD

A regimental history of the War, to be of any value, must be accurate—not merely because it is open to the criticism of the actors themselves—but for the benefit of those who come after; it must be more or less detailed, so as to present a picture of the conditions under which events took place, but at the same time it must be concise; it must be lively, for no one can stand being bored, and most important of all, it must be human and convey the spirit that influenced the actors of all ranks. That spirit, so well brought out in these pages, is, I think, admirably summed up by Field-Marshal Earl Haig in a Foreword written for the history of the 8th Division, in which the Regiment served: "The capacity to fight a losing battle doggedly and relentlessly against odds, and somehow by grit and obstinacy to wrest victory from defeat."

A perusal of the book will, I am confident, satisfy all that the above conditions have been fulfilled with marked success, and while thanking the Committee for the successful issue of their labours, I join with them and all ranks of the Regiment in an expression of deep gratitude to those who have given us materials, time and talents; to Lieutenant-Colonel Whitton for the admirable manner in which the history has been compiled; to Captain A. P. White for the copyright of his unpublished book entitled "The 48th in France and Flanders" which has been extensively used in the compilation of the history of the 1st Battalion; to Major W. J. Jervois for writing the history of the 4th Battalion; to those who have so freely given us their experiences, diaries, correspondence, etc.; and last, but not least, to Colonel Hughes for compiling the list of Honours and Awards, and for undertaking the duties of Editor.

H. Hudson, *General*,

Colonel, The Northamptonshire Regiment.

THE NORTHAMPTONSHIRE REGIMENT, 1914-1918

CHAPTER I.

The 1st Battalion—The Outbreak of the Great War—The Battle of Mons—The Retreat from Mons.

DETTINGEN BARRACKS, Blackdown, where the 1st Battalion of the Northamptonshire Regiment was stationed in 1914, possessed little of the solidity and permanence usually associated with such edifices. The so-called barracks were in truth but a collection of huts erected about the time of the South African War and situated in what may be described as an outlying, bleak and unfashionable suburb of the great camp of Aldershot. The huts had all the disadvantages inherent in such makeshift buildings. Nevertheless, a memory of Dettingen Barracks will for ever be associated with the history of the 1st Northamptonshires. It was from them that the old 48th marched out in 1914 to the great adventure. It was to them that the battalion returned, more than ten years later, to take up the threads of training once more, after the great struggle in Europe and a subsidiary sort of a war in Ireland. Of those who left in 1914 but a handful marched in upon the barrack square. Four years and more of battle and bivouac, of reverse and victory, of blood spilt, of death, wounds and disease had more than once blotted out the battalion, which, however, rose again each time, changed but yet the same.

When an Austrian archduke was murdered in an unknown town in Bosnia on June 28th, no one appreciated the significance of the event. In the general clatter of things nearer home the news caused no more effect than " a tenor solo in a boiler shop." The thrill of horror which ran through Europe soon subsided, and at first the tragedy seemed destined to be but a nine days' wonder.

It was not until nearly a month later that it seemed just possible that the normal routine of training might be rudely interrupted. On July 23rd Austria presented an ultimatum of extreme harshness to Servia, alleging that the assassination was the outcome of anti-Austrian intrigue in that country. Russia took Servia's side; France, by treaty, was bound to stand by Russia. On the other hand, Germany and Italy were leagued with Austria in the Triple Alliance. Five Great Powers were thus immediately confronted with the possibility of war. Before the end of the month Austria was bombarding the Servian capital. The whole of Europe was an armed camp. Deaf to all remonstrance, Germany showed her determination to exploit the situation for her own ends. She refused to give a pledge to respect the neutrality of Belgium. Without haste, but without hesitation, England threw in her lot with France. By August 4th eight nations were now at war. On the one side were Germany and Austria. On the other France, Russia, England, Belgium, Servia, and Montenegro.

Thus it was that in the 1st Northamptonshires and in all other units all training schedules, all programmes of work, and all the hectographed homilies on which the orderly-room had been lavishing enthusiasm became as remote as the Pentateuch. They were swept away at once by the storm of mobilization. A " precautionary period " had been proclaimed at the end of July, and at 6.17 p.m.—as the brigade war diary records with a fine gesture of precision—on August 4th the Army received orders to mobilize.

The Army was now to put to the test the reorganization which had succeeded the South African War. Since then an Expeditionary Force had come into being. Its organization had been completely worked out, and the units of which it was composed were to take the field under the general officers and staffs by whom they had been trained in peace. Its strength had been laid down at some 160,000 of all ranks, and it consisted of six divisions, one cavalry division plus an additional cavalry brigade, and line of communication troops. Each division consisted of three infantry brigades, each of four battalions; possessed 76 guns; and was furnished with the necessary quota of cavalry, engineers and auxiliary services. In this fighting machine the place of the 1st Northamptonshire Regiment was in the 2nd Brigade of the 1st Division, the sister brigades being the 1st and 3rd. Of the 2nd Brigade the other battalions were the 2nd Royal Sussex Regiment, the 1st Loyal North Lancashire Regiment, and the 2nd King's Royal Rifle Corps. The 1st and 2nd Divisions together made up the I Corps.

The mobilization of the Expeditionary Force proved to be a triumph of foresight and organization. Generally speaking, the factors of mobilization were men, material and horses. By the system in force in 1914 the reservists joined at the regimental depot, where they were clothed and equipped and dispatched thence in drafts to the home battalion. Material, such as vehicles, ammunition and harness, was held stored at the peace station. Horses were collected from civilian sources under a scheme by which in time of peace the animals were held available for requisition. The whole business worked extraordinarily smoothly, and by midnight of August 7th/8th the 2nd Brigade was complete to the last button. Recollections of those who took part show that the reservists settled down to military life again very quickly, although there was obvious need to get their feet hard. There is also a note to the effect of " the difficulties we had with the transport horses. These caused a lot of trouble, being unused to the Army limber and the G.S. wagon."

The life of the transport officer during those days

B I

was not a bed of roses. The mobilization store was crammed with brand new harness which had to be assembled, and " it was no easy job making sets complete, and made up entirely of stiff new leather and buckles that would not buckle." The horses were distributed at Aldershot, and as most of them came from farms they required breaking into army ways. One pair particularly resented the battalion cooker, and took it *ventre à terre* across the battalion parade ground until a telegraph pole intervened. The organization of the horse distribution was on a par with the other mobilization arrangements and worked without a hitch. All through the day and night horses kept coming in from all parts. Registration and the veterinary examination were promptly carried out, and immediately afterwards the horses were issued and passed to the military sphere.

The mobilization of the Army Reserve had brought the battalion up to full war strength of practically 1,000 of all ranks, and had left a considerable surplus of trained men for future reinforcement as drafts. The young recruits, of whom there were always a certain percentage in home service battalions, had been sent to the 3rd or Special Reserve Battalion, formerly militia, their place being filled by reservists. Thus all the rank and file of the 1st Battalion were fully-trained soldiers, although comparatively few of them had any experience of actual war. Some of the older officers and other ranks had served with the 2nd Battalion in the South African War, and a few of the senior officers had been with the 1st Battalion in the Tirah Campaign, but the great majority had never seen active service. Most of the reservists had no experience of the recently introduced four company system nor of the platoon organization; and training to introduce them to this new state of things was at once put in hand. Route marches were also undertaken, as the feet of the reservists badly wanted hardening, after factory or sedentary occupation. On August 11th their Majesties the King and Queen motored to Blackdown and inspected the troops there quartered, including the 1st Battalion of the Northamptonshire Regiment.

Although there was no definite treaty to that effect, it was an understood thing that if the Germans ever invaded France the British Expeditionary Force would be moved over to the Continent and come into line with the French. The Germans had entered Belgium on the 4th, and an invasion of France was now a certainty. The British Government therefore decided to send the Expeditionary Force as arranged, but for the moment retained two divisions in the country to act as a stiffener to the Territorial divisions to which the defence of the United Kingdom was mainly entrusted. On August 12th the 1st Battalion Northamptonshire Regiment left Blackdown and marched to Frimley station, where it entrained for Southampton. Here it embarked on the Union Castle liner *Galeka* with the 60th Rifles and details, sailing for an unknown destination.

The following was the organization of the 1st Battalion on embarkation for France :—

Headquarters.

Lieut.-Colonel E. O. Smith.
Major H. H. Norman, 2nd-in-Command.
Captain H. Lloyd, Adjutant.
Captain B. B. Dickson, Machine Gun Officer.
Lieutenant E. G. Warren, Transport Officer.
Lieutenant A. Hofman, Quartermaster.
Regimental Sergeant-Major J. Downs.
Regimental Quartermaster-Sergeant J. Clark.

"A" Company.

Captain R. E. Gordon.
Captain G. W. Hunt.
Lieutenant C. L. Wauchope.
Lieutenant C. H. Bacon.
Second-Lieutenant L. H. B. Burlton.
Company Sergeant-Major A. Cory.
Company Quartermaster-Sergeant B. Eden.

" B " Company.

Captain E. L. Hughes.
Captain E. E. White.
Lieutenant G. M. Fraser.
Lieutenant W. J. Jervois.
Lieutenant G. G. B. Paget.
Company Sergeant-Major J. Willars.
Company Quartermaster-Sergeant P. Church.

" C " Company.

Captain R. B. Parker.
Captain G. M. Bentley.
Lieutenant J. H. Farrar.
Lieutenant E. J. Needham.
Second-Lieutenant A. S. G. Jarvis.
Second-Lieutenant C. G. Gordon.
Company Sergeant-Major J. Good.
Company Quartermaster-Sergeant H. F. Pitcher.

" D " Company.

Captain H. Cartwright.
Captain J. A. Savage.
Lieutenant G. St. G. Robinson.
Second-Lieutenant G. D. Gordon.
Second-Lieutenant A. N. Sherriff.
Company Sergeant-Major C. Murdin.
Company Quartermaster-Sergeant E. A. Phillpot.

After an uneventful crossing, escorted by British
destroyers, the battalion arrived at Havre in the early
morning of the 13th. Having disembarked, the 48th
had a hot march of some miles to a camp on the outskirts of the town. The march was through crowds of
rapturously enthusiastic French people, and to the roars
of " Tipperary "—that haunting marching song of the
Old Contemptibles, as the British Expeditionary Force
was soon to be known from the famous reference by the
German Emperor to the " contemptible little army "
of England. After two hot days spent in camp,
relieved by bathing parades, orders were received on

August 14th to entrain. The march to the station was through miles of coal yards, and as there was a strong wind blowing the battalion reached the entraining place covered with grime. This was in the early hours of August 15th, and through the whole of a swelteringly hot day the troop train moved slowly towards the Belgian frontier, passing through Amiens, Arras, and Cambrai—names now household words but which then possessed little significance. At every station the battalion was given an enthusiastic reception by the inhabitants, and gifts of all kinds were showered on the men. At 1 a.m. on the 16th the train arrived at Etreux, a small station about nine miles south-east of Le Cateau. Here the Northamptonshires detrained and marched to Esqueheries, a village some six miles away. They were now in the concentration area allotted to the 1st Division, and here the battalion stayed five days. Training, route marches, and, in the evening, concerts filled in the time. On the 17th appears the first order of a war type, a platoon being detailed daily on one of the roads outside Esqueheries, with orders to stop all individuals approaching the post and to stop and examine all mounted men. On the evening of the 19th there was a concert on the village green, under the patronage of the *Maire*, at which the local orchestra " persisted in playing ' God Save the King ' at intervals and wound up by playing it twenty times in succession."

So far nothing has been said of the general situation in France and Belgium, and, while the battalion is enjoying its last peaceful days for many, many months, a brief survey will help to make clear the struggle in which the British Expeditionary Force was now about to intervene. To take the Germans first : their plan had been to leave but a small fraction of their armies, in conjunction with Austria, to watch Russia ; and to throw the bulk of the available total against France. The German General Staff were fanatical supporters of envelopment in strategy, and this necessitated throwing the right wing into Belgium. Put very briefly, the German plan can be summarized by saying that south of Metz the left wing of the Germans would act generally on the defensive, while five field armies, pivoting on Thionville, were to make a colossal left wheel, the outer or I Corps passing through Brussels. The swing was to pass outside Paris, and the scoop was to drive the French armies towards the Swiss frontier, where they were to be trapped and destroyed. It was essential that this should be achieved in six weeks. The victorious German armies were then to be railed back through Germany to deal with Russia, whose mobilization was expected to take much longer than that of France.

Like the Germans, the French favoured the policy of the offensive. But they were handicapped by uncertainty up to the last moment as to whether Germany would or would not violate the neutrality of Belgium, and, if so, on what scale. Political reasons, too, caused the French to make their first efforts in Alsace. There is no need to do more than mention the fighting there, for the German advance in strength through Belgium caused a modification in the French plan. The French now decided to stand on the defensive in Alsace while a vigorous attack was to be made by two armies in the Ardennes, so as to strike the flank of the German advance through Belgium. This was to be followed up immediately by an advance of the French Fifth Army (which was assembling in the angle of the Meuse and Sambre), plus the British Army, which was assembling to the left rear of it. The strong fortress of Namur was to serve as the pivot of the right wheel which was to be made by these two armies in Belgium.

Even a casual reference to the map will show that at any moment after August 20th big things were bound to happen in that portion of the theatre of war in which the British Army had arrived. The German I, II and III Armies were on the outer flank of the great left wheel. On the other hand, the French

5th Army and the British were contemplating a right wheel. An encounter battle was therefore bound to occur. Time, however, was on the side of the Germans. They were following out a definite and carefully arranged plan, whereas the French were improvising a new one, and between the French and their ally there was little real liaison. In the original French " Plan 17 " no mention had been made of the British. Now that the latter were coming into the picture they were making great efforts to get forward to a line running roughly north-west and south-east through Mons. But things moved too fast.

Enough probably has now been said to account for the following entry in the war diary of the 1st Northamptonshire Regiment : " 22nd August. Etroeungt. Sudden orders to move, 4.30 a.m." The British Army was now hurrying forward to come up into line with the 5th Army of the French, though as a matter of fact it was now almost too late, for the latter had already been attacked and was giving ground. So far as the 2nd Brigade of the British was concerned, it marched north for about fifteen miles and then halted for some two or three hours near Beaufort. Instructions were now issued for the troops to go into billets, but, late in the evening, further sudden orders were received and the brigade pushed on again. The Northamptonshires had gone into some farm buildings, " a meal was prepared, after which we lost no time in trying to make ourselves comfortable, when to the dismay of everyone the order was passed along to get dressed as quickly as possible, so within two hours of halting we were on the move again, why, and where we were bound for, no one knew." So hurried was the start that some quartermaster's stores had to be left behind under a small guard.

All night long the battalion plodded northwards. The road led through Maubeuge, where large numbers of French troops were seen. Maubeuge was a fortress rapidly becoming obsolete, but it had a garrison of over

40,000 second and third line troops. " It struck us as a great gloomy town, very strong, and its forts looked as if they could withstand a long siege. We did not then know of the power and weight of the German artillery." The small guard left over the stores at Beaufort, saw large numbers of French cavalry pass through the place. These troops were without doubt part of General Sordet's cavalry corps, which was working westward to come up on the left or exposed flank of the British. It did not succeed in so doing until the 26th, but on that day its presence was of the greatest value at the Battle of Le Cateau.

It was during the night march through Maubeuge that the Northamptonshires first heard the guns of war. Just before daybreak a long halt was made at Villers Sire Nicole, and then, at 8 a.m. on the 23rd, the battalion was ordered forward, and it reached Rouveroy, where it went into billets.

Looking at the situation as a whole, the sector from Mons, exclusive, south-eastwards to the River Sambre, was destined to be a kind of " pocket " between two battles. The story of August 23rd is briefly that from Thuin eastwards to the Meuse the French 5th Army was heavily attacked from the north, and during the day its right flank was threatened by the forcing of the Meuse by the German III Army. As for the British Army, its right wing—the I Corps, formed up from Peissant on the right to Mons exclusive. The 1st Division was on the right, with its 2nd Brigade, in which was the 1st Northamptonshire Regiment, in reserve. It was the intention that the II Corps should carry on the line north-westwards from Mons, but this was found to be impossible, and that corps was brought to rest along the Condé Canal, running due west from Mons. The British position was therefore somewhat in the shape of a broad arrow with a marked salient at Mons, and it was against the left corps that the blow aimed by the German I Corps was to fall. Opposite the sector held by the British I Corps the Germans had merely some guns and a regiment of dragoons, and here there was practically no fighting other than some spirited engagements between patrols.

As the Northamptonshires were in reserve and had made a tiring all-night march, all ranks had a good wash in billets and then went to sleep. The battalion was not called upon during the day, and all that could be gathered of the battle was from the sound of heavy firing and from the sight of the Germans shelling the guns of the 1st Division, which were in action east-north-east of Givry. In the evening, somewhere about seven o'clock, three companies of the battalion left Rouveroy and marched up the road towards Givry, halting for some time by the roadside just south of Givry cross-roads. When darkness came on, about nine o'clock, they moved on through Givry and into Vellereille le Sec in support of the Royal Berkshire Regiment. A German searchlight was playing at intervals on the ridge on which ran the road, but the companies got through in a dark interval, and although they came under shell fire they escaped casualties. The remaining company, " D," remained at Rouveroy in divisional reserve. The night passed without incident. At 6 a.m. came orders to retire, and the Retreat from Mons had begun. The total of the casualties suffered by the British in the battle of the 23rd was some 1,600 of all ranks, but of these merely a couple of score were incurred by the 1st Division.

Although the British Army and the French 5th Army under General Lanrezac were supposed to be working in co-operation the actual liaison was sketchy, and throughout the 23rd each was fighting practically a separate battle. So much so that the French 5th Army broke off its fight under the false impression that the British had given way, or were about to do so, whereas as a matter of fact the British held their ground until news of the retirement of the French upon their right left them no option but to retreat also. The object of Sir John French, the British commander-in-chief, was now to fall back until he could occupy another position where he could stand at bay. A line in rear had been reconnoitred for this purpose, in case he should be forced back from the Mons salient. This position rested on the fortress of Maubeuge, on the right, and extended westwards to Jenlain, south-east of Valenciennes, on the left. As a line of defence it was reported to be somewhat difficult to hold, owing to the fact that standing crops and buildings would hinder the siting of trenches and would limit the field of fire in many localities. There were, however, several good artillery positions, and, on the whole, the proposed line had many points in its favour. Towards this line the British Army now fell back.

The Northamptonshires did not get under way until late in the afternoon of the 24th, for the I Corps was charged with the task of covering the retirement of the II Corps, which had had such a gruelling the day before. " D " Company (Captain Cartwright) was ordered to hold a position across the Bavay—Binche road, while the remainder of the battalion was still about the village of Givry. " Throughout the day we saw no enemy, much to the disappointment of the men. Some shelling took place, but there were no casualties. Nevertheless, it was considered prudent to send the battalion transport back at the gallop to get clear of the shell bursts." About this time " D " Company rejoined, and the battalion remained bivouacking in a field until five o'clock, when it turned southwards once again, marching towards Maubeuge, finally billeting near that town, but to the north of it.

The retirement of the transport had been exciting. To save time it was necessary to go across country, and " so we moved at a gallop, with steam pouring out of the cookers like an express train." One of the ammunition carts struck a large boulder and turned " completely turtle," but it was with some difficulty righted by the transport officer, the transport sergeant and the driver. One of the participants in this effort relates how " the shells kept creeping in front of us and seemed to burst just five yards in front of us all the time."

The continued march southwards had obviously begun to make a profound impression on the men. It was the first, and a very significant, indication that all was not going well, and there was considerable disappointment that there had been no fighting during the day. From now onwards the road was crowded with refugees fleeing south. These unfortunate people had all sorts of household treasures with them, and the painful procession of old men, women and children, with carts piled with bedding and packages of every description, and perambulators with three infants abreast, brought home to all the reality of the war.

During the night the British commander-in-chief came to the conclusion that it was hopeless to think of making a stand on the Maubeuge—Jenlain line. All through the day the Germans had been making the most determined efforts to drive in his left flank, evidently with the intention of squeezing the British into Maubeuge. This would not have mattered so much had the French 5th Army been in a position to stand their ground and to prolong the line to the right. But this was not so. That army was still retiring, and it was essential for the British to conform to its movements.

Consequently, on August 25th the Northamptonshires found themselves still marching away from the enemy. On this day the heat, the dust and the hard going on the pavé proved very trying. And this, added to the fact that the battalion was going back without having fired a shot or even having seen the Germans, increased the general depression. Some encouragement was, indeed, afforded by the rumour which spread that the French and British were carrying out a strategic retirement with the view of drawing on the Germans and thus creating a favourable opportunity for an Allied counterstroke. The explanation had its obviously weak points, but it helped to relieve the general gloom. And the discipline of the battalion helped, too. " I would like to add here," writes a company officer, " that the discipline of the men proved wonderful in these trying conditions, and that never once during the long retreat did their courage give way. All they wanted was to come to close grips with the Germans."

Owing to someone's blunder, the 1st Division had to share the road from Hautmont to Dompierre and Marbaix with the French 53rd Reserve Division. In consequence, the troops were on their feet from daylight until nearly 8 p.m., although the distance covered was only about 14 miles. The constant checks, owing to the number of troops on the road, were most trying to men already much worn by fatigue and want of sleep. The 2nd Brigade billeted in Marbaix, which village they shared with the 53rd French Reserve Division.

Whilst the battalion was halted on either side of the road, waiting to be told off to billets, some firing was heard on the road at the east end of the village. This caused some transport horses with their wagons to bolt down the road into the village. There was considerable confusion, increased by the fact that the centre of the road was blocked by the wagons of an R.E. pontoon troop. Order, however, was soon restored, and the men, after this brief excitement, turned in to their billets, thoroughly tired out.

The British Expeditionary Force consisted of six divisions, but only four had taken part in the Battle of Mons, two divisions having been temporarily retained in the United Kingdom. Of these two divisions, one, the 4th, had now arrived in France and was about Solesmes, west of the Forêt de Mormal, covering the retirement of the II Corps. It had been the intention of Sir John French to stand and fight on the line Cambrai—Le Cateau—Landrecies, and during the 25th the ground there had been partially prepared and entrenched.

But during the afternoon he was assailed by grave doubts as to the wisdom of standing at bay for the present. The French army on his right was still falling back. The outer flank of the British was still much exposed, and it was clear that the Germans, with their passion for envelopment, were doing their utmost to roll up the left wing of the Expeditionary Force. Over and above these considerations was the fact that the continual marching in tropical weather was telling on the troops, very many of whom were reservists. Accordingly, Sir John French called upon his troops to make a further great effort to continue the retreat until some substantial obstacle, such as the Somme or the Oise, should be placed between the British and the enemy.

The II Corps, which was on the left, and the Cavalry Division, were unable to comply with this order, and Sir Horace Smith-Dorrien had no option but to stand and fight, a decision which brought about the bloody Battle of Le Cateau. The I Corps, however, continued its retirement in accordance with the orders of the commander-in-chief.

During the night of the 25th/26th orders were issued to the 2nd Brigade to make preparations for an early march towards Landrecies to reinforce our troops, who were heavily engaged there with large German forces. The men were to carry extra ammunition and march as light as possible. Rations were to be issued from the roadside as the battalion marched along.

Accordingly, all greatcoats were collected and placed in a house under charge of Armourer-Sergeant Wright and twelve men.

At 6.30 a.m. on the 26th the battalion marched off in a south-westerly direction to Favreuil, near Landrecies.

Before continuing the story of the 1st Battalion on this day, I must now describe what happened to Armourer-Sergeant Wright and his little party of twelve men. At about 11 a.m. the village of Marbaix, which was then held by the 6th Battalion of the 329th French Infantry Regiment, was suddenly attacked by a strong force of German cavalry and artillery. Armourer-Sergeant Wright at once placed himself under the orders of Captain de Lillers, who was commanding the 24th Company of this regiment and who was in reserve in the village.

Subsequent events are described in the following letter from Captain de Lillers, which reached the 1st Battalion after the war through 3rd Army Headquarters.

Le 2 Fevrier, 1919.

" On the 26th of August, 1914, the 6th Battalion of the 329th Infantry Regiment, coming from Jeumont, on the Belgian frontier, had been sent to Marbaix, a small village of the Department du Nord on the main road from Avesnes to Landrecies. His orders were to reconnoitre the south-eastern edges of the Forest de Mormal, where strong parties of German troops had been reported.

"At the time, I commanded the 24th Company of this regiment. After having sent patrols all over the ground between the village and the canal of the Sambre, I got the order to post my company in reserve on the main square of the village, opposite the church. It was about 11 a.m. The men started eating their meal, taking great interest in a party of a few British soldiers who were busy packing ammunitions on mules, in a sort of big stable.

" Suddenly, the battalion was attacked by an important force of German cavalry supported by artillery, from the directions of north and north-east. My company was under very heavy machine-gun fire, and after a few minutes, having no orders from my battalion commander, I decided to retire from the village, situated in a hollow, from which I had no view and where I feared to be surrounded; I wanted to occupy the hills south of the Avesnes—Landrecies road.

"As soon as the first shots were fired, the N.C.O. in charge of the British party reported to me, asking for instructions; I gave him the order to follow the company, which he did, his men showing the calm and pluck of old, well-trained troops.

"To leave the village in the direction I had chosen, I had to cross the Avesnes—Landrecies road under the fire of hostile machine guns apparently posted on the top of the hill east of the village. I sent out a strong patrol both to cover my left flank and to locate the position of the machine guns as much as possible. Most of the British soldiers volunteered at once to go with this patrol; some of my men who rejoined the company after the show reported with great admiration the gallant conduct of these brave soldiers, who with the greatest contempt for the danger, marched towards the machine guns and were mowed down.

"In the meantime my company were able to cross the dangerous road without any losses, the hostile machine-gun fire being totally inaccurate, the machine gunners being very likely anxious about the movements of my patrol. We joined the rest of the battalion retreating towards Le Vouvion, which we reached late at night, after having seen dark clouds of smoke rolling over Marbaix, which the Germans had very likely set on fire. The following day we marched towards Guise, where we took part in the battle fought on the 28th and 29th of August.

"Having returned to this part of the country in November, 1918, as liaison officer attached to the Third British Army, I took the first opportunity to go back to Marbaix and see the village where I had fought one of my first fights in this war, having the not very common chance for a French infantry officer to get under my direct command a party of British soldiers. The inhabitants remembered perfectly well the fighting of August the 26th, 1914. They showed me the houses burnt by the enemy in the eastern part of the village and told me how they had decently buried the corpses

C

of those who had fallen on that date.   In the cemetery
there is a grave in which nine soldiers are lying.
Their names are as follows :—

" 1. Onimus, Charles, Gendarme, Brigade de
     Clermont (Oise).
" 2. Langlois, Boniface, 329° R.I., Classe 1907, né
     à Limpiville (Seine Infre).
" 3. Buchillet, Emile, 329° R.I., Classe 1905, né au
     Havre.
" 4. Bobe, Alfred, 329° R.I., Classe 1906, N°· Mle.
     856.
" 5. Saunier, Andre, 329° R.I., Classe 1906, N°· Mle.
     2254.
" 6. Francois, Leon, 329° R.I., aucon autre
     renseignement.
" 7. Un inconnu du 329° R.I.
" 8. Thompson, J. M., 11430 1st Liverpool Rt.
" 9. Little, A., 7350, 1st Northampton Rt.

" The two latter evidently belonged to the gallant
men who so willingly joined the 24th Company of the
329° French Infantry Regiment on the 26th August.
The grave is well looked after by the inhabitants, and
the " Secretaire de Mairie " said he has still got some
papers which had belonged to the fallen soldiers."

                    (Sd.) Capt. de Lillers, French Mission.
A.H.Q.
   2/2/19.

Armourer-Sergeant Wright and two or three of this
party rejoined the battalion a few days later. Of the
remainder, one was killed and the others wounded and
captured.
    To return to the 1st Battalion, several hours were
spent at Favreuil, and during this time Captain Savage
and Lieutenant Robinson were sent out to reconnoitre
towards the north. " Here we had our first sight of
the field grey of the German Army."   What appeared

to be a regiment of the enemy was observed moving
across country a couple of miles to the west. Doubtless
this was a portion of the attack against the left of the
II Corps at the Battle of Le Cateau. Nothing, however, was as yet known of the fact that a great battle
was being fought within a few miles. Soon afterwards
the 48th moved off, again acting as rear guard to the
2nd Brigade. No fighting took place, and that night
the battalion billeted at Oisy, the outposts being found
by " D " Company.

It was a trying night. A heavy rain fell, and before
morning it turned cold. The absence of greatcoats was
felt severely, but " in spite of the discomfort everyone
who was not on duty, after partaking of a hot meal
from the cookers, was soon fast asleep." In the early
morning of the 27th the battalion was once more upon
the march, and took up a defensive position a few miles
west of Oisy. It was while thus halted that the
battalion first heard of the Battle of Le Cateau, fought
the day before, and of the gallant defence put up by
the II Corps. In the afternoon the battalion resumed
its march to Wassigny. During the day a column of
troops was seen marching parallel to the battalion and
in the same direction. It was thought that it was
German troops. In Wassigny the battalion was
billeted in various farm-yards, "A" Company (Captain
Gordon) being detailed for outpost duty.

The outpost line was situated about half a mile in
front of the battalion. There was a good field of fire,
both to the front and up a small valley to the right, at
the head of which was a small plantation. Towards
mid-day on the 28th a cavalry patrol came riding in
with the news that Germans in motor lorries were
advancing on the village. Shortly afterwards a small
party of Uhlans was seen approaching. Before the
Germans realized that they were up against an outpost
line heavy fire was opened on them and two saddles
were emptied. *One trooper was made prisoner, and

---

* Belicoo.   His shoulder strap is now in 48th Mess.

C I

was at once a source of great interest to the Northamptonshires. He was a mere lad. The horse he
rode was appropriated by the battalion. Christened
"Uhlan," it did good work almost to the end of
the war.

About half an hour later a German aeroplane came
over, flying very low. Apparently the observer
discovered what he was searching for. A smoke
signal was made, and "along come the shells"—a
procedure to which the battalion was soon to become
accustomed. Shortly afterwards movements were
observed in the plantation in the valley. It was
obvious that the little wood was alive with men, but
owing to the drizzle it was impossible to tell whether
they were friend or foe, "but Captain Gordon, who
was sitting on his horse, after glancing through his
glasses, said 'They are Germans.'" Within a few
minutes the enemy were streaming out of the wood
towards the battalion. Rapid fire was at once opened,
and the German advance was quickly checked. Two
Germans with brassards on their arms were now seen
to leave the wood, carrying what appeared to be a
stretcher. They were accordingly not fired on. "But
we soon found that it was not a stretcher they
carried, but a machine gun. It was getting rather
warm in our position, as the Germans were putting up
a pretty heavy machine gun and rifle fire and the
leaves were falling from the hedge rather thickly. We
had been firing for about an hour, more or less, as one
loses the flight of time during excitement, when I felt
a blow on my left leg; looking down, I discovered that
a bullet had passed through it." The narrator is
Sergeant Hoare, then a lance-corporal, who, by being
wounded, could enable the battalion to say that it had
been well and truly blooded, for this was the first
casualty incurred, with the exception of the losses in
the small party detached under the armourer-sergeant
at Marbaix, in charge of the greatcoats. The battalion
had three other men wounded, and claimed on their

side forty to fifty German troopers killed, wounded, or taken prisoner.

In the afternoon the retreat was resumed, " D " Company doing rear party to the battalion, which was on rear guard. In this operation the company had its work cut out to get clear of the enemy, who were following hard on the heels of the battalion. After a long and hot march Hauteville was reached about 9.30 p.m., and the companies went into billets. The men by this time were feeling the effects of the incessant marching, and feet were getting sore.

During the evening the Scots Greys came by, after covering the retirement of the brigade during the day. This fine regiment had been working with the 1st Division during the retreat, and in conjunction with the rest of the cavalry had done wonderful work. On this particular day the Greys had experienced much fighting, and they looked war worn, though in fine trim, as they filed by, their horses scrubbed with some wash to give them a khaki appearance and thus lessen their visibility. As they passed, with many empty saddles showing the sacrifices they had made, the men of the 48th lined the road and cheered again and again. " I cannot speak too highly of our cavalry during those days " writes an officer of the battalion who served in the Retreat from Mons.

At 3.30 a.m. on the morning of the 28th the Northamptonshires left Hauteville and marched to some high ground near Thenel, on the River Oise and north of Ribemont. Here the battalion entrenched and took up a defensive position, facing north, to cover the retirement of the remainder of the division across the river. At about 12.30 p.m. the battalion came under shell fire and could see masses of Germans in close order coming down the slopes opposite. The Germans did not press the attack, and the Northamptonshires withdrew in good order across the Oise to Ribemont, where they had their first real meeting with their allies, for part of the French 5th Army was now in touch.

Close to this place the battalion halted for dinners, and then took place one of the longest and most trying marches of the retreat, to La Fère, where the battalion arrived about midnight, men staggering and hardly able to move from fatigue. The battalion bivouacked that night cheered by the news that the following day would be a day of rest. Even the unemotional war diary of the brigade bears witness to the strenuous march of the 28th with the words, " Weather very hot. Burning sun. Men very exhausted but marching well. Rations none too plentiful. Very little sleep, owing to early starts and arrivals in billets after dark." The following day, however, to some extent made up for things. The battalion spent it in resting and cleaning up generally, and in spite of the terrific heat it was a real repose for the men.

On this day the pressure on the British began to be somewhat relaxed, and their position had sensibly improved. From the latter point of view the two wings, separated by the detention of the II Corps at the Battle of Le Cateau, were once more reuniting. The pressure was relaxed owing to the formation of a new French Army—the 6th—on the British left and also owing to a fine attack made by the French 5th Army on the pursuing Germans at Guise. Further, Sir John French arranged with General Joffre that the British should make a further short retirement towards the line Compiègne—Soissons, promising, however, to do his utmost always to keep within a day's march of the 5th and 6th French Armies.

However, to get back to the 1st Northamptonshire Regiment. It left its bivouac before dawn on August 30th and marched through the Forêt de Coucy. The country on this day's march was pretty in the extreme, with wood-covered hills. After a hot and fatiguing march the battalion billeted at Anizy-le-Château for the night. There all ranks had comfortable accommodation, the officers, who were put up in a private hospital, actually enjoying the luxury of beds with sheets.

" We left this place with regret " next morning about
5.30 a.m., and marched through Soissons. The heat
was again very trying, and after doing fifteen miles
the battalion went into bivouac near Corcy. About
this time rumours began to gain ground to the effect
that the Germans were closing in upon Paris and that
the Allies were everywhere in retreat. Another very
early start was made on September 1st, still southwards, but now apparently in the direction of Paris.
During this day there were various alarms and reports
to the effect that large bodies of Germans were
advancing, screened by the numerous woods. Dispositions were made for defence, but nothing happened and
no enemy appeared.

And now occurs in a narrative an important statement : " It seemed as if any enemy movement was
across our front, *i.e.*, from east to west." Mark these
words, reader, for they are the overture to the Marne,
one of the decisive battles of the world, and, as the
Germans themselves say now, " the turning-point " of
the war. In the next chapter the remark will be
explained, and it is merely sufficient to call attention to
it now.

During the afternoon of this day, September 1st, the
Northamptonshires moved off again, and, as part of the
rear-guard of the division, took up a covering position
about Mareuil. Outposts were put out as usual, and
the battalion assisted in blowing up sundry bridges
over the River Ourcq. " I remember," says a corre-
spondent, " that here we felt as if we were at last
cornered and trapped, for we heard guns firing from
what seemed to be all round us, so much so that it
appeared as if no hole were left for us to slip through."
The work of assisting the engineers went on till late at
night, and then the battalion once again headed south,
about 2.30 a.m. on the morning of the 2nd. It was the
anniversary of Sedan, a day on which a big German
attack might not unreasonably be expected. It proved
another very trying march, very hot and dusty and no

chance of getting anything to eat until the evening.
But the men stuck it in splendid fashion, and the
battalion got to bivouac just north of Meaux. There
is a note in a diary to say that "this continual retirement without fighting is undermining the *moral* of the
men, making them lifeless and depressed."

For twenty or thirty miles north of the town, right
back almost as far as Compiègne and Villers Cotterets,
every road was crowded with khaki-clad horse, foot,
and artillery. The troops were preceded and accompanied by an unceasing stream of fugitive French
civilians, for everywhere the villagers, on learning of
the approach of the Germans, had collected such of
their scanty possessions as were easily portable and
were fleeing south. An eyewitness has left on record
a striking picture of the flight. "It was a sad sight.
There were huge wagons of grain; there were herds of
cattle, flocks of sheep; there were wagons full of household effects, with often as many as twenty people sitting
aloft; there were carriages; there were automobiles with
the occupants crowded in among bundles done up in
sheets; there were women pushing overloaded hand-
carts; there were women pushing baby carriages; there
were dogs and cats and goats; there was every sort of
vehicle you ever saw, drawn by every sort of beast that
can draw, from dogs to oxen, from boys to donkeys.
Here and there was a man on horseback, riding along
the line, trying to keep it moving in order and to
encourage the weary." Yet the *moral* of the men,
though shaken, still stood firm, and the same observer
paints the British soldier of those strenuous days as
"ragged, footsore, bearded, dirty and unkempt, gaunt-
eyed from lack of sleep, but upheld by that invincible
spirit which is the glory of the British race."

In transport and food the Northamptonshires had
difficulties to contend with, but good organization and
the resources of the Army Service Corps eliminated
actual hardship. The battalion horses stuck the retreat
excellently, thanks to the good horsemastership of the

transport officer and his subordinates. Stray horses were utilized when possible—and to a good transport officer " stray " horses come to hand in a remarkable manner. Spare shoes became short, but the supply was made up from dead horses passed on the road. As for food, the battalion always managed to get something to eat, chiefly bully beef and biscuits. The cookers were a godsend. On the whole the men fared better, perhaps, than the officers. There was only one officers' mess cart, and this was found insufficient to provide and carry food, and a second cart was accordingly collected.

On September 3rd the Northamptonshires moved once more. The start was made at 4.30 a.m., and the battalion marched some ten miles to La Ferté, on the River Marne. The sudden change of direction gave rise to much discussion, and there were many rumours flying through the battalion. Fighting now seemed imminent. The battalion took up a position north of the town, having a fine field of fire. Through glasses Germans could be made out in the far distance. Again they were marching across the British front, and large bodies could be seen moving from west to east. After some hours the Northamptonshires moved back across the Marne at La Ferté, where the bridge was being prepared for demolition as the companies filed over it. Finally, the battalion went into billets at Romeny, a little village just south of the river.

South again on the 4th. An early start, 3 a.m., but the battalion had an easy day, doing only some six miles and going into billets at Aulnoy, north of Coulommiers. The Northamptonshires were now in the fruit district, and " officers and men were given as many pears, apples and peaches as they wanted." The weather was still scorchingly hot. About four o'clock in the afternoon the battalion was turned out, as reports had come in that the Germans were advancing in force, but except for the artillery, who got some good targets, there was no shooting for anyone. Another alarm came about midnight. The battalion stood-to, and soon rifle and machine gun fire was heard. It is believed that a German officer and some eight men who formed a patrol were killed or wounded. At about 2.30 a.m. on the 5th the battalion was once more *en route*, this time to the south-west. The march ended at Bonnay, some sixteen miles off, where billets were found. Here a draft of 99 men, under Lieutenant Mylne, joined the battalion, which more than brought the 1st Northamptonshire Regiment up to strength, for the losses during the retreat did not exceed seventy.

During the evening Lieutenant Robinson was detailed to report at divisional headquarters to take down orders for the 2nd Brigade. " It was a moment I shall never forget. Sitting round a big table, we heard for the first time from General Lomax, our divisional commander, that we were once again to take the offensive. The faces of everyone were lightened. Such things as fatigue and depression were forgotten."

It was one of the great moments in history. The sequel was the Battle of the Marne.

CHAPTER II.

THE 1ST BATTALION—THE BATTLE OF THE MARNE— THE PURSUIT TO THE AISNE.

ROUGHLY speaking, the war had now been in progress for just a month. Victory upon victory had been secured by the Germans. Nevertheless their situation at the beginning of September, 1914, was by no means free from anxiety. The principle underlying their plan of operations had been that France was to be brought to her knees within six weeks; but although two-thirds of that period had now expired the French and British Armies were keeping their opponent at arm's length. It is true that the German great left-wheel had been a success. The movement was well up to the scheduled time-table. The outer German army was almost at the gates of Paris. On the other hand, the very successes of the Germans had got to their heads. The great machine was somewhat dislocated, and army commanders had been endeavouring to achieve and exploit individual successes rather than to conform to one general plan. Further, the ever-lengthening lines of communication were adding to the supply and transport difficulties of the invaders, and slowly but surely sapping their strength. Maubeuge, too, still held out, and the retention of this fortress by the French denied the use of a valuable line of railway to the Germans. The inevitable wastage involved by a rapid advance in trying weather had made itself felt. The cavalry horses were sorely in need of rest. British musketry had exacted severe toll at Mons and Le Cateau. Nor was there any depth in the advance. Troops had been perforce left in Belgium to mask Antwerp, in which fortress the Belgian Army had taken refuge. A corps was immobilized by the siege of Maubeuge. Worse still, two corps had been sent off post-haste to East Prussia to deal with the Russian invasion there, and of these corps one had been subtracted from the right wing, where every man was urgently required. A further demand was made on the right wing to send troops—including seventy heavy batteries which had been earmarked for the investment of Paris—to take part in an attack on Nancy. In a word, the Germans were now discovering that they had " bitten off more than they could chew." And, unfortunately for them, von Moltke was a weak commander without much back-bone, whereas Joffre was determined, imperturbable, and a ruler of men.

After the Battle of Le Cateau on August 26th, General von Kluck, the commander of the German I Army, fell into a serious error. He was convinced that the British II Corps—or, indeed, the British Army, for he conceived that the whole of the Expeditionary Force had been opposed to him—was retiring west-wards to the coast, instead of southwards as was actually the case. By pursuing westwards he thus not only allowed the sorely-mauled II Corps to escape, but he increased his distance from the German II Army of General von Bülow. The latter was roughly shaken up by the French 5th Army at Guise on August 29th, and he found himself committed to an advance on Paris while out of touch with the I Army on his right and the III Army on his left. Becoming anxious for his situation, he sent out urgent wireless appeals to the I and III Armies to close inwards to his aid. General von Kluck, tired of beating the air, gladly complied, and thus forced German Supreme Headquarters to revise their original plan. The advance against Paris was definitely written off. Trusting that the newly-formed French 6th Army, which had fallen back on Paris, would be chained to the capital; and convinced that the British Army was incapable of any other action at present than of licking its wounds, the Germans decided to ignore these armies and to make the left flank of the French 5th Army the new objective of the German right wing.

It was this new plan which caused the appearance of German troops marching across the British front, as already related, from west to east. This obvious change in the German plan had been reported to General Galliéni, the military governor of Paris. He was in a difficult position. He knew that General Joffre did not intend to turn and fight until the Seine had been crossed. On the other hand, there was the German I Army making a flank march across the north-east of Paris; " trailing its coat," so to speak, under the very fortifications of the capital; actually inviting attack; and providing a temptation almost impossible to resist. General Galliéni realized that an opportunity not often vouchsafed in war had come. He placed his 6th Army in position to attack the German I Army, and communicated at once with General Joffre. The French commander-in-chief saw at once that the time had come. He determined to stay his retreat and to attack at the earliest moment.

The Allied armies now occupied a line which can be visualized by imagining a ribbon suspended from Paris and Verdun at the extremities and sagging in the centre. On the left, north-east of Paris, was the French 6th Army. Next came the British Army, which lay behind the Grand Morin, covered by its cavalry, the I Corps (in which were the Northamptonshires) being on the right. Working still eastwards came the French 5th, 9th, 4th and 3rd Armies, the last named holding on to Verdun with its right hand, so to speak. Facing this long concave line were five German Armies, the I being on the right. For the purpose of this history it is not necessary to go outside the area occupied by the French 6th Army, the British, and the French 5th Army. The first two were to attack eastwards and the last-named from south to north, the idea being to envelop and bite off the German right wing. The attack was to begin on the morning of September 6th.

The Germans, meanwhile, were frantically trying to evolve a new plan, into which there is no need to enter, as it never came off. Sufficient is it to say that General von Kluck, in defiance of the new orders, kept pushing across the Marne.

During September 6th the British Army saw but little fighting. The explanation is simple. The French 6th Army was pushing forward to the Ourcq, with Château Thierry as its ultimate goal, and was driving in General von Kluck's right flank guard. That general at once began to withdraw troops across the Marne to deal with the danger to his right rear. In other words, his army began to face west instead of advancing south, and the British, instead of attacking the front of the German I Army, were merely feeling an improvised left flank guard. The day therefore calls for little remark, and as a matter of fact the 2nd Brigade was in reserve. The battalion bivouacked for the night at Pezarches, the line held by the British at evening being from left to right, Crécy—Coulommiers—Choisy.

In the area to which the description of the battle is limited the fighting was hard and bitter on September 7th, with the exception of that portion in which the British found themselves. The reinforcements hurried off to strengthen the Germans on the Ourcq had now left a comparatively small force to oppose the British troops. The task of holding back the army of Sir John French was now being carried out mainly by a cavalry screen, reinforced, as was the German custom, by Jäger battalions. A change was made in the direction of the British advance, the new route being north instead of east. The British cavalry everywhere acted with great vigour, and by the close of the day the British position was roughly as follows: The III Corps, on the left, was about La Haute Maison. In the centre the II Corps lay about Chailly and Jouy-sur-Morin. On the right, the I Corps (less 3rd and 4th Brigades) was south of the Grand Morin from Jouay-sur-Morin to

Siméon, the Northamptonshires being the right flank battalion. It did not fire a shot, nor did it see a German. It left its bivouacs about 9 a.m. and halted for a long time near Mauperthuis, where the ground was "strewn with dead horses." After this halt the battalion turned eastward and marched through Chailly to St. Siméon, where it bivouacked about 8 p.m. "On this march we passed German bivouacs which were strewn with empty bottles and broken transport carts, which gave us to understand that they had moved much quicker than they had expected. The villages we passed through were very much damaged, and the furniture had been thrown into the street by Germans.

On September 8th the Northamptonshires continued their advance, this time as rear-guard, and consequently once more it saw no fighting. The march began about 7 a.m., and a long halt was made at La Tretoire. The 1st Brigade was this day sharply engaged at Sablonnières, and the fighting was clearly audible. All day long the thunder of the French guns right and left could be heard, although it was hard to realize that fighting was in progress from Paris to the Swiss frontier, and that one of the world's greatest battles was being waged along that immense front. The Northamptonshires passed the night on outpost duty near Rebais. On the following day the advance was resumed at 6.30 a.m., and after moving forward a few miles the battalion was halted until 1 p.m. Two hours later the Marne was crossed at Nogent. A further march of some half-dozen miles brought the battalion to bivouac.

And so ended September 9th. And so ended the Battle of the Marne. By evening the whole right and right centre of the great German line were falling back. The area into which the British Army had been pushing was in reality a dangerous gap in the German front, imperfectly filled by cavalry. The German I and II Armies were widely separated. On the Ourcq, General von Kluck had as much as he could do to hold off the French 6th Army, and General von Bülow, the commander of the II Army, was exceedingly anxious about his exposed right flank. There had been Homeric fighting from Paris to Verdun, and thence in a subsidiary but co-related series of battles right down to the Swiss frontier. But the waves of battle had surged right and left of the Northamptonshire Regiment. War is sometimes an odd thing, and Fate works often in streaks. Present at Mons, the battalion had not been engaged. It went through the great retreat with but a handful of casualties. It advanced over the decisive sector in one of the decisive battles of the world apparently without firing a shot. It was as if Fate were just "nursing" the 1st Northamptonshire Regiment for a fuller vengeance. This, indeed, was so. And if a hundred years hence a bloodthirsty reader may become impatient at the narrative up to this point, he is asked to bide his time. Before he shall have read another hundred pages he will have blood—rivers of it, and will see the old 48th not merely decimated, but practically wiped out of existence.

The very next day, September 10th, Fate put a tick opposite the 1st Northamptonshire Regiment in her tablets. The advance was resumed—or to be correct the pursuit was undertaken—and the 2nd Brigade, which was acting as advanced guard to the division, moved on Courchamps. Early in the morning the divisional cavalry brought back word that a German rear-guard was holding a position north of the village of Priez. The advanced guard was ordered to attack, the front line consisting of the Royal Sussex and the Loyal North Lancashires—the latter on the right—the 1st Northamptonshire Regiment to follow in support. Lieutenant-Colonel Osborne-Smith ordered "B" (Captain Hughes) and "C" (Captain R. B. Parker) Companies to deploy, with "B" Company on the left and astride of the road, the remaining two companies to follow in support.

Priez lies in a shallow valley formed by the little River Alland, which is crossed at right-angles by the Courchamps—Priez road, up which the advanced guard had been advancing. The position held by the Germans was a low wooded ridge on the far side of the stream. The country south of the Alland, and over which the attack was to be made, was grass land, unenclosed and flat until about five hundred paces from the village, where it slopes gently down to the stream. The country on this side was sparsely wooded, but there was a large copse on the left of the road just where it begins to drop to the river. As the Northamptonshires approached the copse they could hear in front a considerable volume of artillery and rifle fire, and our guns were also in action to the left rear. Shells now began to burst on the battalion, and it was clear that the copse was being used as a ranging mark by the enemy. Meanwhile the Royal Sussex had occupied Priez without much difficulty, and had begun to mount the slopes beyond, when they came under a fairly heavy artillery fire. The morning had been wet and the Sussex men were wearing their waterproof sheets, so that when they began to retire our gunners appear to have mistaken them for Germans advancing, and opened fire upon them. For a time the British advance was checked. Shells continued to fall among the brigade, and several casualties were sustained, the adjutant (Captain Lloyd), Captain Hughes, and Lieutenant Jervois being wounded, curiously enough in the ankle in each case. Major Norman and Captain Bentley also received slight injuries. Captain Hughes was hit immediately his company began to advance from the copse, which, owing to the German shell fire, had become distinctly unhealthy. As " A " Company advanced in support of " C " a curious incident occurred. The latter company put up a covey of part-ridges, and a German shrapnel, bursting overhead at that moment, brought down two of the birds, which were promptly retrieved and put into the pot that night.

D

The British guns were now doing good work, and the 1st Brigade having been pushed up to support the right of the 2nd the advance was resumed, covered by the artillery fire. Inasmuch as the German force was a rear-guard, and as it had fulfilled its duty of imposing delay on the pursuers, it withdrew before the full-dress attack, and the Northamptonshires occupied the ridge from which the Sussex had been shelled. The German heavy guns continued to fire for some time, but without much effect, and the Northamptonshires maintained their hold on the south side of the ridge. Towards evening " A " and " D " Companies moved forward to occupy another ridge east of Rassey village, which lies about two miles north of Priez. During this move forward a German cyclist scout emerged from some houses and tried to bolt, but he was immediately shot down by Company Sergeant-Major Phillpot. No opposition was now encountered, and the outpost companies entrenched for the night, the remainder of the 2nd Brigade bivouacking near Rassey.

The losses sustained in this affair by the battalion were 3 men killed and 25 wounded, including 5 officers. Most of the casualties were caused by the heavy artillery fire while the battalion was deployed on the south side of the valley and before it moved forward. The Royal Sussex, after their check, pushed forward and captured a considerable number of prisoners. In the Northamptonshires, Lieutenant Robinson now took over the duties of adjutant.

Altogether during this day the British captured 13 pieces of artillery, 7 machine guns, about 2,000 prisoners, and quantities of transport. The Germans left many dead on the field. The fighting in this sector was confined mainly to the British, for neither on the right nor left did the French 6th and 5th Armies meet with much opposition.

Early in the morning of September 11th the pursuit was resumed, the 1st Northamptonshire Regiment leaving its position about 5 a.m. There was practically no fighting throughout the day, and the three corps of the British Army crossed the Ourcq—which here flows from east to west, and therefore at right-angles to the northerly march of the British. The cavalry got up to the River Aisne, with its main body on the line Braisne —Soissons. The Northamptonshires billeted for the night in Coincy, after an uncomfortable day, for the weather had turned very wet. On the 12th the battalion left Coincy at 7 a.m. and marched to billets at Paars, two companies going on outpost duty. During the afternoon it had become probable from the opposition encountered by the centre and left British corps (the II and III) as well as by the French 6th Army west of Soissons, that the Germans had, at any rate temporarily, arrested their retreat and were apparently about to make a stand.

The Battle of the Marne had to some extent bewildered the Allies, and the sudden change to becoming the pursuers instead of the pursued had led not only the rank and file, but even the higher commanders, to a rather unjustified optimism. It was thought even in high quarters that the Germans might possibly be retiring out of France altogether, or rather, if the pursuit were kept up, that this might be brought about. There was little, indeed, in the actual result of the Marne to justify this conclusion. No great number of prisoners or trophies had been taken; in no portion of the colossal field had the Germans been decisively beaten; they broke off the battle at their own time and their retirement had been orderly and well carried out. What had really occurred, although it was not known until afterwards, was this. The Germans, during their advance, had earmarked a position north of the Aisne as a line on which to fall back in case of necessity. And, so far from contemplating the evacuation of France, they had swung back their whole line so that while their left still remained in the neighbourhood of Verdun, their right was near Laon. Although all this was not known at the time,

D I

it was at any rate clear that the Aisne would now have to be crossed and the position north of it would have to be carried. And a very formidable position it looked.

To begin with, the Aisne was no mere stream, but a regular river nearly sixty yards broad, and although the current was sluggish the depth in the centre was at least fifteen feet. At the moment, however, the river itself was invisible, but there was nothing invisible about the heights which rose on the far side. There was a steep line of wooded hills rising some four hundred feet from the valley, broken into numerous spurs and re-entrants. After the plateau-like, or, at most, undulating terrain over which the battalion had been moving now for some days, the Aisne heights, when first seen, gained in prominence and seemed to take on almost the appearance of mountains. Certainly they gave the impression of affording an ideal line on which the enemy might offer very serious opposition indeed. By the afternoon of the 12th Sir John French had his army almost up to the river, and accordingly, on the following morning, Sunday, September 13th, he ordered his troops " to advance and make good the Aisne."

On the morning of this day of September 13th, the day on which the Battle of the Aisne really opened, the British Army was in position south of that river, between Soissons on the west and Bourg on the east, with outposts on the river itself. The prevailing tone in the respective headquarters was one of optimism. The Marne had been a welcome surprise. The Belgian Army appeared to be well established in Antwerp, and a fine sortie—directed by the King of the Belgians—had considerable effect, undoubtedly delaying the march of the German IX Reserve Corps and of the 6th Reserve Division. The news from Russia was also not unfavourable. The British Army was about to be reinforced by the 6th Division, which had landed at St. Nazaire—the new base—and was hurrying up to the front, having been railed as far as Coulommiers. On the left of the

British the French 6th Army had reached the 'Aisne, after some opposition, and beyond them French cavalry were working round by Compiègne to threaten the German communications. On the right of the British the French 5th Army was on the line Cormicy —Rheims—Verzy, and beyond them again the 9th and 4th Armies had made good progress.

It was in these circumstances that in the early hours of Sunday, the 13th, the British attacked all along their front. On the right was the I Corps, the 1st Division of which, pressing hard upon the heels of the Germans, approached the Aisne at Bourg. Here it was reported that the enemy were in force. After the cavalry had been sent forward the 2nd Brigade was ordered to advance and cross the river. An aqueduct spanned the river at this point, and it was found to be intact. By it the crossing was effected without difficulty, no serious opposition being offered by the enemy. As a matter of fact, although in other portions of the British front the Germans shelled the crossings and had snipers and machine guns in the woods, they did not seriously contest the river line. Their position was on a plateau on top and some distance from the edge. It suited them better to allow the British to emerge on to this tableland, where they would have a strong enemy entrenched position in front and an unfordable river in their rear.

Having crossed the river the 2nd Brigade pushed forward to a point south-east of Moulins, where the Northamptonshire Regiment, " very tired, came to rest in a farmyard." After a halt of about an hour positions were taken up at various points on the high ground around, " A " and " D " Companies being sent to occupy a hill about three-quarters of a mile north of the village. Here they came under heavy rifle and artillery fire from the enemy, who was evidently in considerable force on the ridge beyond. The advance was not pressed, " A " Company remaining on outpost duty on the hill during the night, while " D " returned to Moulins, where the battalion was billeting, with orders to be ready to turn out at a moment's notice. It had become clear that the Germans intended to offer an obstinate resistance to any farther advance. So far, the 48th had been engaged only in rear-guard or advanced guard actions in which, by the rules of the game, one side or the other was certain to break off the action when it got too hot. Now, for the first time, the battalion was confronted by hostile forces determined to stand their ground and to maintain their hold upon the strong natural position which they had occupied.

The opposition encountered by the II and III Corps, in the centre and on the left respectively, had been much more severe than that met with by the I Corps on the right, and by the evening of the 13th it was still uncertain whether the enemy was making only a temporary halt, covered by rear-guards, or whether he intended to stand and defend the position. With a view to clearing up the situation Sir John French ordered a general advance, the I Corps being ordered to cross the line Moulins—Moussy by 7 a.m. On the right of the corps the general officer commanding the 1st Division directed the 2nd Infantry Brigade and the 25th Artillery Brigade (less one battery) under Brigadier-General Bulfin, to move forward before day-break in order to protect the advance of the division up the valley to Vendresse. An officers' patrol sent out from the brigade reported a considerable force of the enemy near the factory north of Troyon, and the brigadier accordingly directed the King's Royal Rifles and the Royal Sussex Regiment to move at 3 a.m. The Northamptonshire Regiment was ordered to move at 4 a.m. to occupy the spur east of Troyon. The remaining battalion of the brigade, the Loyal North Lancashire Regiment, moved at 5.30 a.m. to the village of Vendresse, where it was in reserve. The road to Vendresse runs between wooded downs on either side, and the idea was to bring the rest of the division along it so soon as the heights right and left had been cleared by the 2nd Brigade.

At 4 a.m. General Bulfin's brigade advanced. The 48th moved forward to the hill where " A " Company had remained during the night. " D " Company resumed its old place on the left of " A," while " B " (Captain White) Company continued the line to the right, an interval of some 900 yards being left between these two companies. Meanwhile the 60th Rifles and the Royal Sussex moved round to the left of the hill and advanced against the German position.

It was soon realized that there was a hard nut to crack in the shape of the sugar factory which stands near the cross-roads on the Chemin des Dames, north-west of Troyon village. The factory itself was very strongly held with machine guns, and was flanked by two batteries of artillery. For a quarter of a mile on either side were German trenches, on the one side running along the Chivy road and on the other along the Chemin des Dames, the two forming an apex at the factory itself. In addition, the enemy had four pieces of heavy artillery behind their line. The approach to this position was over turnip and beet fields, very wet and sticky. The day was a particularly unpleasant one. There was a cold and persistent rain from the north-west right in the faces of the attackers, accompanied by a kind of fog which made it impossible to see more than a couple of hundred yards ahead. The poor visibility reacted on the guns, and the 25th Artillery Brigade and the divisional artillery were unable to render any effective support until about nine o'clock.

In spite of a most gallant attempt the Royal Sussex and the 60th could make no impression on the factory, and the brigadier ordered up the Loyal North Lancashires in support. Even with this reinforcement the attack was unable to make headway, and on the arrival of the 1st Brigade the Coldstream Guards were moved up to support the right of the 2nd Brigade, the remaining three battalions supporting the left.

Meanwhile the 48th was remaining on its hill, the men peering through the driving rain and endeavouring to make out what was passing on their left front. About 11.30 a.m. orders came to support the attack by an immediate advance. Accordingly " C " Company moved forward into the gap between " A " and " B," and then " C " and " B " advanced together, the 1st Queen's, which had been brought up from the 3rd Brigade, being on the right. The advance was carried out in a most spirited manner, but the intensity of the German fire made it impossible to obtain possession of the ridge. On the left of the Northamptonshires desperate fighting took place round the sugar refinery, which was once stormed by the Loyal North Lancashire Regiment after a terrible and heroic struggle, but was subsequently abandoned. When dusk fell, " B " Company of the 48th had forced its way up to the Chemin des Dames, while " C " Company lay a little south of the road. " A " and " D " Companies were now ordered forward to fill the gap between the left of " C " and the right of the North Lancashires, " C " Company being brought back into battalion reserve. The advance had not been accomplished without severe casualties. Captain White and Lieutenant Paget, of " B " Company, had both been killed, while Lieutenant Mylne, who had joined the battalion with the second reinforcement a week earlier, was badly wounded. Three other officers were wounded, and the casualties among other ranks were 102. The total losses in the brigade were nearly 1,000, of whom 600 were missing.

The battalion dug itself in for the night on the slope of the ridge, " each man making cover for his head and a hole to crouch in, this being considered to be a temporary measure, but proved to be a stoppage." An unwelcome feature of the day had been the activity of the German heavy artillery, which employed projectiles hitherto not met with by the battalion. Their characteristics were a huge crater formed and an immense vertical column of thick black smoke which rose on the impact of the shell. Christened at once " Black Marias," " Coal Boxes," and " Jack Johnsons," they gave the British troops a foretaste of what the Germans had in store. As the war went on, " Jack Johnsons " became very *vieux jeu,* but when they were first encountered they had a very intimidating effect indeed.

The next two days were spent in improving the hastily contrived trenches, which were as different from the system of the later stages of the war as a child's digging on the beach is from the underground railway system of London. The artillery was active on both sides, but no actual attack was made. The rain was active, too, for it came down in torrents and made life a misery. On the 15th Captain Gordon was killed leading his men into some advanced trenches.

Thursday, September 17th, was an eventful day. About 1.30 p.m., amid pouring rain, the Germans launched an attack against the right of the 1st Division. A counter-attack was ordered, and in that sector occupied by the Northamptonshires it took the form of a bayonet charge by " C " Company, which drove the Germans from some trenches which they had occupied. While leading the attack, Captain R. B. Parker was killed. The struggle continued with varying fortunes until nightfall, when the Germans were finally driven back.

It was during this day that what was known as the " white flag " incident occurred, which gave rise to much comment at the time. The Germans, three days earlier, had inflicted heavy loss on the Royal Sussex Regiment by a simulated surrender, followed, while the attackers were thus taken off their guard, by a heavy and suddenly-opened fire. On this day, September 17th, another such incident took place. In " A " Company, Captain Gordon had been killed, and on the following day Captain Ward Hunt, the second captain, had been wounded. The command of the company then devolved on Second-Lieutenant Burlton, whose *ipsissima verba* are now given about an incident of which there are several other and inaccurate accounts.

" At about 3 p.m. or a little later, we saw a line of our troops deployed and advancing. And hardly had we spotted them, when, to our unbounded joy, we saw the enemy in front of us making signs of surrender by putting their hands up. Their fire stopped, and I ordered mine to do likewise. I stood upon the parapet and called for an officer to meet me. An individual —I think a private—who spoke English, responded to the call, and I went out some forty yards ahead of my trench to make the necessary arrangements. On my finding out he was not an officer, I ordered him to return and to tell his officer to replace him. A sergeant, or under-officer next turned up, but was also returned as ' not wanted,' after which an officer did materialize. He appeared to find great difficulty in understanding me. I agreed to accept surrender, but, as a preliminary thereto, naturally ordered him to make his men lay down their arms. Our conversation took place half-way between the opposing trenches, and to my annoyance I saw a large number of the enemy debouch from their trenches before my arrangements were completed. Most of them had their rifles, but many had not, and many had their hands up. I tried to make the Boche officer understand that I would order my men to fire if his men continued to advance with their arms. All this time the enemy continued to advance, and the officer appeared quite willing to surrender, but unable to grasp my idea about his men putting their rifles down as a preliminary. I found myself being surrounded by the advancing Germans, and, as there was no officer in our own trench (Second-Lieutenant Jarvis was in a state of concussion and non-effective), I could not afford to remain out in No Man's Land, which was rapidly being overwhelmed by the advancing Huns. I was, at the time, quite sure of their *bona fides* as to surrender, and did not want to open fire for two reasons (I do not know how far I calculated these reasons at the time, but their validity was certainly in my mind). Firstly, I thought it was a *bona fide* surrender, as many of the enemy came without arms and with hands up; and, to make the illusion complete, some of those who were armed delivered their rifles over to some of our Tommies, who had come out on their own to meet them. It would have been a dirty business to have opened fire on men who were advancing with their arms because they did not understand English. Secondly, I had a message delivered verbally to me by one of my men, ' From the General, do not fire.'—I remember that message most distinctly; its incongruity did not strike me at the moment, and I thought it a genuine one. It came down from the right of our line from a quarter in front of which the enemy had also put up their hands. By this time I was back on the top of my own trench with the Boche officer and the under-officer, the Huns, about 400 strong, already amongst us, and in many cases surrendering their arms to Tommy Atkins and being warmly shaken by the hand. This situation passed very quickly, however, for a German quite close to me shot one of my men dead, and the officer, on my saying that if he did not order an immediate cessation of his fire I would order mine to open, informed me that I was his prisoner. We then all set to in earnest, so to speak, and at point-blank range, of course; no accuracy of shooting was necessary—the men used their butts and bayonets lustily. We were, however, far outnumbered, being but some seventy odd, I believe, against 400. Then the most wonderful thing happened. The Queen's (I think) on our right, seeing we were in trouble, and seeing that the Boches were, for the most part, standing on our parapet and firing down into us in the road, turned on their machine gun and the spectacle was one never to be forgotten. They fairly enfiladed the Huns on our parapet, and the execution can only be compared to that of a harvesting machine as it mows down wheat. A regular lane was cut—those Boches on their side of the lane (perhaps some hundred strong) made their best pace back to their trenches; those on our side of the lane threw down their arms and surrendered; but we declined their offer, and, in fact, I think only kept one prisoner—a souvenir, no doubt."

Captain Savage, who had just been sent from " D " Company to take over the command of "A" Company, arrived on the left flank of the company during this incident. He went out with an officer of the 60th to parley with the Germans opposite him. After an apparently inconclusive talk, he and the officer of the 60th walked back to our own trenches, but, before getting there, were fired on. The 60th officer escaped unhurt, while Captain Savage was shot in the back and killed. Seeing what had taken place, the battalion machine gun section and that of the 60th Rifles also opened fire and the Germans fled back to their lines. Second-Lieutenant Gordon also lost his life in this affair. The casualties on this day amounted to 161 of all ranks, and in addition to the officers already enumerated Major Dobbin, Captain Ward Hunt, Lieutenant Fraser, and Second-Lieutenant Burlton were wounded between the 14th and the close of the 17th September.

Several officers and men of the battalion were mentioned in despatches for gallantry in the actions and engagements already narrated in this history. For the fighting on the Aisne Lieutenant-Colonel E. Osborne Smith was brought to notice for his skill, coolness and marked ability in handling his battalion, and for the ease with which he controlled it in difficult circumstances. Lieutenant Needham was commended for having led his company with skill and coolness when all the other company officers were either killed or wounded; and Second-Lieutenant Burlton for his coolness and skill in leading his men and for the valuable service rendered in rallying them after the confusion of the white flag incident. Of non-commissioned officers, Company Sergeant-Major H. F. Pitcher and Sergeant F. Johnson were mentioned, the former for the coolness displayed after taking command of his company after all the officers had been disabled. The despatch also records the valuable services of Lieutenant G. St. G. Robinson, who was now acting as adjutant of the battalion.

"Still raining" is the opening remark in the war diary for September 18th, though some excitement is yielded by a short notice of an enemy attack during the night. This was rather a half-hearted affair, and was easily driven back. The next day the battalion was relieved by the 18th Brigade of the newly-arrived 6th Division, and marched back to Pargnan, a village just north of the river. Here it went into billets for a sorely needed rest, and here officers and men wrote home their experiences, gratefully opened parcels of cigarettes, chocolate and other comforts, and took the opportunity of ridding themselves of the accumulation of chalk, mud and filth which they had gathered on their clothes and their persons during the preceding days. In the officers' mess there were evidences of the toll which a great war levies. In just over a week four officers had been killed and thirteen wounded.

It is inevitable that when a battalion is resting and licking its wounds the impression should grow that the fighting is over, and there is a paragraph in a narrative of this period in a battalion record to the effect that "the Battle of the Aisne, in the proper sense of the word, may be said to have ended on September 20th, though occasional local attacks took place during the next few weeks." This is, however, not quite the case, as a reference to Sir John French's despatch will show. During the night of the 21st the Germans made a violent attack on the II Corps, which, however, was repulsed. Between the 23rd and 26th there was a bit of a lull, but on the latter day there was "a very marked renewal of activity." There was heavy artillery firing on both sides, in which four six-inch howitzer batteries, just arrived from England, retaliated on the German "Jack Johnsons." From the 26th to the 28th the Germans

made one last great effort, culminating during the night
of the 27th/28th in a most determined attempt to
capture the trenches of the 1st Division, but without
success. Thereafter, chiefly owing to a growing shortage
of shells on either side, the battle petered out. In it the
48th Regiment had played its part. When the
commander-in-chief visited the brigade at Paissy on
September 22nd, he testified his appreciation with the
words : " I shall never forget the four regiments
composing the 2nd Brigade."

What may be called the centre of gravity of the
Western Front was now about to be shifted north-
westwards, and the euphonious French place-names on
the Aisne were to be replaced by harsher sounding
Flemish words. What has been called, though not
quite accurately, the " race to the sea " had begun.
While the 48th was on the Aisne the French had been
gradually reinforcing their left, north of Noyon, to
which the Germans replied by a corresponding extension of their right, with the result that the British
Army, which had been originally on the left of the
Allies, now began to find itself embedded in the centre.
There were several objections to a continuation of this
state of affairs. The British line of supply from St.
Nazaire now ran across supply lines of several French
armies : this was awkward, and might be even more so
if the Allies had to retire from the Aisne position, a
contingency which was not impossible. And what
might be nothing more than an inconvenience so long
as the Allies held their ground on the Aisne, might be
something much more serious if a retirement should
take place. Feeding troops in a retreat is always
difficult, but when lines of supply cross the difficulty
would perhaps become insuperable. The drawback of
the situation had been for long patent to Sir John
French, and there was another reason which made the
British commander-in-chief wish to move his army—
his anxiety for the Channel ports. Sir John French
later placed on record that he was genuinely alarmed

lest the enemy might make a powerful attack against those ports while the main forces of both sides were locked in a kind of stalemate in the interior of France. About the middle of September he had begun to conceive the idea of disengaging from the Aisne and moving to a position in the north-west, where he could defend the Channel ports and also be in a better position to co-operate with the Navy in keeping open the Straits of Dover, which were vital to us. General Joffre admitted the force of Sir John French's arguments, and consequently the opening days of October saw the British Army in process of moving westwards from the Aisne.

The withdrawal was carried out in instalments, so to speak, the cavalry, II and III Corps gliding away, leaving the I Corps, with the French, to hold the line. As a matter of fact, the 2nd Brigade remained in the Aisne position until October 17th. By that time operations had completely stagnated, and a period of trench warfare had begun. Both armies steadily laboured at the work of improving and strengthening their trenches, barbed wire was put up—though nothing like the maze of entanglements that developed in the later stages of the war—and a more or less regular system of reliefs was instituted. When they were out of the trenches, the Northamptonshires usually stayed in the caves near Paissy.

Shelling continued with some frequency. The Germans at this time adopted the plan of indicating the position of our trenches to their gunners by dropping a smoke bomb from one of their aeroplanes on the spot where their aerial observers imagined our lines to be situated. Hence came into being a fragment of verse, which continued to have a considerable vogue in the 48th long after the Germans had abandoned this practice :—

> " When the airman in the sky
>   Drops his signal from on high,
>   You'll be ' coal-boxed ' by and by,
>   Never mind !"

Occasional local attacks were made by the enemy, but they were invariably repulsed with little difficulty. Lieutenant Wauchope was badly wounded by a shell splinter on September 27th, a day on which two attacks were made by the Germans, but generally speaking the casualties at this time were not heavy. A reinforcement draft consisting of 8 officers and 200 men, which arrived on October 9th, helped to swell the depleted ranks of the battalion. Among the officers were Captain W. R. Russell, from the 2nd Battalion; Captains F. Pope, Darwell, and Sir F. V. L. Robinson, of the Reserve. Second-Lieutenant K. McClure, who came up with this draft, was the first officer with no military service prior to the outbreak of war to join the battalion. At about this time Company Sergeant-Major Phillpot, Company Quartermaster-Sergeant Eden, and Sergeant Leach were awarded commissions for their services in the field. The last-named went to the 2nd Manchester Regiment, and a few weeks later won the Victoria Cross in an engagement near Festubert.

On October 15th orders were received by the 2nd Brigade to prepare for a move. The unusual activity prevalent in the British lines in consequence of this order aroused the suspicions of the Germans, who anticipated an attack. Twice during the following night the enemy opened heavy rifle and machine-gun fire against an imaginary attacking force. Next day the officers of the French troops who were detailed to relieve the Brigade visited our trenches and expressed their satisfaction at their condition, which certainly had been improved considerably during the past four weeks. The actual relief took place on the night of October 16th/17th. There was considerable delay and confusion, as the German artillery opened fire upon the relieving troops, caused several casualties among them, and delayed their advance for an hour and a half. When finally the French did arrive, at 10.30 p.m., it took them no less than five hours to effect the relief. This was a serious matter for the Northamptonshires, who had eleven miles to march to their billets at Vauxere, mostly over country under enemy observation. However, a morning mist saved the situation, the Aisne was recrossed without difficulty or danger, and by 7 a.m. the battalion was at Vauxere.

At 3 a.m. on the morning of the 18th the Northamptonshires entrained at Fismes, about four miles from Vauxere. The train, proceeding via Amiens and Etaples, arrived at Cassel station at about 11 a.m. Here Captain D. W. Powell rejoined the battalion from the Royal Flying Corps. The 48th detrained and marched up the hill into the town, where they went into billets. It was the first time for nearly two months that they had rested away from the sound of the German guns.

CHAPTER III.

1914. THE 1ST BATTALION—THE FIRST BATTLE OF YPRES AND THE CLOSE OF 1914.

WHEN Sir John French decided to pull the British Army out of the line on the Aisne, and to move it round to the extreme left, Antwerp was still holding out, and the Belgian Army, which had fallen back to it, was very much " in being." The general plan of the Allies was, therefore, to extend their left so as to gain touch with Antwerp, in which case the fortress would form an admirable *point d'appui,* while at the same time the Channel ports would be covered, and the German lines of communication would be threatened. But in the first days of October events moved with disconcerting rapidity. The bombardment of Antwerp had already begun, and, in spite of efforts made by England to send marines and an improvised force called the Royal Naval Division, the place fell on the night of October 8th and 9th, and the Belgian Army made its way to the Yser.

At this time the British II Corps was in the neighbourhood of La Bassée, the III was about Hazebrouck, and the I Corps was expected to begin to arrive about October 17th. Antwerp having fallen, a modification of the Allied plan was necessary. It was decided to attempt to gain the line Lille—Courtrai on October 13th. Another serious complication had now to be faced. On the 12th Lille fell into the hands of the Germans, who, like ourselves, had been hurrying troops from the Aisne. Consequently, in that sector of the front marked by La Bassée on the right and Nieuport on the left, the operations of the Allies were rather of the nature of a series of improvisations.

So far as the 1st Northamptonshire Regiment is concerned, its story is bound up with the I Corps.

While they were being railed round from the Aisne, the
II and III Corps had been heavily engaged in the new
sector. Sir John French had begun to feel anxious
about the situation. There was reason to believe that
large reinforcements were streaming across Belgium to
strengthen the German right, and against this access
of strength the Allies could oppose no corresponding
weight. Along the Yser was but an insufficient number of
French troops—many of whom were *Territoriales*. The
Belgian troops which had escaped from Antwerp were
tired out. On the right of the Belgians were the newly-
arrived 3rd Cavalry Division and 7th Division, and
both of these were in sore need of rest and refit. It was
clear to Sir John French that the enemy was threatening
Ypres and the Yser, and no less clear was it that if the
threat succeeded the seaboard would be theirs and the
Channel ports would be lost to the British. He determined to retort by a corresponding offensive, and
accordingly hurried the newly-arrived I Corps northwards, hoping that with the assistance of the French
and Belgians on the Yser, and of Sir Henry
Rawlinson's force, the enemy might be cleared out of
Bruges and Ostend and driven from Ghent. But by
this time the Germans had started their big push, and
the Allies were at once thrown upon the defensive.

We left the 48th resting in billets at Cassel, but the
respite was destined to be very short-lived. The
remainder of the 2nd Brigade had arrived at Cassel by
the 19th, and at 5 a.m. on the 20th the whole marched
away to Poperinghe, and thence to Elverdinghe. The
Battle of Ypres had now begun, but as yet the enormous
numerical superiority of the Germans in this part of the
line was not known, and the idea generally prevalent was
that the 1st Division was to advance towards Thorout.

On October 21st, the 2nd Brigade, which had become
corps reserve, was ordered to march to Pilckem. Owing
to the congested state of the roads, a detour was made,
and the brigade went by way of Ypres, then a very
different place from the battered mass of ruins which it

E I

became later. On arrival at the ill-fated town at about 11 a.m., the brigade was halted, as news had come through of an attack from the south-east. Reserves were rare and precious things in those early days, and there was a natural reluctance on the part of the Higher Command to commit them irrevocably to one part of the line when their presence might be more urgently required at the opposite extreme. However, the danger from the south-east was averted, but a slight modification of the original plan was made, the 48th alone proceeding to Pilckem, and the remainder of the brigade only about as far north as Boesinghe.

At about 7 p.m. the Northamptonshires arrived at Pilckem, which is a small hamlet about one and a half miles south of the Bixschoote—Langemarck road. The morning of the next day was spent, like every other spare moment available, in cleaning rifles, clothing, and equipment. In the afternoon German shells began to fall in and near the village, and the battalion at once occupied some trenches close at hand, which had been dug by the French. Meanwhile, north of the line of the Bixschoote—Langemarck road, the 1st Camerons (1st Brigade) were with difficulty holding back an attack by overwhelmingly superior forces of the enemy, who were endeavouring to break our line at what must now be described as the northern extremity of the Ypres salient. After a most gallant defence, the Camerons were finally forced to abandon their trenches, and shortly after 7 p.m. the 48th were ordered up to their assistance.

A lane from Pilckem comes up from the south-east, and crosses the Bixschoote—Langemarck road nearly at right angles. At the cross-road thus formed is a small group of buildings, centreing round an inn. About half a mile farther in the eastern or Langemarck direction, the road from Bixschoote crosses a stream. Half way between the stream and the inn, on the northern side of the road, is a mill. The country here is flat and fairly well wooded. When the Northampton-

shires arrived on the scene, the Camerons had been
driven right out of their trenches, which lay about 800
yards north of the road, and were endeavouring to make
a stand to the west and south of the inn, now in the
hands of the enemy. " C " and " D " Companies were
at once pushed up on the right of the lane leading to
Pilckem, and succeeded in retaking the mill and in
driving the Germans out of the sunken road, which
they then occupied, connecting up on the right with the
Black Watch and on the left with the remnants of the
Camerons and a company of the Coldstream Guards
who had also come up to reinforce the Camerons.

It was now resolved to attack the inn before daybreak,
and this task was entrusted to " A " Company, now
under the command of Captain Russell. The attacking
force, acting in conjunction with the Camerons, reached
the inn, but, being unable to force an entrance in the
face of the heavy fire of the enemy, they were then
compelled to retire. Captain Russell lost his life while
leading this attack. Throughout the night fighting
continued, the Germans being in superior and rapidly-
increasing numbers. By daybreak on the 23rd the
60th Rifles and the Loyal North Lancashires had come
up on the left of the line, which had been seriously
threatened by the enemy, while The Queen's advanced
through the 48th and the Camerons to attack the inn.
This time the assault was successful; the inn was taken,
and about 350 Germans were captured with it. Meanwhile " B " Company, which had been in reserve
behind a hedge west of the lane, had sent a platoon to
reinforce " A " Company, as the latter company had
suffered many casualties.

October 23rd was spent in improving the hastily-dug
trenches that the 48th had made by the side of the
road. The German artillery was busy throughout the
day, battalion headquarters and the reserve company in
particular being subjected to an extremely heavy fire.
Our own gunners found great difficulty in obtaining
suitable positions for the British artillery, owing to the

flat nature of the ground. 'At 6 p.m. that evening the enemy attacked all along the line, and succeeded in regaining possession of the inn. Another attack was made on " C " and " D " Companies during the night, but it was repelled.

Shelling continued intermittently through the next day, the reserve company again being the chief sufferers. In the afternoon German shells set fire to the mill that stood in the vicinity of the centre companies of the 48th. Houses and haystacks were on fire in all directions, and when dusk fell the whole countryside was lit up by bright jets of flame. At 6 p.m. the enemy made another determined general attack, which was preceded by heavy artillery, machine-gun, and rifle fire. But the men of the 48th, hungry and exhausted as they were, held their ground stubbornly, and after an hour and a half the Germans, who had sustained severe losses from the well-directed fire of the defenders, retired in disorder.

It had been announced that the battalion would be relieved by the French that night, and during the temporary lull that followed the repulse of the German attack the relieving force came up. Everything was going smoothly, when suddenly the burning mill, which had been smouldering quietly for some time, flared up into a sudden blaze, illuminating the whole landscape. At once the Germans opened artillery and rifle fire, and although very few casualties were incurred, the relief was delayed for about an hour, and it was not till about 3 a.m. that the last company reached the village of Pilckem. Here tea was served to the tired men, and, when the whole brigade had assembled, it marched off to Ypres, which was reached about 6 a.m. The remainder of the day was devoted to a much-needed rest, for everybody was in a state of absolute exhaustion after the strenuous exertions of the past three days.

The casualties sustained in the fight near Pilckem were about 150 in all. In addition to Captain Russell, whose death has already been recorded, Captain Lochrin (the regimental medical officer) and Captain Bentley were both killed. The last-named officer lost his life just as the relief of his company, " C," was being completed. In addition, Captain Pope was so seriously wounded as to be permanently incapacitated for active service, while Captain D. W. Powell, Captain Sir F. Robinson, Lieutenant E. J. Needham and Second-Lieutenant B. Eden were all wounded. The Northamptonshires were thus deprived of the services of several of their most valuable company officers at a time when the need for them was most pressing. The Battle of Ypres was only just beginning, and many days of stern fighting awaited the old 48th.

At that time Ypres " was a lovely place, hardly touched by shell fire "—to use the words of one enthusiast, who must have radically altered his opinion when he saw that unfortunate city during the later stages of the war. The battalion was billeted in a reformatory school on the outskirts of the town, but it was not to enjoy this comfort for long. The Northamptonshires remained merely for twenty-four hours in their billets, and at 8 a.m. on October 26th they marched out along the Menin road to Hooge, where they halted for some time, finally bivouacking in a field by the roadside.

From La Bassée to the sea the great battle was raging, and, at this stage, the main feature of it was that the thinly-held British line was in perpetual danger of being broken by enormous masses of attacking Germans. Hence it came about that the scanty reserves, even at a time when they were supposed to be resting, were continually marched this way and that so as to be ready to give instant support to a threatened portion of the line. Thus during the next few days the Northamptonshires were hurriedly moved from one position to another as the needs of the situation dictated. October 27th saw them bivouacked in a wood near Harenthage Château, just south of the Menin road and a mile and a half east of Hooge. On the

28th they moved to dug-outs on the western edge of Polygon Wood. Next day they returned to their former position near the château. All this time the fighting in front of them was continuing with an ever-increasing intensity.

At 9 a.m. on October 30th, the Northamptonshires and the Royal Sussex were ordered to move to a small wood which was known in later years as Bodmin Copse. Bodmin Copse lies south of the Menin road and about a mile and a half due west of Gheluvelt. Here the two battalions, which now came under the orders of the 7th Division, took up a defensive position. Trenches were rapidly dug, the 48th occupying the southern and eastern edges of the copse, while the Royal Sussex held the northern side. " B," " D " and " A " Companies of the Northamptonshires were from right to left in the front line, while " C " remained with the battalion headquarters on the western side of the copse. South of Bodmin Copse, and connected with it by a track, lay the irregularly-shaped wood which was afterwards called Shrewsbury Forest. On the right of " B " Company, entrenched in a strip of open country with several cottages in their immediate front, were the 2nd Gordon Highlanders, a battalion of the 7th Division.

Saturday, October 31st, was the critical day in the Battle of Ypres. At an early hour in the morning the Germans began a heavy bombardment of Gheluvelt, and by about mid-day the village was in the enemy's hands. The Germans were about 200 to 300 yards from the battalion, but except for a continuous rifle fire there was no actual attack made during the morning, although, of course, intense gun and rifle fire was heard to the north, indicating the German attack along the Menin road by Gheluvelt. During this phase the battalion suffered a number of casualties, including Captain Cartwright, who was seriously wounded. Then the morning wore away until about 1 p.m., when the commanding officer received a message directing him to report at brigade headquarters. Accompanied by his adjutant, the commanding officer repaired as directed, and was there informed that, in consequence of the situation on the left, it would be necessary to withdraw slightly the line of the 1st Northamptonshire Regiment. The necessary orders were soon issued, and the withdrawal began.

Running from the position of the battalion back to Shrewsbury Forest was a sunken lane which afforded a kind of covered way to shelter the retiring companies. At first the withdrawal was not seriously interfered with, but the Germans were pressing on with great determination, and, as the Gordons had retired, the 1st Northamptonshires were subjected to a very heavy enfilading fire, while at the same time the Germans were following the rearmost company very closely. It was now that most of the casualties were incurred. Second-Lieutenants Sherriff and Jarvis were killed; and Second-Lieutenant Phillpot was wounded, and about 100 other ranks were struck down. None the less the retirement was carried out in good order, and finally the whole battalion reached the cross-roads in Shrewsbury Forest, where it rallied, re-formed, and awaited further orders. Soon it was led to form a line along the front of the forest. " I remember," writes the adjutant, " how difficult it was to get this line formed, as the Germans were already through part of the wood and pressing our brigade back." While this fire fight was in progress the adjutant was sent back by the commanding officer to report the situation to the brigadier. The brigade headquarters were in a ride in the forest to the left of the battalion. A cottage hard by was in flames; the wood was filled with the smoke of rifle and shell fire; and " things in general looked very serious."

Brigadier-General Bulfin, having received the report, directed the battalion to hang on at all costs, and declared that help would be sent. Meanwhile, in the front line plans had been made for a counter-attack, and as the triumphant Germans poured through the forest the 48th, together with the Royal Sussex and Gordons, with loud cheers charged them with the bayonet. The issue was not long in doubt. 'After a few minutes' hand-to-hand fighting the enemy broke and fled back to Bodmin Copse, leaving many of their number, dead and dying, behind them. " I have never seen so many German dead at any other time of the war," writes one officer of the battalion, who had plenty of opportunity later of making the comparison. " They were lying in heaps in a shallow ditch which ran on both sides of a ride in the wood." Two hundred were actually counted, and there were more lying scattered about at different points.

The Northamptonshires followed up their successful charge by an attempt to recapture Bodmin Copse, but their farther advance was held up by machine-gun fire from the cottages. The retreating Germans now rallied, and the struggle continued during the greater part of the night. It finally proved impossible to retake the copse, and the battalion entrenched themselves in an irregular line along the northern edge of Shrewsbury Forest, " D " Company being on the right, with " B " on the other flank.

This position was held during the greater part of the following day, the Grenadier Guards being on the left of the battalion and the Irish Guards on the right, the Guards Brigade having been moved up on November 1st with the intention of retaking Bodmin Copse and the remainder of the position vacated by our troops on October 31st. It was soon seen that this was impossible, and the idea was given up. The battalion came under the orders of General Lord Cavan. " D " Company was once driven from its trenches by the artillery fire of the enemy, but a German attempt to occupy the position from which our men had been forced was frustrated by the accurate and rapid rifle fire of those who still held their ground. Towards the evening of November 1st it was decided to straighten the line, as the part held by the left of the battalion formed a dangerous salient. After nightfall, trenches were dug in a straight line running through the middle of Shrewsbury Forest, and were occupied without difficulty. A section of the trenches occupied by " A " Company, which was now on the left, lay beyond the wood in open country. A welcome reinforcement, consisting of Captain Coldwell (of the Reserve), Captain Crowe (of the Royal Warwickshire Regiment), Second-Lieutenant Whitehouse (of the Royal West Kents), and 60 men, arrived during the night and was at once sent into the trenches. Captain Darwell and Second-Lieutenant R. H. Marshall had been wounded during the struggle for Bodmin Copse, and Lieutenant Warren in the course of the following day, so the question of officers was becoming a very critical one. Brigadier-General Bulfin was wounded during the day.

On November 2nd the Germans shelled the exposed trenches on the left of " A " Company, Second-Lieutenant Whitehouse and several men being killed. At night, several attacks were launched against the trenches, which were now only a short distance from those of the enemy, and had for protection in front nothing but a single strand of barbed wire. But the men, though wearied by continual fighting and badly in need of sleep, never relaxed their vigilance, and each German onslaught was met by a well-directed burst of rifle fire, before which it melted away.

No attack took place on November 3rd, but shell fire continued throughout the day with scarcely any intermission. Just before dawn on November 4th, the enemy, after a particularly heavy bombardment, again attempted to carry the trenches by assault, but once more they were beaten back by the rifle fire of the defenders. During the night of November 4th the battalion was relieved by the Royal Sussex, and went back into close support. There was no respite from the continual shelling, however; indeed, the support line suffered almost more than the advanced positions. Seven men lost their lives from hostile shell fire on November 5th, among them Company Sergeant-Major

Good, who had done excellent work ever since the beginning of the war.

On the night of November 7th the 1st Northamptonshire Regiment again occupied the front line trenches, where they were relieved a day later by the King's Own Scottish Borderers. The battalion then moved back into local reserve, and went into dug-outs just south of Hooge. On November 9th Lieutenant-Colonel Osborne-Smith was evacuated to hospital, and Major Norman assumed command of the battalion. That evening the battalion—or rather, what was left of it, for by now it was sadly depleted in numbers—moved to the north side of the Menin road and occupied a trench in the support line which had previously been held by a Zouave regiment. Here it again came under heavy shell fire, Captain Crowe being killed. As Captain Coldwell was evacuated to hospital about this time, the shortage of officers once more became acute.

November 11th witnessed the great attack by the Prussian Guard—the last desperate attempt of the Germans to break through the line still held by the unconquerable remnant of the British Army. Soon after 9 a.m. the Northamptonshires received word that the enemy had forced their way through the 1st Brigade near Polygon Wood. The 48th were moved off to reinforce the line at this point, and occupied the eastern edge of Nonne Bosschen Wood. Polygon Wood was situated some 500 yards to the west of them, a tract of open country lying between. On the north, the two woods were nearly connected by a copse that lay between them. On the south, the road to Reutel fringes the skirts of both woods, and is lined by a hedge on its northern side. At 11 a.m. orders were received to advance into Polygon Wood. " D " Company, on the left, moved forward through the copse and sustained comparatively little damage, but the remainder of the battalion came under a deadly fire from the right flank, where the Germans were in force. The enemy's machine gunners had occupied some houses south of the Reutel road, and from these they were able to enfilade our advancing lines with considerable effect. The 48th thereupon wheeled to the right, took up a position along the hedge, and engaged the enemy, who were now advancing in force. Just at this time Major Norman was killed, and his adjutant (Captain G. St. G. Robinson) wounded. The latter officer was subsequently awarded the Military Cross for the gallantry which he had displayed in this battle. The command of the battalion now devolved upon Lieutenant Farrar.

Although the rifle fire of the Northamptonshires checked the frontal advance of the Germans, the position was one of extreme danger, as the left flank was very exposed. Second-Lieutenant Vandal, of the Royal West Kent Regiment, who had been attached to the 48th shortly before the move from the Aisne, was killed during this part of the engagement; Second-Lieutenant R. Davison was wounded. However, the arrival of the Oxfordshire and Buckinghamshire Light Infantry on the left secured that flank, and the Northamptonshires entrenched themselves along the line of the hedge and prepared to resist a fresh attack.

None came. The German attempt to break the British line on November 11th had been their last effort. This day's fighting was the closing act of the First Battle of Ypres. Both sides were utterly exhausted by close on a month of sustained and bitter fighting, which had thinned their ranks, drained their supply of ammunition, and left them no available reserves to be used for a further effort. Although the French commander on the Yser contemplated renewing the offensive after his troops had had a period of rest and retirement, General Joffre felt that the operations on the Flanders front had reached a fitting termination with the repulse of the enemy's last desperate effort. The defensive was therefore enjoined. The battle of Flanders was at an end. The Channel ports were saved. And the opposing armies, their front stabilized along all the line from the North Sea to Switzerland, settled down with the approach of winter to trench warfare. For four more days the 1st Battalion held the trenches that they had constructed behind the hedge, then on the night of November 15th they were relieved and marched back to Vlamertinghe.

The fragment of a battalion that entered Vlamertinghe on the morning of November 16th presented a spectacle very different from the 48th that had marched away from Blackdown so cheerfully barely three months before. A subaltern of the Special Reserve was now acting as their commanding officer, and the only combatant officers besides Lieutenant Farrar were Second-Lieutenant Lewis, of the Royal West Kents, and Second-Lieutenant C. S. Cowley, who had just rejoined. Lieutenant Hofman (the quartermaster) and Lieutenant Adie (the medical officer) were still with the battalion. The entire strength of the rank and file was about 350. Like their officers, they were unshaven, ragged, dirty, and utterly exhausted.

In some ways it may be said that the First Battle of Ypres marks the end of the old 48th. From that time onward the regular officers and men of the battalion who had left Blackdown were always a minority, and an ever-dwindling minority at that, in the 1st Northamptonshires. Yet throughout the war a certain leaven of those who had taken part in the campaign of 1914 remained in the battalion, and endeavoured, not without success, to instil into the newcomers something of the splendid regimental traditions that had brought the old 48th so gloriously through the great Battle of Ypres.

Captain Thunder had arrived at Vlamertinghe on the 15th with a draft of 100 men for the regiment, and as senior officer he took over command when the battalion came down from the line during the night of November 15th/16th. After a short rest the march was resumed to Westoutre, everyone very tired after the hard spell in the line. That night the battalion billeted in Westoutre, and on the following day it marched to

Strazeele. The road was very congested with French infantry, guns and transport moving up to Ypres, " and if we got off the *pavé* the mud was very deep and the going heavy." Owing to this and to the congestion, the march took a considerable time. Strazeele was far from proving a haven of rest. To begin with there was a heavy fall of snow, which in places lay five to six inches deep, and "the billets were horrible, most stables or chicken-runs or anywhere we could find shelter." "Remained in billets" is the entry for November 18th. The brigadier saw all commanding officers during the morning and gave the welcome intelligence that the battalion was to start refitting and reorganizing—a procedure actually laborious but almost a rest cure in comparison with life in the line. In the evening Captain Humphrey joined with a draft of 300 men. There was no accommodation for them, so they were billeted in the church, which at any rate was an improvement on the chicken-runs and stables.

On the 19th the Northamptonshires marched to Hazebrouck. Before they left, the *curé* of Strazeele thanked the commanding officer for the good state in which the men had left the church. At Hazebrouck the battalion started refitting. Hazebrouck was a large town, with excellent facilities as regards baths, which were much appreciated. It had amenities, too, or as one chronicler puts it, "the evening was for our own pleasure, which we never forgot."

Successive drafts of officers and men had brought the 48th once more to something approaching full strength, but the officer question was serious. The majority of the junior subalterns now joining the battalion were undergraduates or other young men of a similar type, who had undergone some form of O.T.C. training, but whose service in the Special Reserve dated only from the beginning of the war. The rank and file, on the other hand, contained a large proportion of re-enlisted and Section D men. The heavy demands for drafts had denuded the 3rd Battalion of almost all the younger

Army Reservists and the best of the Special Reserve. The young soldiers who had joined since the beginning of the war had not received sufficient training to render them fit to be sent out, while comparatively few of those who had been wounded in the earlier engagements had as yet fully recovered from their injuries. Thus, in order to bring the reinforcement drafts up to the requisite strength, it was necessary to include some men whose advancing years unfitted them for the rigours of a winter campaign.

The month at Hazebrouck passed very pleasantly. Training took place daily, but it was not of an exceptionally strenuous nature. On November 28th Sir John French inspected the battalion (" we waited for two hours in pouring rain before they arrived "), when he congratulated it on " having borne the brunt of the fighting and borne it well." His Majesty King George inspected the 2nd Brigade on December 3rd, and expressed to Captain Thunder his satisfaction at seeing the men looking so fit after their trying time. Major Dobbin rejoined the battalion on the 16th and took command, with Lieutenant Farrar as adjutant. Captain Thunder shortly afterwards became staff captain of the 2nd Brigade.

On December 19th the battalion received a warning to be ready to move at short notice, as a general outburst of activity was taking place in the line. At 7 a.m. on December 21st, the 48th were taken away from Hazebrouck in a long string of motor omnibuses, and arrived at Vielle Chapelle about noon. The period of rest was over, and once again the 48th had to face the rigours of the front line. The new scene of their activities was the district near Festubert, to the north-west of La Bassée. The Indian troops had here been driven from their trenches by the enemy, and an immediate counter-attack was necessary to regain the positions that they had lost.

From Vielle Chapelle the battalion marched to Le Touret, together with the Loyal North Lancashires.

On its arrival at this hamlet, which was close behind the line, orders were given for a night attack upon the trenches that the enemy had captured near La Quinque Rue. As the ground on which the operations were to take place was entirely unknown to everyone concerned, the task assigned to the two battalions was an extremely difficult one. The attack was launched at about 7 p.m., " A " and " D " being the leading companies of the Northamptonshires. The latter suffered severely. Captain H. H. O'Brien was wounded in the face at the very beginning of the attack; 2/Lieutenant J. T. R. Pastfield, attached from the Middlesex Regiment, was killed while leading his men to the assault ; 2/Lieutenant Wainwright was mortally wounded. By 10 p.m. the greater part of the lost trenches had been retaken. The total casualties incurred were about 60.

In accordance with the orders given the previous evening, the Northamptonshires were withdrawn from the recaptured trenches before dawn, the task of garrisoning them being left to the Loyal North Lancashires. " D " Company of the 48th, which was now commanded by Major W. O. Cautley, of the Suffolk Regiment, remained to complete the left of the line, the rest of the Northamptonshires going back to billets a mile or so in rear. It was fortunate that they remained so close at hand, for before they had been in their billets two hours they were hurriedly summoned out again. The North Lancashires had been driven from their trenches by a German attack, and a dangerous breach had been made in the line. Major Cautley had withdrawn his company some 600 yards to a line of trenches, which he was holding with the help of men from various units. The three remaining companies took up a position in support of " D " and remained there until relieved by the 4th Brigade after nightfall.

In a Special Brigade Order issued a few days later, Brigadier-General C. B. Westmacott stated that he desired " to take the opportunity of congratulating

F

'D' Company of the 1st Northamptonshire Regiment on its gallant and steady behaviour during the action of December 22nd. The manner in which, under Major W. O. Cautley, it resisted the German attack, and the steadiness with which it finally withdrew in the face of superior numbers, and eventually occupied a position in rear to cover the gap made in the line, was worthy of all praise and adds fresh laurels to the fine records of the old 48th."

Major Cautley was subsequently awarded the D.S.O. for his conduct upon this occasion. 2/Lieutenant T. C. Fulton, who also distinguished himself in this engagement, received the Military Cross. Sergeants Lodge and Pippet, and Private Cockerill, all three of "D" Company, were awarded the D.C.M.

After being relieved by the 4th Brigade, the battalion went back to Essars, where Christmas Day was spent in billets. Next day they relieved the 6th Brigade, who were holding the trenches east of Givenchy. The weather was now exceptionally severe, and many of the devices which were discovered later to mitigate the hardships of the trenches in winter time were then unknown. The misery suffered by some of the older men from the wretched conditions of the Givenchy trenches beggars description. The officers, generally speaking, were younger and better provided with appliances to make the rigours of the climate more endurable, yet, even so, no less than five of them were invalided home with "trench foot" during this period.

CHAPTER IV.

WHILE the 1st Battalion of the Northamptonshire Regiment was submitting to the first round of the process of extermination which was to last throughout the war, the 2nd Battalion arrived on the Western Front. When war was declared the old 58th was stationed in Mustapha Barracks, Alexandria, Egypt, and little over a month had passed since it had played an Austrian man-of-war's team at football and entertained them also. So soon as a state of war had been declared the battalion set about training the Europeans residing in Alexandria for their part in the conflict, and mopping up many spies round the place. Several officers were home on leave, some of them having travelled on a German East Africa liner, which omitted Southampton as a port of call and proceeded straight to Hamburg. Luckily the three Northamptonshire officers got off at Marseilles and travelled across France. Most of the officers of the 2nd Battalion in England rushed to Blackdown to endeavour to wangle an attachment to the 48th, "having collected very scratch kits from Moss Brothers and other places." Eventually they were shepherded to the 3rd Battalion at Weymouth, there to await the arrival of the 58th from Egypt.

The original Expeditionary Force had consisted of one cavalry division, six divisions " of all arms " and some line of communication troops. Within a month the whole of this force was in the field, the 6th Division being the last to come into line—on the Aisne on September 16th. It was, of course, soon evident that an army of such dimensions, in a struggle of such magnitude, was about as much use as a celluloid fan in hell. The first step was to expand the regulars. A

7th Division had been raised at home from unallotted units. To an 8th Division the colonial stations mainly contributed. And three divisions of British troops from India, to which were allotted the numbers 27, 28 and 29, were put under orders. In addition, there were purely Indian divisions now in France. Over and above these there were fourteen Territorial divisions, of which a large part had accepted liability for service overseas, and Lord Kitchener had called for 500,000 recruits for the New—or " Kitchener," or, more briefly, " K "—Armies. The 2nd Battalion Northamptonshire Regiment was to form one of the units of the 24th Brigade of the 8th Division.

In Egypt there arrived, towards the end of August, a Territorial division from home to take over the garrisoning of that country. The 58th assisted it to disembark, and then its own turn came to embark for the seat of war, joining the Worcestershires, from Cairo, on board the ss. *Desiardo*. Protection was supplied by an escort of French cruisers as far as Marseilles, to which port the *Desiardo* was taken in error. Two or three days were spent there, whilst the authorities discussed whether the troops were to go over-land or not. Eventually the voyage was resumed to Gibraltar, unescorted. From thence the transport was escorted by H.M.S. *Carnarvon*. Off the coast of Spain she carried out target practice, the transport towing the target about a quarter of a mile astern. The subalterns of the battalion, who were detailed to mark, were much impressed at the accuracy of the shooting. In due course the battalion arrived at Liverpool, where it entrained for Winchester.

The camp there was situated in Hursley Park, and the surrounding country was alive with game. A well-thrown stone often caused a casualty, and many a bird found its way into the company messes. Towards the end of October the weather became very wet. The camp was soon a sea of mud. Heroic efforts were made to ladle the stuff into waterproof sheets and to remove it, but this, if anything, made matters worse. The Sherwood Foresters, who were in the brigade, had just come from Bombay, and suffered very much from the weather, as they had to live in foreign service khaki drill for over three weeks, there being no service dress available. Luckily the 58th had this kit with them.

The division was visited and lectured to by Sir Henry Rawlinson, who came over from France "full of the troubles which had overtaken the 7th Division." That division had landed at Zeebrugge and Ostend, and had suffered very severely before it joined up with the remainder of the British Army round Ypres. Out of some 400 officers, over 340 had become casualties. "We went to the lecture feeling very cheerful, but came away feeling as if we had had a good thrashing, and that apparently we had no chance of beating the Germans."

This was soon to be put to the test. On November 3rd and 4th, the division marched to Southampton. By this time, the first enthusiasm for the war had evaporated and the march through the streets evoked no cheer from the inhabitants.

The ship allotted to the 58th was an ex-cattle vessel, the *Turcoman,* and "the smell inside her was positively fearsome." There was practically no accommodation for either officers or men, and sleep was to be had only in the alleyways between decks. About 8 p.m. on the 4th, the vessel cleared for Havre, where it arrived without incident early next morning. The 58th marched into a camp above the town, and two or three days later entrained for the front. Thirty hours of tedious travelling brought the battalion to Merville, where it detrained, moving into billets at Vieux Berquin. On arrival in France the 2nd Battalion was organized as follows :—

Headquarters.

Lieutenant-Colonel C. S. Prichard.
Major C. E. Higginbotham, Second-in-Command.
Captain H. Power, Adjutant.

Lieutenant R. Mayes, Quartermaster.
Lieutenant U. Rastrick, Machine Gun Officer.
Lieutenant B. O. Smyth, Transport Officer.
Lieutenant O. Ryan, Medical Officer.
Regimental Sergeant-Major G. Lee.
Regimental Quartermaster-Sergeant W. R. Collins.

"A" Company.

Captain J. I. Wood-Martin.
Captain O. Oakes, Yorkshire Regiment (attached).
Lieutenant St. L. C. Stocker.
Lieutenant S. H. Sprey-Smith.
Second-Lieutenant G. A. Parker.
Company Sergeant-Major Morris.
Company Quartermaster-Sergeant Smith.

" B " Company.

Captain L. J. Robinson.
Captain L. A. Haldane.
Lieutenant A. D. Middleton.
Lieutenant R. E. Lucy.
Second-Lieutenant C. Z. de la P. Beresford.
Second-Lieutenant E. B. L. Rushton.
Company Sergeant-Major Carvell.
Company Quartermaster-Sergeant Buckby.

" C " Company.

Captain A. G. C. Capell.
Captain C. D. Elston.
Lieutenant S. H. Beattie.
Lieutenant R. D. Lake.
Lieutenant G. T. Shaw.
Second-Lieutenant C. Belding.
Company Sergeant-Major Palmer.
Company Quartermaster-Sergeant Jackson.

" D " Company.

Captain C. R. J. Mowatt.
Captain C. H. R. Watts.
Lieutenant H. W. Jackson.

Lieutenant W. G. A. Coldwell.
Lieutenant O. K. Parker.
Second-Lieutenant G. D. Gordon.
Company Sergeant-Major A. Fisk.
Company Quartermaster-Sergeant C. Asplin.

The expression, "Going up into the line," had now become current, and its use signifies the change which had come over the Western Front. Open warfare had given place to close; mobile operations were replaced by static; "trench warfare" had come to stay. The 58th duly went into the line. Some amusement was caused by the capture of an alleged spy by "C" Company, "at which the company commander rather specialized." In this case, the spy was dressed in a dark blue greatcoat, and on being interrogated could only mumble indistinctly. The hearts of the spy-chasers burned within them with excitement and revenge, but a further examination by the light of a torch revealed a private of the Suffolks wounded in the mouth and on his way to the nearest first-aid post.

The first tour in the trenches lasted seven days. During the first two days it rained heavily, and throughout the last five there was a succession of sharp frosts and snow. The trenches—very shallow, and filled with straw, which made the subsequent deepening a very laborious affair—had been originally dug by the Lahore Division, now on the right of the 58th, and in order to secure some trace of warmth and shelter the Indians had burrowed under the parapet in many places. The men of the 58th sometimes ventured to enlarge these recesses, but with disastrous results, for the parapet kept falling in here and there. Loopholes were constructed wherever possible and were "blinded" with mud. In some places the German line was only seventy yards away, so that casualties in the 58th were frequent, the majority, of course, being head wounds. Worse even than the risk from a sniper's bullet was the suffering caused by the weather and the mud. Sleep was possible only from exhaustion : cooking had to be carried out individually. Judging by later standards, shell fire was negligible, but the proximity of the enemy made movement in and out of the line possible only by night, and consequently the wounded had to remain in the trenches all day owing to the absence of communication trenches. During this first tour, Captain Elston was seriously wounded, and Lieutenant-Colonel Prichard—who, however, refused to go sick—was hit through the arm. On relief, the battalion moved into brigade reserve billets at Red Barn for three days.

The men took off their boots, for the first time for seven days, before dropping off to sleep. On waking, over one hundred men were unable to put them on again. Their feet had swollen to such an enormous extent that to do so was impossible. The sufferers had to go sick with frost-bite or " trench feet," as it came officially to be called. The second tour in the line was almost as severe an experience as the first. True, there was little frost, but it rained almost continuously. The loopholes in the parapet had proved dangerous, so notches were cut along the parapet, and casualties were thus reduced. The first officer death casualty in the 58th now occurred, Lieutenant Rastrick, the machine gun officer, being killed. Some new gadgets of war now made their appearance. Jam tin bombs were issued—" Tickler's Artillery," as they were named by the men, from Mr. Tickler, the jam manufacturer. About this time, too, the 58th got their first stove-pipe trench mortar. After three or four rounds, " it assumed the shape of a soda-water bottle and we left it alone." On relief this time, the battalion moved back to divisional reserve at La Gorgue.

During the brief rest, everything possible was done to get the stiffness out of the men, but, as nearly all were crippled with frost-bite, marching, in the real sense of the word, was out of the question. When marching up to the trenches, to relieve, it was sometimes found necessary to have " slow marching parties," called " lame ducks." Lieutenant Parker was put in charge of one of these, and his reminiscences throw a vivid light on conditions of that terrible winter of 1914-15. " We set out for the line two hours ahead of the company. Marched two hundred yards or so, then fell out on the side of the road, and, sitting down, put our feet up against trees or anything as high as possible to get the blood out of them. Stayed like this for two minutes or so and then marched again. When moving about the line in mud and water over one's boots, feet gave little trouble, but a road surface was killing."

How trying were conditions in the line will be realized when it is stated that all officers and non-commissioned officers as well as 75 per cent. of the men had to be on duty all night (14 hours). During daylight, officers had four hours off for sleep by company arrangements, and sleep was to some extent rendered possible by the issue of sandbags. These were filled with straw and one foot was thrust into each of two sandbags allotted. Messing was still an individual enterprise, but some attempts were made to cook by sections or platoons, using the men's canteens. " My men," writes a platoon commander, "found a huge black kettle one night. This was hung over a smouldering fire in the centre of the platoon sector, filled with water, and a large quantity of tea and sugar emptied into it. When men came along during the night, after taking a mug of tea from it they had to replenish the kettle with water from their bottles." Another platoon commander found a few men cooking on a small fireplace. Asking how they had made it, he was told that they had found three things like bricks. Fortunately he suspected " the bricks," as on examination they turned out to be hair-brush bombs, well muddied. Milk was, of course, unprocurable, but, to the universal joy, a goat was found—by this time, the verb "to find " had acquired a sinister significa-tion. It proved strangely reluctant to yield any juice, and, although various experts were called in, there was " nothing doing " and the dry and ungenerous animal was set free. The conditions in the trenches were now

exacting a severe toll from the personnel. One platoon
about 50 strong was reduced in three hours to 19 men,
with only one sergeant and two lance-corporals left of
the N.C.Os. Sickness from exposure was responsible
for 60 per cent. of the loss.

Of actual fighting there was but little. " Our sojourn
on this sector during the latter part of 1914 was broken
by only one real scrap. That was when we relieved
the Worcesters on one occasion. We discovered that
Fritz had sapped up to our part of the line and was
only a few yards away. Immediately the Worcesters
heard of this, they made arrangements to clear Fritz
out and went over one night, clearing the whole sap at
the point of the bayonet." There is mention, too, of
raids on a small scale. And there was one occasion
when a supply of portable wire entanglements was
brought up and hastily put in position in the dark.
They remained in position next day, but the second
dawn showed that " Fritz had them all in front of his
section of trenches." This was, of course, a little too
much, and " of course, they had to come back."

The year had now worn on to Christmas Day, and
in both armies there lingered a tradition that troops
facing each other from trenches but a few yards apart
should observe some kind of " Truce of God."
Generally speaking, the initiative was taken by the
enemy. On the Armentières sector the truce began on
the evening of the 24th, when the Saxons opened pro-
ceedings by chanting " Play the game, play the game.
If you don't shoot, we won't shoot," and so on *da capo*.

Thus ended 1914. The confident prophecy that the
war " would be over by Christmas " was dismally
unfulfilled, and it was becoming clear even to the most
unthinking that much blood would have to flow before
the goal was won. Nevertheless, in England the
prevailing sentiment was one of inane optimism. The
old Regular Army had been practically destroyed, but
—outside the ranks of the remaining professional
soldiers—a sure and early triumph was everywhere
expected. And, although the losses in the Old Army

had been terrible, the country, as a whole, had not
been brought face to face with reality, chiefly because
in pre-war days the Army had in a sense been a class
and a caste apart. Hundreds of thousands of civilians
had flown to arms, had swamped the recruiting booths,
and at the end of 1914 were being steadily trained so
far as shortage of arms, ammunition, clothing, camp
equipment and professional instructors would allow.
But other millions were still content to look on. In
London at the end of 1914 were still to be seen in
thousands young, lusty chauffeurs, strapping young
clerks, and stalwart vendors of lace and ribbons in
drapery establishments east and west. Some, indeed,
were at pains to show a vivid pro-Ally feeling, and
youth found an outlet for its expression by darting
about on motor-cycles with inefficient silencers and the
flags of the Allied Powers waving defiantly on the
handlebars.

There was a most amazing credulity in accepting as
gospel idiotic calculations made by " well-known
strategists "—sometimes civilians—in the Press. It
was proved by these experts in the most convincing
manner that Germany was at the end of her tether;
that her supply of men was running out; that her ranks
were filled by old fat men in spectacles or by very
emaciated boys; that she was already robbing the
cradle and the grave; that she had no more money;
that her people at home were starving; that the soldiers
at the front hated fighting and had to be flogged into
battle by their officers; that the German officers were
nothing like so good as had been thought; that they
cowered in dug-outs while the fighting was going on,
and spent the rest of their time getting drunk. Meanwhile, the remnants of the Old Army, patched up by
hastily and partially-trained reinforcements, were
standing in the mud and slime of the trenches and
silently enduring, in that awful winter of 1914-15,
sufferings to which the horrors even of the first
Crimean winter in some respects would have seemed a
veritable picnic.

CHAPTER V.

EARLY MONTHS OF 1915. THE BATTLE OF NEUVE CHAPELLE.

AFTER the glorious resistance of the French and British troops in the First Battle of Ypres, the war entered upon a new phase. War of movement had now become impossible, for, owing to the construction of a continuous barrier from the North Sea to the Swiss frontier, mobile operations now gave way perforce to trench warfare. For this class of warfare the Germans were considerably better equipped than the British. Not only had they studied and profited by the lessons of the Russo-Japanese War to the extent of making provision for hand grenades, searchlights, trench mortars and pistol flares, but they were also enormously favoured by conditions of terrain. The ebb and flow of attack and defence had left the Germans in Flanders almost everywhere in possession of the higher and drier ground, while in the lower strips water was found at a few feet and in some cases a few inches below the surface. In this latter terrain, the construction of adequate trenches was a physical impossibility, and, in such makeshift protection as could be got, the conditions were terrible. Lying in sodden and sometimes water-logged trenches, exposed to the fire of a vastly superior artillery, and opposite an enemy with weapons not at our disposal, the British infantry was called upon to endure as severe a test of constancy as occurred throughout the whole war.

In a previous chapter, the 48th were left in trenches at Givenchy, and it is there that the New Year of 1915 found them " All quiet : weather bad," as the war diary tersely states for January 1st. The following day, they were relieved by the 1st Battalion Coldstream

Guards and went back to billets at Annequin, a village some three miles south-west : their stay here was short, for, on the 3rd, the 48th shifted its billets forward a mile or so to Cambrin, and next day they were for the trenches again, relieving a battalion of the 60th Rifles in trenches just east of Cuinchy.   Here a junction of a line from the south with the main Lille—La Bassée—Bethune railway formed what was known as the Railway Triangle.   The trenches here were found to be much drier than those occupied in the previous tour.

The weather had now definitely improved, and the following two days are logged as " quiet," a term which, however, implies no cessation from noise, for there is clear evidence that our artillery was particularly active, and the term " quiet " may usually be taken as indicating simply a freedom from annoyance by the enemy's guns or infantry, or an absence of any definite operations.   The halcyon spell was, however, too good to last for long.   On January 10th, the 60th Rifles carried out a small local attack, the 1st Northampton-shires being detailed as support.   The small operation was successful, even though the Germans made a counter-attack in the evening, when " C " Company of the 48th was sent up in support.   The casualties in the Northamptonshires were slight, but the battalion had to mourn the loss of one of its officers killed—Lieutenant A. L. Airy.   The next day, the 2nd Royal Sussex relieved and the 48th went back to its billets at Cambrin, from which village for ten days or so it played Box and Cox with the 60th Rifles, the two battalions exchanging billets for trench in succession. A kind of " stand easy " ensued on the 21st, when the whole brigade was relieved by the 1st Brigade, and went back to the comparative civilization and rest afforded by Bethune.   But after three days, it was necessary to move forward again to Cambrin owing to a slight reverse which had been suffered by the 1st Brigade.   The so-called " rest " now definitely came to an end, for on the 27th the battalion once more relieved the 60th at Cuinchy. On this day, 2/Lieutenant Campling was wounded in the wrist while supervising the construction of a trench to connect our lines with those of the French on the right. He had been promoted from the ranks of the 58th. The battalion at this time had among its subalterns several warrant officers and N.C.Os., including 2/Lieutenants Clark, Pitcher and McNaught. The services of these experienced veterans were of especial value now that the majority of the subalterns were young officers with only a few months' service.

January 29th was the Kaiser's birthday, and his generals hoped to make him a present of the Cuinchy position. Accordingly, after a trench mortar bombardment, an attack was launched against our front line, which was then held by " D " Company under Major Cautley, and " B " Company under Captain Dickson. This attack, being met by a well-directed rifle fire, was easily repulsed with considerable German casualties. Our losses during the day were about 20 men killed and 25 wounded. 2/Lieutenant Nelles of " B " Company, a young officer with barely a month's service, was shot through the head and killed while delivering a message to Major Cautley; 2/Lieutenant Pillars of " D " was wounded.

This was the last episode of importance during the battalion's stay in the Cuinchy area. On January 30th, the 2nd Brigade was relieved. A few days were spent in Bethune, where the battalion was inspected by Major-General Haking, who had assumed command of the 1st Division after Major-General Lomax had been mortally wounded near Ypres. The 48th then marched to Allouange, where they remained throughout the month of February, reorganizing and training.

Some idea of the havoc wrought by the abnormally bad conditions of the trenches that winter may be gathered from the fact that during this period of rest nearly 500 men were drafted to the battalion to bring it up to strength again. Two officers who have been mentioned before, Captain Mylne and Captain Sir F. Robinson, rejoined the battalion about this time, while Lieutenant Bourdillon replaced Lieutenant Adie, the medical officer, who was invalided home. Colonel Osborne Smith rejoined the battalion for a few days, but his health again broke down, and Major Dobbin once more became commanding officer, with Major C. R. J. Mowatt, who had joined the battalion at Cuinchy, as second-in-command, and Captain Farrar as adjutant.

For the first eight days of March, the battalion was in billets in Oblinghem, a village two miles north-west of Bethune, whence it was shifted to Locon, the 2nd Brigade now being in Army Reserve. On the 14th, the 2nd Brigade relieved the 3rd in the Festubert sector and for a week the 48th were in and out of the line in the usual way. On March 22nd, the 1st Brigade was relieved at La Quinque Rue. Here the battalion had to take over a very long strip, but everything was very quiet, and at the end of the month the 48th were in billets behind Locon.

During these months, the 2nd Battalion was in the neighbourhood. The axis, so to speak, of the positions of the 48th was the line Béthune—La Bassée, while the 58th was generally about Estaires, a mere ten miles to the north. The conditions, climatic and topographical, were therefore more or less the same, and if the war diary of the 48th is undoubtedly rather meagre for this period we can fill in the picture from the distinctly more generous flow of information yielded by the pen of the adjutant of the sister battalion.

The new year found the 58th in billets at La Gorgue. At that time, the burning question was boots, for dry feet were impossible in the water-logged trenches, with the usual foot covering. The adjutant decided to deliver himself of a monograph, in which the virtues and vices of all classes of boots then in vogue at the front should be set down in detail. Gum boots had their advantages, but, as the adjutant pointed out, they were useless when the surrounding water was higher than the top of the boot. A new pattern ammunition boot was also examined, but as, equally with the old, it admitted water freely, it had no special claims for recognition. The adjutant concluded that waders required some beating, " as the water is often more than knee-deep." The memorandum apparently never got further than the orderly room. There is the pencilled remark on it, " Not worth sending on," in rather colonelish script. But it is pinned to the war diary, and the information in it is of considerable value as giving the historian a good idea of what trench conditions were like at the time.

There is a note that January 6th passed "quietly," but that the term is merely comparative is shown by the reference to a continuous fire from the British guns. There is a reference, too, under this date to "a trench cannon known as Archibald and which fired a jam-pot bomb." This seems to be one of the earliest mentions of the nick-name which in course of time came to be associated entirely with anti-aircraft guns. The casualties for the week were 5 killed and 18 wounded, in the latter being included Lieutenant S. H. Sprey-Smith. Water at this time was an enemy no less objectionable than the Germans. The communication trenches were in a dreadful state and most of the battalion when relieved preferred the risk of moving back across the open to wading knee-deep by the safer way. And so back to a two-day spell in billets—Red Barn this time. " Weather awful. Incessant rain," are words which tell their own story.

When the 58th went back to the line on the 9th to relieve the 1st Worcestershires, the heavy rain had made the trenches in an awful condition. In places the water was waist deep, and, in order that the line should be tenable at all, it was decided to build parapets behind the fire trenches. In the worst sectors, breastworks were erected. Another 33 of the battalion had now to be written off, 11 killed and the remainder wounded.

Three days of this misery were endured, and then there was a similar spell of rest in billets at La Gorgue. At least, so much rest as was compatible with "wire cutting day and night, and practice in throwing bombs and grenades." But, at any rate, there was firm ground to stand on, and the war diarist records with gratitude "a very peaceful three days."

This cheeriness received a sharp set-back on the 18th, when the battalion went into the trenches once again, to find that the dreadful weather conditions were aggravated by a heavy fall of snow. There was a distinct set-off, however, by an issue of seven days' leave to a proportion of officers and men. Until the end of the month, there was just the usual in and out of the line, exchanging trenches for billets and *vice versa*. Grenades were now coming well to the fore and threatened to become almost a stunt. Grenade and bomb-throwing practice became frequent. A grenadier company was formed in each brigade, the 58th contributing 28 other ranks under Lieutenant G. A. Parker. The weather conditions can be summed up by the ominous words, rain, frost, thaw; there was, indeed, a bright moon at night, but its brilliance had the effect, unfortunately, of interfering with reliefs. A novelty was tried towards the end of January by bringing up wagons as close as possible on relief nights. The distance to billets at La Gorgue was about five miles and the men were offered the choice of being carried on wagons or by "Shanks's mare." Only a dozen or so chose to walk. Not much time was actually saved, but the men's feet gained considerably. About this time, the strength of the battalion was about 500 of all ranks; the sector was a "quiet" one, but there was still a steady drip of casualties, 5 killed and 15 wounded being a normal week's bill. February brought about a slight change for the better all round. The weather began to improve, and the losses went down a bit, the total for the month being 12 killed and 30 wounded, with 88 evacuated from the line as sick.

G

Trench feet still claimed victims, but the malady was yielding to treatment. Incorrectly diagnosed as frost-bite, the disease was found to result from cold and wet in the extremities, aggravated by tight boots and putties, which brought about a poor circulation of the blood.

On the whole, the first two months of 1915, though full of discomfort, were " quiet " so far as fighting was concerned. A stagnation was the immediate result of the trench warfare which succeeded the great effort of the Germans to seize the Channel ports in the closing days of 1914. This stagnation was now about to come to an end.

The advent of trench warfare had convinced many students of war that to carry serried lines of defence bristling with barbed wire and obstacles must prove a costly and bloody business. These brains sought eagerly for a way round the barrier which would lead to a speedier and less expensive victory, and so began the controversy between Easterners and Westerners which endured while the war lasted. It was proposed to transfer the bulk of the British Army to the Balkans and to fight one's way into Central Europe by a back door. Such an enterprise, although there were many obvious objections to it, was one in which the command of the sea enjoyed by the Allies, and secured for them by the British Navy, might have been exploited to its full extent. An operation derided by the ignorant as a " side show," would possibly have merited the description in history as a maritime strategic counter-stroke of the highest value. It is not, however, here intended to argue the vast question of such operations in general nor this one in particular. All that need now be said is that the Balkan project was condemned, but that an immediate result of the controversy was the inception of the Dardanelles adventure.

General Joffre was an out-and-out Westerner. He laid stress on the fact that the Germans were in occupa-tion of a large slice of France, that near Noyon they were barely fifty miles from Paris, and that on the Somme they were but twenty miles from Amiens, the point of junction between the French and British Armies. He maintained that the security of the Western Front must be a paramount consideration in Allied strategy, and that to secure the position in the West it was necessary to drive the enemy further back. His method to ensure this end was to attack on the Western Front at the earliest possible moment and with the maximum of force. With these views Sir John French, the British commander-in-chief, was in general agreement. His first proposal aimed at a combined naval and military attempt against the Belgian coast, but when this was found to be impossible of fulfilment he set himself wholeheartedly to co-operate with General Joffre's plans. Wishing to give his troops a wider experience of an attack against entrenchments, and being desirous of ascertaining the effect of a super-bombardment by artillery he delivered an attack on Neuve Chapelle with his First Army.

Sir John French's object was to obtain a more favourable position for his share in the major operations to be undertaken in conjunction with the French. The present position was not wholly satisfactory, for the British had been thrust off the Aubers Ridge, during the fighting of October and November, 1914, and had been forced into the water-logged region below. To recover the ridge was essential if the hold of the Germans on the Lille—La Bassée line was to be loosened. By the capture of Neuve Chapelle on October 27th, 1914, the Germans had driven a salient into the British lines and it was here that the British commander-in-chief now decided to make his effort with the IV and Indian Corps, minor diversions being made at the same time to the north and south of the main attack.

On March 7th, the 58th went into the trenches in front of Neuve Chapelle to hold the front line for the two days before the attack, which it was known would

G I

probably take place on the 10th.   Strict orders were
given not to remove any wire, but rather to put more
out, so that " the Hun might not smell a rat."   For
some weeks previously, extensive preparations had been
going on.   Scaling ladders, bombs, etc., had been
brought up in large quantities.   Guns came into
existence in concealed positions in a manner almost
uncanny.   " Officers of all descriptions were doing
weird things such as laying lines of wires, drawing
maps and making plans of trenches."   Somewhere about this time, all the officers were sent
for by Major Higginbotham, the second-in-command,
and " told a few facts and told to get out our maps "
—and pretty useless maps for an attack they were in
1915, without " squares," so that arbitrary numbers
had to be given to important points.   A day before the
10th, " everybody had the best of everything, including
clothes and rations, mails, etc.   Everyone was talking
about the battle and the number of miles we were
going to make the first day."

During March 9th, the necessary operation orders
were issued and the gist of them was as follows :
The IV Corps and the Indian Corps were to carry
out a vigorous attack on the following day, the attack
to be preceded by an artillery bombardment at
7.30 a.m.   The village of Neuve Chapelle was to be
attacked and carried by assault and a subsequent
advance was to be made to a named line, not given
here, as it was fated to have but an academic interest.
Of the troops engaged, the 7th Division would operate
on the left, the 8th Division in the centre, and the
Meerut Division of the Indian Corps on the right.   The
two latter were chiefly concerned with Neuve Chapelle,
the 8th Division attacking it frontally, while a simultaneous attack was to be made by part of the Indian
Corps on the south-east corner of the village.

The commander of the 8th Division decided to place
the 23rd and 25th Brigades in front line and to use
the 24th Brigade (less a detachment) as divisional

reserve. That detachment was under the command of Lieutenant-Colonel Prichard, and consisted of the 2nd Northamptonshire Regiment, the 5th Black Watch and some machine guns of the 4th Cameron Highlanders. It was at first to remain in " B " lines, as a portion of the British trenches was called, which would come under the orders of Lieutenant-Colonel Prichard from 11 p.m., and he was to report direct to divisional headquarters.

The night which was devoted to the necessary final preparations for the first great attempt at a " breakthrough," was passed in an eerie stillness. The night was fine and the troops moved to their proper stations untroubled by either rifle fire or artillery, and waited for dawn. In their position in " B " lines, the 58th were in support of a battalion of the Royal Berkshires, " and our job was to build roads for our artillery." Everyone was in fine fettle and hope ran high, stimulated by a final message from the IV Corps commander, Sir Henry Rawlinson, who reminded his men that " The eyes of the world will be watching your movements during the coming battle."

Punctually to the second the British bombardment opened at 7.30 a.m. on the 10th, developing an inferno of fire hitherto unknown in the history of war. The noise was terrible—" like a thousand express trains roaring through a tunnel," as one narrator puts it. The German line immediately disappeared in clouds of black and yellow smoke, from which leaped up now and then great clods of earth, broken planks, and fragments of Huns—" our guns simply blew everything to pieces." The excitement among the troops was great. No bombardment such as this had ever been witnessed before, and many were the delighted interjections. " That's the stuff to give them," as chunks of the German line went sky-high. The enemy guns dropped some shells among the British, " but no one paid any attention to them. We were too excited for that." And the frightful hurricane of noise was

almost maddening in its stimulation.   So much so,
that the historian is rather surprised to find in the war
diary of a higher formation the nonchalant entry:
"Bombardment started.   Considered disappointing.
No windows broken.   No need for cotton-wool in the
ears."   A rather artless admission that higher formations are sometimes out of reach of and touch with the
battle line.   The battle line did not bother much about
cotton-wool.

The storm of fire could not, of course, last for long.
The ammunition supply sufficed only for thirty-five
minutes of this intensive shelling.   At 8.5 a.m., the
barrage slowed down and lifted, and the attacking
troops scrambled up their ladders and "over the top."
The men of the 58th were lining their parapet eagerly
watching the progress of the assaulting troops, but a
fierce burst of rifle fire broke out from the German
trenches, causing them to take cover once again,
but not before an officer had time to note the following
impression : "The Berks went forward at a walk on
our left and the Indian troops on our right.   I can
still see an Indian running along the top of the Hun
parapet loosing off into the trench below."   The
enemy's guns were now firing rapidly, dropping shells
of varying calibre amongst the reserve troops, and the
crackle of rifle fire was still intense.   In "B" Company alone there were soon some twenty casualties, and
hundreds of wounded were passing on their way to the
rear.

So far, the day was promising well.   The 25th
Brigade carried Neuve Chapelle without much difficulty, joining hands with an Indian brigade which had
over-run the ground between the village and the cross-
roads south of it known as "Port Arthur."   Many
prisoners were taken, and it looked as if only reinforcements were needed to enable a substantial advance to
be achieved.

Shortly after the attack had been launched, "C"
and "D" Companies of the 58th were sent forward

to assist the 25th Brigade in digging trenches beyond
Neuve Chapelle facing the Bois de Biez, but were later
ordered back to assemble at a place called Sign Post
Lane.   Meanwhile, about 8.30 a.m., " A " Company
had been told off to clear a barricade in the German
lines on the road leading into Neuve Chapelle.   After
the barricade had been removed, Sergeant Wilkes
collected about half a dozen Germans who were walking
towards our lines.   " I had proceeded about four or
five yards when one of the wounded, lying on the
ground, a German officer, fired his revolver, hitting
one of my men in the knee.   We promptly collared
the German officer and I am afraid that he had a very
rough passage."   The ground here showed that in this
sector the attackers had had a terrible time.   It was
strewn with the dead of the 2nd Scottish Rifles, the
right-hand battalion of the 23rd Brigade.   Here a fold
in the ground had concealed the German wire, and it
was untouched by our artillery.   Against this, the
Scottish Rifles had gallantly rushed, but in the attempt
nearly every officer, including the commanding officer,
was either killed or wounded, and more than half the
battalion fell.   Nothing daunted, the survivors had
forced their way under a withering fire, through all
obstacles into the enemy trenches, clearing them with
bullet, bomb, bayonet and butt.   Some of their dead
could be seen impaled upon the German wire.   The
sight was a ghastly one, and almost as ghastly was the
appearance of the German dead and wounded, bulging
eyes, terror-stricken features, and bodies yellow from
head to foot with lyddite.

From the records consulted, it would seem that " B "
Company came up about eleven o'clock.   It certainly
passed over the sector strewn with the gallant dead of
the Scottish Rifles, and, in one narrative commenting
on the failure of the artillery to destroy the wire, there
is this terse tribute to the infantry battalion : " They
had done their damnedest, for ' No Man's Land ' was
covered with dead."

The 58th was now set to dig a communication trench up to the captured enemy position and to bring up stores of all sorts.   Several casualties were incurred in this operation and the battalion became much scattered.

It was now about one o'clock.   It was clear that reinforcements were urgently required, but explicit orders had been issued that reserves were not to be put in without sanction of corps, and this fact, coupled with the increasing difficulty of maintaining communication with the front line, rendered the putting in of reinforcements a slow task.   At 1.5 p.m., divisional headquarters inquired of the 24th Brigade as to the situation generally, and whether it warranted collecting the 2nd Northamptonshire Regiment, whereupon the brigade communicated with the commanding officer, who replied that he could collect his battalion in about an hour.   It was now decided to collect the brigade, with a view to putting it into the fight, and by 3.40 p.m. it was assembled.

The original orders were that the 2nd Battalion Northamptonshire Regiment were not to be used as reserves.

Their rôle was to hold the line the night before the attack, removing barbed wire, etc., while the rest of the brigade had a night in bed out of the trenches to fit them for duty as reserves on the morrow. The battalion consequently had had no sleep and had been working all night and all day until 1 p.m.   They were tired out and should never have been taken for this attack, but one of the other battalions of the brigade could not be found, and the 2nd Battalion were asked to take their place.

At twenty minutes past four, the 24th Brigade advanced.   In the front line were the Northamptonshires and Sherwood Foresters, the former on the left. The Worcesters formed the second line, and as a third line, but echeloned somewhat to the right rear, were two companies of the East Lancashires.   It appears that the advance was to be made in a south-easterly direction with the left on the Bois de Biez. In the 58th the order of advance was that " A " and " C " Companies were in the front line, with " B " and " D " in support. Shortly after five o'clock, the 24th Brigade reached point 18 apparently without outstanding incident, but here the 58th, who were, it will be remembered, on the left, were unable to get touch with the 7th Division, who were to come up and pass through the 8th. The commanding officer sent back a message to brigade headquarters to this effect, and added that he was remaining at point 18 for the present. A reply was quickly received, directing the Northamptonshires to move as soon as possible.

It had now fallen dark and it was impossible to see what was happening, but the advance was carried out in accordance with orders. The battalion had been perforce drawn up in practically a solid mass with no space even between companies. " Occasional bullets sang over us, and I can see one man now who got one through both cheeks." The battalion now shook itself out. " A," " C " and " D " Companies moved off into the darkness without a sound, while " B " Company extended and lay down. " Soon we found ourselves advancing by short rushes. The rifle and machine gun fire was intense. Very lights continually flashed in the air and in the pale light I could see great-coated men rushing short distances, getting down, and, after a short pause, up and off again. We were not firing, for it soon became evident that there were other British troops in front. During our rushes, we passed many dead and wounded."

" On we went into the darkness, moving automatically when it came our turn to rush. There was no excitement. Everyone seemed to know what was expected of him, and did it without thinking. The value of our hard peace-time training was impressed on me that night. The commanders were there, but the advance was carried out so perfectly that there was no necessity, I suppose, for commands. Every time we rushed, the terrific din of musketry seemed to increase in intensity, dying down a little as we rested. A good many went under during that advance, which, so far as I remember, was about a mile. Suddenly we found ourselves mixed with other units. We had reached the front line. Some confusion followed, but before long they faded into the night, leaving us alone. We immediately began digging in. There were a few shovels lying about, but the majority set to work with their entrenching tools, and in an hour had made some reasonable head-cover. Every man dug the sort of hole he fancied, but mostly it was a long, shallow hole that was dug, owing to the deeper ones filling with water. These shallow holes were the cause of many casualties later.''

That is how the advance on the evening of March 10th appeared to a platoon commander of "B" Company. A stretcher-bearer of "C" Company narrates it as follows: " Our battalion was ordered to proceed before dusk. We were split up by now, and our front became difficult to understand and when it was quite dark nobody knew what was happening and casualties were getting heavy. I followed my company until we reached a very thick wood. Here we met the enemy in full force with new reinforcements and still in their battalion formations. Others were digging very rapidly. With sufficient men near this spot thousands could have been captured, but our men were scattered by this time and the orders were given to dig as quickly as possible. Why we were not captured remains a mystery to me, but I think that they were at a loss as well as ourselves regarding the situation.''

The above account can do no more than give an impressionist picture of the advance of the 58th during the evening of March 10th. It might be expected that the battalion war diary would present it with more diagrammatic accuracy of detail, but as a matter of fact the story there merely amounts to the statement that the

advance was about 1,000 yards; that the battalion dug
in some four hundred yards beyond the village; and
that casualties were heavy. But the scantiness and
aridity of the war diary are due to no lack of ability
or industry on the part of those whose duty was to
compile it. They are due to the fact that in the three
days' battle the 58th was practically exterminated.
Ninety per cent. of its officers were put out of action;
the colonel was wounded; the adjutant was killed. The
historian knows from experience that a bloody battle
will mean bald battalion records.

A comparison of various narratives with the
messages, to and fro, which are duly logged in the
brigade and divisional archives, establishes one fact
beyond doubt, and it is this. The darkness when it set
in made the whole thing a kind of blind man's buff.
Thus at about a quarter to six the 58th sent back a
message to say that " it is very dark and impossible to
see what is happening." Twenty-five minutes later a
report was received by brigade from the Worcesters
to say that the Northamptonshires were slowly
advancing but that "it was impossible to see." In the
narrative of a company commander there are the words,
" it was dark except for a burning farm in the Bosch
area." The same officer describes the digging-in:
" Power, the adjutant, came along and told us to dig in
where we were," and with a fine gesture, indicative of
the difficulty of fixing the exact hour, states that it was
"about 8? 9? or 10? p.m." " What I *did* know was
that if the company didn't dig like hell, they'd be well
shot up when it got light next morning, and I must say
the company dug well enough."

Obviously there was no use in barging ahead in pitch
darkness until at any rate some kind of reorganization
had been attempted, and the commanding officer went
back to explain personally to brigade headquarters the
nature of the situation and the proposal he recommended for dealing with it. Lieut.-Colonel Prichard
told them that the situation was very complicated.

Units of the 24th Brigade were mixed up with those of the 7th Division. The 58th had reached a point about 300 yards from the enemy, who were holding some houses in front and were also firing into the battalion from the right rear. Touch had been lost with the Sherwood Foresters on the right. The darkness was baffling. The ammunition supply required replenishing. In these circumstances, and chiefly on account of the way the battalions were mixed up, Lieutenant-Colonel Pritchard gave it as his opinion that an attempt to rush the houses in front of his battalion was not likely to lead to success, and he recommended that the advance should be postponed till dawn, when a bombardment by our guns would pave the way for the attack by the infantry, who in the meantime should sort themselves out. It is clear that this report, coupled as it was with clear evidence that the Germans had been reinforced, carried weight. At 11.20 p.m. the division issued orders that the 24th Brigade should advance at 7 a.m. on the 11th against La Cliqueterie, in which operation it would be supported by the 25th.

About 3 a.m. on the morning of the 11th a German patrol jumped into the trench of " A " Company, and before fire could be opened on them the intruders surrendered to the commander of one of the platoons—Sergeant Wilkes, who took the prisoners to the company commander, Captain Wood-Martin. While Sergeant Wilkes was explaining about the capture, firing started, and he was wounded through the arm and leg and the prisoners were detailed to carry him back, under escort, to the first-aid post.

March 11th was ushered in by a foggy morning, and the day continued dull and misty, a factor which was to have a serious influence on the battle, for the weather interfered with artillery observation. In accordance with orders the advance was to be resumed at 7 a.m., the 24th Brigade being instructed to gain the line La Russie—Peitre. The front line of the brigade consisted of the Sherwood Foresters on the right, with the

Northamptonshires directing on the left. As has been said the weather hampered the artillery, and in fact the bombardment was of very little use. The advance was tried, but in vain: "At the given hour (after this parody of artillery assistance) my men went over the top, but before they had gone ten yards they were all flat."

The 58th were now in a re-entrant formed by a " dog's-leg " bend formed by a change of direction in a road north-east of Neuve Chapelle. The German position was here very strong, and it was clear that some vigorous artillery bombardment was essential. The Worcesters, who were in second line, managed to get a message back to brigade to the effect that the Northamptonshires were held up in front, and that assistance from the artillery was essential. This message was transmitted to divisional headquarters, where it arrived at 7.40 a.m. The general situation was now by no means reassuring. The chances of substantial progress, already reduced by the arrival of strong German reinforcements, were further diminished by the weather conditions, which made aerial observation for our artillery impossible. This, combined with the interruption of telephonic communication between forward observing officers and batteries, prevented the co-operation between artillery and infantry needed to reduce the numerous machine-gun posts formed by the houses which studded the area north of Neuve Chapelle. Moreover, the Germans, in addition to throwing in reserves, had brought up much additional artillery.

Divisional headquarters attached very great importance to the capture of point 86, which was the numeral assigned to the bend in the road facing the 2nd Northamptonshire Regiment, and a message was sent off at 8.45 a.m. to the 58th to say that " Point 86 *must* be captured." As a matter of fact this message never reached its destination, and there is a note in the brigade war diary as follows: " Message *not* delivered," the italics occurring in the original. Meanwhile, while brigade headquarters had been engaged on the discussion which led to the abortive message above referred to, a second report was on its way from Lieutenant-Colonel Prichard, which, although timed at 7.35 a.m., did not reach its destination until nearly two and a half hours later. In this message the commanding officer stated that the artillery bombardment had been ineffectual, that the German breastwork along the roads forming a re-entrant in front of the 58th was practically untouched; that it was impossible to leave the trenches; and that an attempt which had been made at 7 a.m. had to be abandoned after a few yards had been traversed. A similar report, it may be mentioned, was received from the 1st Worcestershire Regiment.

Although the narrative of the doings of the 58th on this March 11th, 1915, has so far been concerned with little more than half an hour of time, already several discrepancies in various narratives at his disposal have struck the historian between the eyes. Thus the mortal wound received by Lieutenant Gordon is described, below, by an eye-witness as having been received about 7 a.m., while the battalion war diary gives this occurrence as having taken place in an advance five hours later. And the battalion war diary wounds Lieutenant Coldwell several hours before the actual casualty as testified by that officer himself.

To go back once more to the beginning of this March 11th, and to dissect the body of narratives in greater detail, it seems that " C " Company was on the right, with " B " Company on the left; but " D " Company " somehow got amalgamated with the front line " either during the night or very early on the 11th. Everyone dug in—that much is certain, at any rate. " B " Company " occupied the complete width of a field, being bounded on either flank by a ditch and a thin, scraggy hedge. In front of us, about 800 yards away, was a wood, and the enemy was occupying the front fringe of it." This narrative by a non-commissioned officer of " B " Company goes on to say that " the day (11th) passed without incident," but a perusal of what actually did occur will probably show that by March, 1915, some of the veterans had become such gluttons for fighting that the words " without incident " are apt to convey a wrong meaning.

"About 7 a.m. Gordon and I "—it is Lieutenant Coldwell, of "D" Company, who gives the information —" were looking over the top of the trench with a view to our line of advance, when a bullet took him straight through the throat. I gave him a morphia pill—poor devil, it was quite hopeless, but I think it kept him out of pain. He died about 11 a.m. or thereabouts." Apparently, immediately after this our guns opened up, but the effect was not very great : " it was a thoroughly poor show; honestly it was only a few 18-pr. shells that they put over, and the German guns replied far more vigorously on us." The next thing was the advance, and according to the battalion war diary "'C' Company and part of ' A ' attempted to renew the attack, but were repulsed." It is clear, however, that, *pace* the war diary, "D" Company also took part. "' D ' Company went forward. We ran into a hail of German bullets. . . . The O.C. company shouted at me to come back, as the attack was cancelled. I came back to him and he either told me or showed me a message to that effect—I forget which. Anyway, we stayed where we were, except those who had been hit. . . . ' D ' Company lay pretty low all that morning; the slightest movement above the parapet, such as it was, attracted German bullets, and we lost a fair number of men. We got breakfast as best we could; some people had " Tommy's cookers " on the go. We spent the rest of the morning and the early part of the afternoon in trying to dig deeper and in being shelled by the Germans, who had obviously got their guns into position again."

Time now tangles itself up badly, and it is possible merely to make an attempt to piece together the various sources of information, official and otherwise, at the historian's disposal and to fit them more or less roughly together. It is certain that the reports sent in from the front line, including those of Lieutenant-Colonel Prichard, convinced the people in rear that further artillery action was absolutely essential, and it was decided that a bombardment of thirty minutes' duration should begin at 1.45 p.m., after which the infantry advance should be at once resumed. Unfortunately it was now ten minutes past one, which left only thirty-five minutes in which to warn the battalions of the 24th Brigade, and as a matter of fact only two companies of the Worcesters got the message at all. This is frankly admitted in the brigade war diary. And so it came about that when Lieutenant-Colonel Prichard received a message from a company officer of the Worcesters to the effect "We have *got* to attack. Will you give orders?" the former was distinctly in the dark as to what was meant. He sent back a reply to say that as the artillery had made practically no impression on the German breastwork any advance now would be a useless waste of life. His prescience was amply justified. The Worcesters gallantly tried an attack. It lasted for about fifty yards, and when that space had been traversed the attackers had been mown down as if by a scythe.

The 2nd Northamptonshire Regiment, however, did its share of further attacking, although the diversity in the records leaves us in some doubt not only as to the exact time but as to whether this further attack took place before or after the artillery bombardment which began at 1.45 p.m. The attack in question was carried out by " D " Company, and, according to the battalion war diary, it began at 12 noon. From a narrative supplied by Lieutenant Coldwell, of the company, this hour seems earlier than the actual fact, and there is ground for believing that the afternoon was half spent when the attempt was made. The verbatim extract now given below will give the details of this attack.

"About 3 (?) p.m. I saw an officer slinking up a ditch

behind us; he came level with my bit of trench and I recognised him either as Major Inglis (Devons) or as a major in the Worcesters—I can't remember which now, but I fancy it was Inglis—anyhow, the Devons were close behind us. He told me that the whole line was going to attack again—was I ready? I remember saying, ' Give me a few minutes, sir, and I'll let the men know.' So I told all I could get hold of that as soon as I said ' Go ' and got out of the trench we would all go forward to what looked like a mound some 150 to 200 yards ahead. I can see Inglis looking at his watch now, and my saying to him, ' All ready now, sir.'

" Off we went; dead silence for three or four seconds, and then came the German bullets, and that, as far as I am concerned, was the end of the attack of ' D ' Company—practically everyone who left my bit of trench was blotted out. I know I hadn't gone more than twenty yards when I was hit through the leg (afterwards I discovered, in hospital, that counting the hole in my leg I had five bullets through various parts of my clothing). I can't say for certain, of course, but I think that practically everyone who left the trench round me were hit. Sparrow (Lieutenant), however, was untouched. I can't remember what company he was with or how he came to be close to ' D ' Company's attack. Anyhow, it was one of the most gallant things I have ever seen. On he went, with ' half the German Army!' shooting at him, but he didn't appear to be touched until he had gone about 100 yards, when I saw him fall. I rather fancy his servant was with him, too, but I can't remember. Sparrow was collected later on ; he got over his wound, and was killed later in East or West Africa.

" It was pretty patent that this attack was a failure. The Germans let fly a good deal of rifle fire, mainly directed at those who were lying out in front. I got one through the seat of my breeches; it also went through my shirt—I felt it, and thought it was a spent

H

shrapnel bullet. (I never discovered what it was until weeks later on, in hospital, when I came to look at my breeches.) The Germans then started to shell our line and things were decidedly unpleasant, so those of us that could made a painful crawl back to our line.

" I remember talking to a wounded man close to me as he lay out there. He was badly hit and he wanted me to finish him off, but I was too much of a coward to do so, with so many of our own people about. He didn't belong to us, and I can't remember his regiment, though I did get his name and I mentioned it to Captain Towse, V.C., whom I saw some days later when I was in hospital. (Towse, as you know, was doing all he could to find out names of killed, missing, etc., in his rounds of the hospitals.) This man must have been killed soon after I saw him, as I remember a shell which appeared to burst slap on top of him. As a matter of fact this particular shell prompted me to seek the corner of our own trench."

For the remainder of March 11th the day seems to have been, relatively speaking, "without incident," other, that is, than a heavy and continuous shelling and " a continuous crackle of musketry from the enemy, which caused us to keep our heads down." Some touches of narratives of non-commissioned officers and men are not without interest as throwing a light on the conditions of this day and on the impressions made on those who had to endure them. One contributor states that the Germans " had collected hundreds of thousands who were quite fresh "—a statement which at any rate indicates that the enemy resistance had stiffened considerably. There is a human touch in a description of the enemy shelling, in the following : " It appeared as if I were the only one there, with the exception of hundreds of cries and groans from all sides." One who acted as medical officer's orderly apologizes—but with a touch of professional dignity which implies reproof—for inability to supply copy, for the reason that " my work was done slightly away from the hustle of the firing line." Let it be said, though, at once, that the medical and stretcher personnel worked like heroes : and these words mean much. " Our doctor was simply a marvel, and he worked himself to his last ounce; his name was Lieutenant O. Ryan. I don't think he was still the whole time."

By midnight the strength of the 2nd Northampton-shire Regiment had been reduced by casualties to 12 officers and 320 other ranks. The story of the doings of the battalion during this March 11th is perhaps confusing; nevertheless the main points stand out clearly, and the action in which the 24th Brigade was concerned will be better understood if a brief glimpse is taken of the battle as a whole. Put in a nutshell, the case was this. The British effort had practically spent itself; the initial surprise had been discounted by weather conditions on the 11th; the attack slowed down and stopped against the strong reinforcements which the Germans had thrown into the fight. The Lahore and 7th Divisions came under heavy fire and suffered severely in crossing ground in rear of the advanced troops, sometimes without even reaching the front line. The 7th Division beat back counter-attacks and added considerably to the tale of prisoners, but made no real progress. The 8th Division could do no more, but until the right of the 8th could come forward to cover it the Indian Corps could not tackle the Bois de Biez.

Digging, more digging, deepening and connecting trenches—these, with the evacuation of the wounded, were the unceasing task of the 58th during the night of the 11th/12th. So passed the night, and when dawn broke " a stir ran through our line and everyone felt that something big was about to happen." The Germans were about to counter-attack. Through the misty dawn a grey wall of troops suddenly loomed into view about four hundred yards away. Instantly the 58th opened rapid fire, but although men fired until the rifles scorched and burnt their hands, no thinning in the German ranks was at first apparent. On came

H I

the grey wall, presenting a target impossible to miss, but it reaches now the ground but 200 yards from the trenches of the 58th. At this distance grey forms are seen every moment to fall prone, but the advance still continues. " Suddenly the advancing line began to thin out, and almost at once faded completely away. It was now light, and all we could see was the wounded moving. The German counter-attack had failed."

An attempt was now made to take advantage of the confusion into which the Germans had been thrown and of the loss of *moral* which the musketry of the 58th had brought about. Lieutenant-Colonel Prichard ordered an attack, which was carried out with such vigour that part of the battalion reached the German trenches and actually occupied them for a time. In this gallant effort Captain Wood-Martin and Captain Stocker lost their lives. It was found impossible to retain the captured trenches, and a withdrawal was ordered. This was successfully carried out, but the battalion had to mourn the loss of its adjutant, Captain Power, who was killed. " Power was a terrific loss to the regiment, an example of all that an officer and soldier should be." So writes a brother officer. No soldier could have a nobler epitaph.

All the officers in " B " Company were killed, and there follows now a narrative from a platoon commander as to how that company fared. " About half an hour after the German counter-attack No. 8 Platoon, on the extreme left, sent along to say that only two or three of the platoon were left, and could we send along some help? A bit later No. 7 Platoon reported that No. 8 were all dead. I happened to be looking along to the left—I was in No. 6 Platoon and right in the centre of the company—when I saw the khaki hats of two men of No. 7 shoot into the air, and the men fall dead. Then I saw what was happening. Someone was sniping into our shallow trench from the left or left rear. It was impossible to locate him, for the noise was terrific, and my only surmise is that the counter-attack had been successful on the other

side of the hedge and ditch on our left, and that a party
of the enemy was occupying a portion of trench there.
And so the annihilation of " B " Company went on.
The man on my left was shot through the head, the
same shot snapping off my bayonet. That I should be
next I had not the slightest doubt, but it was not to be,
for when everything quietened down I found myself
with two others still alive. The night, when we three
moved over to the right, we found ten others unhurt
who had been protected by a slight bend in the trench.
Every officer had been killed. The C.S.M. (Fisher)
took command. That night we tried to find the officers
to bury them, but it was impossible to find any but
Captain Robinson, the officer commanding company.
The thirteen of us then consolidated the right-hand
portion of the trench. The commanding officer
(Prichard), who was at battalion headquarters with ' C '
Company just the other side of the ditch, gave us orders
to hang on to our position at all costs, and this we
prepared to do."

Late at night the wearied survivors of the 58th were
relieved by battalions of the Devons and Middlesex. A
further loss was suffered when Lieutenant-Colonel
Prichard, who had passed through all the fighting
unscathed, was wounded while talking to the brigadier.
It fell to Captain Smyth, who had been with the transport, and Lieutenant G. A. Parker to take the remnants
of the battalion out of action. The casualties had been
terrible. Seventeen officers had fallen, of whom nine—
or more than half—were killed. In other ranks the
casualties numbered 414, with 102 killed, 203 wounded
and 83 missing, and, as is ever the case, many of the
last number might be written off as dead. Severe as
were the casualties actually, relatively they were even
more so, for the strength of the battalion at the opening
of the battle seems to have been but 19 officers and less
than 600 other ranks. Practically speaking, the 58th
had been wiped out, but with such relentless precision
was the machinery of drafts and reinforcements now
working that by the end of the month the battalion

had practically its full quota of officers and was some
550 strong. This is, however, to anticipate slightly.
The battalion, or what existed of it, was withdrawn to
billets for a well-earned rest.

The Battle of Neuve Chapelle lasted into March 13th,
but by that date the fighting had diminished much in
intensity, and the day was spent almost entirely in
consolidation. On the whole Neuve Chapelle had been
somewhat of a disappointment, and certainly so in view
of the high hopes which had been entertained. The
Germans had been able to pour in reinforcements and
the road to the high ground on Aubers Ridge was
barred. Tactically, however, the British had slightly
improved their situation round Neuve Chapelle, and if
this had been at the cost of over 12,000 casualties there
was consolation in the fact that the German casualties had
been even more severe, and that over 1,700 prisoners
had been taken. Looking back at the battle with the
advantage gained by comparison with later attacks,
then unfought, it is obvious that attacker and defender,
the former particularly, had much to learn. The
arrangements, schedules, time-tables, orders and instructions for Neuve Chapelle seem amateurish and sketchy
when read with those of battles three years later.

A word of warning may here be given to those who
may be anxious to supplement the restricted narrative
of the battle, given above, with fuller accounts and
larger maps. The warning deals with place names.
The French are an economical—nay, a parsimonious—
people, and in nothing is this spirit more marked than
in names of places. They use the same designations
over and over again. A gazetteer of France will reveal
an extraordinary number of Bailleuls and Armentières.
The Rouges Croix and Rues du Bois are as the leaves
of Vallombrosa. Les Epinettes are as the sands of the
sea. Rue du Bois is frequently mentioned in detailed
accounts of the battle. Actually there are four of them
all within a few miles of Neuve Chapelle. And the one
given in the 1 over 100,000 map is not the one connected
with the battle.

CHAPTER VI.

1ST AND 2ND BATTALIONS—AUBERS RIDGE.

WHILE the 2nd Battalion was being so terribly handled at Neuve Chapelle, the 48th were holding the line at Festubert. This was the first time that many of the men had been under fire, for now about half the battalion was composed of young soldiers, who had joined since the beginning of the war. Though raw and inexperienced compared with the seasoned veterans with whom they were serving, they were mostly men of excellent physique and considerable intelligence— really good fighting material, as they were soon to prove.

The so-called " trenches " near Festubert at this time were not, in the strict sense of the word, trenches at all. It would be more correct to describe them as sandbag barricades; for by now both armies had discovered that it was virtually impossible to prevent trenches from being flooded out in this district, owing to the swampy nature of the soil. The seven weeks spent by the battalion in this part of the line were not particularly eventful. The spells of duty in the line were broken by short periods of rest in villages and hamlets a few miles behind. The casualties sustained were few in number, and, as the weather had now greatly improved, there were fewer cases of sickness. During this period the principal duty of working parties was the construction of a new front line closer to the enemy's breastworks. The method by which this was accomplished was as follows : Fatigue parties, protected by a covering force, left the front line after nightfall with sand-bags already filled. These were piled up to form a semi-circular breastwork in No Man's Land. A detachment was left during the day to garrison this " grouse-butt "—as the

breastworks were popularly termed. They employed
the day in filling piles of empty sandbags which had
been left out for this purpose. On the following night
these in turn were placed in position, and the " grouse-
butt " was extended laterally. Ultimately, the various
" grouse-butts " were connected one with another, and
a new front line thus formed.

All these measures foretold a new attempt to break
through the enemy's defensive system, and many were
the speculations hazarded as to when the great event
was to occur. Even the enemy ventured upon a guess,
for on one occasion a board was displayed above their
breastworks, bearing the following inscription :—

> WE ARE SAXONS!
> YOU ARE ANGLO-SAXONS.
> WHY SHOULD WE FIGHT?
> WAIT TILL MAY 15TH.

The general opinion among the older soldiers of the
rank and file was that " the poor old 1st Division has
about done its whack, and this show is going to be done
by Kitchener's Army." This view, which had its basis
in the fact that the division had taken no active part in
the Neuve Chapelle offensive, was unduly optimistic, as
the event proved.

On May 2nd the battalion left the trenches and moved
back to Oblinghem, where it went into army reserve.
Preparations were made for a long stay, and plans for
a boxing competition and other similar amusements
were already on foot, when on May 5th orders came to
be ready to move at half an hour's notice. A slight
rearrangement in the organization of the battalion had
taken place a week or two before. Major Cautley had
become second-in-command of the battalion; Captain
Farrar took over the command of " D " Company;
while Capt. G. St. G. Robinson, who had come from
the 2nd Battalion on April 9th, resumed his old position
as adjutant.

Although in some respects the Battle of Neuve

Chapelle had been a disappointment, sufficient success had been achieved to warrant the hope that, profiting by experience, a second effort would lead to better results. At Neuve Chapelle the British had not fully mastered the question of the use of reserves—when to put them in and how to bring them up by roads blocked with the debris of battle and over ground scarred by trenches and torn by shell fire; but at any rate the lesson had received consideration. The French and British held firmly to the importance of the offensive, and the former were busy with preparations for a great assault on the Vimy Ridge, to be carried out in connection with an attack by the British round Fromelles. The Germans, however, were not an enemy to be caught napping. Opposite the British they had strengthened their position so that only the heaviest artillery could produce any effect upon them. Parapets many feet thick and backed by concrete were proof against 18-pounders, and afforded complete protection against anything but a direct hit to the machine-guns placed in pits sited at the ground level, which swept No Man's Land with a grazing fire. Worse still, from the Allies' point of view, the Germans made a strategic counter-stroke in the Ypres salient, which had been skimmed of French troops for the attack on Vimy. Here the Germans made use of a new weapon—poison gas, and by their fierce attack not only compelled General Foch to send back some of the troops borrowed from the salient, but exhausted portions of the meagre supply of ammunition which the Allies had been husbanding for their own offensive.

The attack by the British was originally fixed for May 8th, but was postponed till the following day— May 9th, a day for ever memorable to the 48th. The task was entrusted to the First Army, whose mission was to break through the German line, to gain the La Bassée—Lille road between the former town and Fournes, and thence to advance to the line Bauvin— Don. So much for the general idea, and we can omit

further detail until we come to the 1st Division, which
was to attack with the 2nd and 3rd Infantry Brigades,
the 1st Guards Brigade being the divisional reserve.
As for the attacking Brigades, each was to have two
battalions in front line; one in second line, to perform
the duties of what were known later in the war as
" moppers-up "; and two more in brigade reserve, the
extra battalion present with brigades being due to
attached Territorial formations. A certain definite
sector of the German front was allotted to the division,
this being in turn sub-divided for the two leading
brigades. At 5 a.m. the bombardment would open on
the enemy's wire, and at 5.30 the fire would be maintained for ten minutes on the enemy trenches. The
infantry would then assault, *i.e.*, at twenty minutes
to six.

Before this Battle of Aubers Ridge the 48th was up
to strength in officers and men, and the adjutant of that
time has put on record his opinion, " I don't think the
battalion, since the early days of 1914, had ever presented a finer appearance, or had ever again such a fine
type of man." The *moral* of the battalion was particularly high, and all ranks were in good spirits and eager
for the coming battle. Hope ran high, especially as
regards the expected devastating effects of our heavy
artillery. " This was going to work wonders, we were
told, and our artillery support would be adequate. I
remember Major-General Haking, our divisional commander, stressing the point." This optimism was
particularly noticeable as the battalion paraded and
moved off to take over its position during the evening of
May 7th. Then came the order that the attack was
postponed for twenty-four hours—an anti-climax and a
bad omen.

The 48th took over on the following evening the line
from the 1st Battalion The Black Watch, of the 1st
Brigade. The relief took place without special incident. The line here was mostly sand-bag parapet.
The ground was low and flat, with several small

streams and ditches between the battalion and the Germans, whose trenches were some 300 yards away. The night was a busy one. There were bombs to be fuzed—a long and cumbersome business in those days, and " the usual one hundred and one things one had to do prior to an assault. Every one was up and ready at daybreak completing the last details and arrangements. There were various kinds of stores to be carried— scaling ladders, bridges, wire cutters, bombs, progress flags, etc. Morning, when it dawned, was fine and clear, and, in the opinion of an artillery observing officer, " ideal for the purpose."

At 5 a.m. precisely the British bombardment began with 18-pounder field guns and 9-inch and 15-inch howitzers. The noise was terrific, and there was a confident expectation in the infantry that the damage to the Germans would be reflected later during the assault. For half an hour the tornado continued, being directed chiefly upon various enemy batteries and strong points in rear of his line. Then at half past five every gun was turned on to the German " trenches "— which as a matter of fact were like the British front line, sandbag breastwork—the 18-pounders being employed upon the enemy wire. The arrangement in the 1st Northamptonshire Regiment was that two companies were in front line, with two in support; the latter and battalion headquarters were to move into the front trench when the leading companies had advanced to the assault.

During the ten minutes' pounding of the German front line, the two assaulting companies—" B," under Captain Dickson, and " D," under Captain Farrar— had climbed out of their trenches, preceded by bombers and ladder-carrying parties. The companies then moved forward, but it was at once apparent from the artillery and rifle fire directed against the attackers that our bombardment had not succeeded as had been hoped. In spite of this, however, the advanced companies were able to get to within 100 yards of the German

breastwork.   The order was now given to lie down until
the cessation of the bombardment at 5.40.   Meanwhile
the two supporting companies, "A" and "C," under
Captain Mylne and Sir F. Robinson respectively, had
moved up from the support to the front line and had
climbed over the parapet, advancing to the support of
"B" and "D." Major Cautley, as second-in-
command, went forward with the attacking companies.

For ten minutes the hail of projectiles upon the enemy
line continued.   At 5.40 a.m. it ceased abruptly, and
the Northamptonshires rose from the ground and
rushed to the assault.

What followed was less a battle than a massacre.
The artillery had done little damage to the enemy's
breastworks, and, save at one point, had failed to
destroy his wire.   Even while the bombardment had
been at its height some rifle and machine-gun shots
were fired at the battalion from the loopholes
in the German breastworks.   These loopholes were
sited at the bottom of the parapet and so arranged as to
bring a cross and enfilade fire with devastating effect.
When the bombardment ceased the enemy lined their
defences and poured in a deadly fire at close range.
Before this terrible hail of bullets the Northamptonshires fell in scores.   The two leading companies did
indeed succeed in reaching the wire, and Captain
Dickson gallantly led about twenty of his men up to a
gap that had been made in the breastworks.   Here,
however, they were all shot down.   Captain Farrar,
too, was killed while leading his company to the
assault.   Major Cautley was hit in the arm, and while
his wound was being bandaged by his servant, Private
Bates, a second bullet ended the gallant officer's life.
It was hopeless to attempt to force a way into the
enemy's position, and the handful of officers and men
who yet remained unhurt flung themselves to the
ground.   The assault had failed.

The support companies going over the top met with
no better fate, and were all mostly shot down before

going very far.   Battalion headquarters had meantime moved into the front line, and during this move Colonel Dobbin was knocked out for a time by an enormous lump of earth thrown up by a bursting shell.

On the right of the 48th was the 2nd Battalion of the Royal Sussex Regiment, and their experience was identical with that related above.   The Germans had not been caught napping.   They had made all arrangements for repelling the attack, and when the two remnants of the battalions of the front line flung themselves prone the Germans shouted out derisively, " We expected you yesterday morning "—showing that they had been forewarned of the date actually intended.   It is curious to read in the narrative of the divisional commander, who was watching the attack from the top of a building in rear, the words, " So far as I could see, it only wanted a bit of push to get the battalions to assault."   But it was soon brought home to him that the whole of the 2nd Brigade was definitely held up, and although for the moment he thought of strengthening it with the Guards Brigade for a second effort, the project was abandoned as useless.

At 8.20 a.m. the Guards were ordered to relieve the 2nd Brigade, which was to withdraw and re-form behind our breastwork, but any such movement was impossible by daylight.   Throughout the day the survivors lay huddled together behind what little cover could be found in the narrow No Man's Land.   They were exposed to a pitiless rifle and machine-gun fire, to which they were unable to make any effectual reply. The Germans seem to have been particularly vindictive this day; the slightest movement on the part of a wounded man was the signal for a fusillade.   To add to the distress of the battalion, the German artillery began a counter-bombardment which was directed primarily against our front and support lines, but which incidentally wrought much havoc amongst those lying down close to our wire.   These men were now ordered to attempt to crawl back, and some succeeded in doing so. Second-Lieutenant Pitcher did good work by keeping battalion headquarters in touch with the men lying out in front, while Lieutenant Bourdillon, the medical officer, displayed great courage in endeavouring to bring in the wounded. Both these officers received the Military Cross, while Private Austin, who rendered valuable assistance to the medical officer in his work of rescue, was awarded the Distinguished Conduct Medal.

Between three and four o'clock the British artillery again opened fire, and this second bombardment was followed by another attack, the 1st Brigade assaulting the enemy's breastwork. This attempt failed, as the earlier attack had done. A handful of the Black Watch managed to break into the German defence, but were unable to maintain their position there. During this attack many officers and men of the 2nd Brigade who had been lying out since early morning rushed forward and joined in the assault.

And so the day dragged slowly on. Not only was the enemy fire directed against the troops lying out between the British and German lines, but, in addition, our front and support trenches were shelled heavily throughout the day. Any attempt to move out of the front trenches was received by intense rifle and machine-gun fire, so much so that it was difficult to look over the parapet. Captain Upton, the adjutant of the 2nd Battalion of the 60th, met his death in this way, being shot through the head as he was standing alongside of Captain Robinson, the adjutant of the 48th. Out in No Man's Land several men were seen to have their clothing on fire, the work apparently of incendiary bullets. Then at last came the blessed dusk, and those who were still alive made their way back to their own lines, after lying in the open for over fourteen hours. The Black Watch rendered splendid service, and an officer of the 1st Northamptonshire Regiment thus writes : " I remember how extraordinarily fine their men were in helping to bring in our wounded. Time after time they went out and brought in a wounded man, suffering heavy casualties themselves. I would also like to mention our medical officer, Lieutenant Bourdillon, in this connection. He remained out all night attending to those still alive."

In the evening the regimental sergeant-major received orders from a staff officer to take up rations and cookers to the village which the 48th had left so cheerfully twenty-four hours earlier. Meanwhile the commanding officer and adjutant had brought the remnants of the battalion out of action, " and we found that all the survivors could be collected in one barn." The men were given " as much hot tea and food as they liked and as much rum as was good for them."

Never before had the 48th suffered so many casualties in a single day. Besides Major Cautley, Captain Dickson and Captain Farrar, whose deaths have already been recorded, Lieutenant T. G. Powell, Lieutenant C. S. Cowley, Second-Lieutenant H. Thompson and Second-Lieutenant R. Davison were killed, while Second-Lieutenant K. E. Monro was mortally wounded. Captain Mylne, Captain Sir F. Robinson, Lieutenants Attwater and Champion, and Second-Lieutenants J. A. Nye, T. C. Fulton, H. H. Forbes, A. L. Norman and J. Clark were wounded; a total of 8 officers killed and 9 wounded. Only Lieutenant C. H. Bacon and Second-Lieutenant Pitcher returned unscathed of all the officers who had crossed the parapet. The loss in officers was even greater than it appears at first sight, for of those who were wounded, only two were ever fit for active service with the battalion again—Lieutenant H. St. J. Attwater and Second-Lieutenant J. Clark. The former had a remarkable escape from death, a bullet lodging in the muscles around his heart; the latter was wounded in the arm, and was able to make his way back to safety through a gap blown by a German shell in our breast-work. In Captain Farrar the battalion lost the only combatant officer who had been with the 48th ever since they first landed in France. The casualties among the

non-commissioned officers and men reached the appalling total of 541. Unfortunately, a very large
percentage of these were killed.

The attack made upon the German position on
May 9th has sometimes been called the Battle of Aubers
Ridge, sometimes the Battle of Richebourg, but in the
1st Northamptonshire Regiment it was always referred
to by its date, never by the locality in which it took
place. It is in some respects the darkest page in the
long records of the old 48th. One does not so greatly
begrudge the lives lost on the Aisne or in the woods of
Ypres; there something was achieved, a position taken
or a position held. On May 9th the lives of many
brave men were thrown away because the artillery
preparation for the assault was insufficient. Yet the
gloom of this sad story of wasted endeavour is lightened
by the memory of the magnificent courage and devotion
to duty shown by the officers, non-commissioned officers
and men of the 48th who went forward so gallantly to
their death on May 9th. And here we leave the
survivors of the 48th resting at Le Touret, while we
follow the fortunes of the 2nd Battalion in this bloody
Battle of Aubers Ridge.

The 2nd Battalion took part in the attack made by
the IV Corps on the left. The general idea in that
quarter of the field was that a break-through should be
made in the neighbourhood of Rouges Bancs. This
was to be carried out by the 8th Division—in which was
the 58th—and the 7th Division, following up, was to
pass through the 8th, exploit the gap, and so on. That
was the idea. Actually things did not pan out quite
in that way, as we shall see.

From about May 1st, the battalion was billeted just
behind Sailly-sur-le-Lys. The gap caused by the losses
at Neuve Chapelle had been filled with some of the
earliest of the New—or " Kitchener's "—Armies, and
the days were spent, significantly enough, in lectures
on the attack and instruction in first aid. It was
impressed upon all ranks that in the forthcoming battle

a stream twelve feet wide would be met in " No Man's Land," " so every morning we had the troops out jumping, or trying to, twelve feet in marching order." Apparently not much secrecy was observed about the forthcoming operation, for there is a naïve account of how detailed instructions were given " in a field full of peasants " and a statement, not to be wondered at, that " all the villagers knew a lot of forthcoming events." All this, however, was overlooked in the confidence which reigned everywhere. Hope surged high. The commanding officer (Lieutenant-Colonel Mowatt) was frankly enthusiastic about the preparations that were being made to lay out the Huns. " Boys," he said, " we'll just pick 'em out like periwinkles." Eleven years later, a surviving but disillusioned non-commissioned officer writes sadly as follows : " He was, to say the least, unduly optimistic."

On or about May 4th, company and platoon commanders were taken up for a " look-see " visit. It was a glorious spring day. The trees were bursting into bloom in front of and behind the front line. There was no trench, but merely a breastwork of sandbags, and the jumping-off place for the advance of the 2nd Northamptonshire Regiment was an orchard about mid-way between Petillon and Rouges Bancs. The ground about was untouched by shell fire and the grass was long and green ; a quiet spot such as the 58th had not yet experienced, and those who now visited it found themselves envying the occupants who had spent the winter there.

The advance by the 8th Division was to consist of a right attack, a left attack, and a reserve. The 24th Brigade was in the right attack. A very detailed programme had been drawn up, setting forth the various phases of the battle, but here it will be sufficient to say that at Zero + 50—to use the barbarous jargon of the war—on May 8th the 2nd Northamptonshire Regiment (having been preceded by two other battalions of the brigade) would leave the friendly orchard and

I

attack in a direction generally south by west, its objective being first a salient at a point in the enemy trenches to which the distinguishing number 372 had been assigned, and after that a sector lying beyond and between two points numbered 368 and 361.

During the night of the 7th-8th, the battalion left its billets to move to the orchard, but before it had proceeded far "a motor-cyclist fetched us back, the show being postponed for a day." It was currently reported afterwards among the rank and file that the postponement was due to the fact that the Germans were not quite ready and that, with the courteous idea of allowing them time to complete their preparations, the date was altered by one day. This much, however, is certain : the Germans knew all about the projected attack and were expecting it on May 8th.

However, the battalion eventually left Sailly at 10.15 p.m. on May 8th and took its place in the column of route of the brigade. Shortly after midnight the orchard was reached. "D" Company under Lieutenant Parker had been sent on ahead and had dug trenches and cleared away the wire round the orchard. When the battalion came up in the darkness, " A " Company joined " D " in front line, while " B " and " C " occupied trenches in rear. From each company twelve men were detailed to carry tools : this party remained with " C " Company. There were also detailed from each company six men to carry rations and ammunition. This party was under the sergeant-major and stayed near brigade headquarters.

At the first sign of dawn, the German machine guns woke up and began ripping the sandbags from the breastwork in front of the orchard. "This was not very encouraging," as a narrator correctly remarks : it also showed that the Germans probably knew what was coming and were getting their blow in first. Since the battle of Neuve Chapelle the 58th had been practically reconstituted and for a very great many this day was the first real baptism of fire. Several of the

surviving non-commissioned officers looked curiously to
see how the new hands would shape, but the result of
the scrutiny was reassuring.   As one veteran remarked,
"they hadn't the training of the men of Neuve
Chapelle, but they had guts and they were extraordinarily enthusiastic."   It was a day when enthusiasm
was valuable indeed.

In the growing light, the men of the 58th could now
peer over the top and see to some extent the nature of
the task which confronted them.   The German line of
breastworks was about 400 yards away.   A fourth of
that distance from the battalion was a stream
and thin hedge enclosing the orchard; then a stretch
of green; and from that right up to the German line a
high patch of bright yellow mustard flowers.

At 5 a.m. the bombardment opened and two features
of it were instantly noticeable.   In the first place, in
volume and noise it was much inferior to the inferno
of Neuve Chapelle.   Secondly, there was an
unpleasantly large number of "shorts."   And throughout this display, the German machine guns were
systematically ripping the top row of sandbags of the
Northamptonshires' breastwork to smithereens.   The
German fire actually increased in volume during the
continuance of the bombardment.   For fifty minutes
this went on, the officers, non-commissioned officers and
men of the two front companies standing with their feet
on the first rungs of the ladders—waiting.

At ten minutes to six the fire of the artillery lifted.
At the sound of a whistle the men of "A" and "D"
Companies instantly scrambled up the scaling ladders.
Here and there a man fell backwards into the trench.
Others collapsed on top of the breastwork.   The
remainder, "D" Company being on the right, dashed
forward.   Immediately a terrific enfilade fire was opened
by machine guns from the left front.   Men fell in
dozens, but in spite of heavy losses the survivors
gallantly pressed forward.   Lieutenant Parker with
about thirty men of "D" Company actually got up to

I I

the German breastwork. "A" Company were nearly all wiped out. A few minutes later, "B" Company under Lieutenant Middleton tried to move forward in support, but met with the same terrific fire and could do nothing. Then at half-past six "C" Company under Captain Jackson, with two machine guns under Lieutenant Lawrence, were ordered to advance and push home the attack. But in the face of the withering fire it was impossible to carry out the order and, indeed, the company was unable to proceed much beyond the orchard. The casualties were very heavy. A message was now sent to brigade headquarters with information about the heavy machine-gun fire from the left and left front, and about 8 a.m. "C" Company was withdrawn. The machine guns, however, remained in position in the orchard till about eleven o'clock, when they, too, had to be removed.

Several attempts were made to gain touch with the front line, but communication was impossible and the view was much restricted by trees. Then Private Lapham volunteered to go in person. In spite of the heavy fire, he made his way up to the front and brought back word that very few of "A" Company had reached the German line and that in all under Lieutenant Parker were some thirty at, or actually on, the German parapet. A report was now sent in to 24th Brigade Headquarters to say that the battalion could make no further progress. The general situation of the 58th was at this moment almost identical with that of the sister battalion a few miles to the south : a few were up in the enemy's line ; the bulk was scattered, dead, wounded, or untouched, and praying for night, in "No Man's Land." A residuum with battalion headquarters was in trenches and being heavily shelled.

Here is the experience of a survivor—a platoon sergeant of "B" Company—and not Napier nor King-lake could have told the story better :—

"I saw (I couldn't hear) the captain blow his whistle. I blew mine and darted to the ladders. A man here and

there fell back into the trench.   Others collapsed on
the top of the breastwork.   I ran on through our wire.
The crack of rifle fire and the rattle of the machine guns
had now reached a terrible intensity.   A run of about
70 yards and I was alone, and dropped down in the
long grass and started collecting as many as I could
of my platoon.   I got about 15 and started off again.
At the stream I had about two with me.   Down in the
grass again, crawling here and there trying to find
people still unhurt.   I got a dozen or so, a mixture of
all platoons, and pushed on in the storm of bullets.
I was alone again before I reached the yellow patch,
but I went on into it, for it was about 18 inches high
and afforded some cover from view.

    " I crawled about in that yellow patch, searching for
unwounded troops to take on.   I found a few, perhaps
20, of all companies, and two more senior N.C.Os.
I found no officers, and from enquiries found that they
had all been hit.   I discussed the situation with the
other N.C.Os., and found that their companies had
suffered as badly as mine, and I felt convinced at that
time that not more than a dozen of ' B ' Company were
unhit.   We decided that with so few men it would be
useless to go on, and keeping our small party together
we stayed where we were and awaited events.

    " During the advance the Germans had been plainly
visible over their parapet, firing steadily.   Their wire,
we could see from our position, was untouched.

    " After a couple of hours an orderly crawled up to us
with a message from the C.O.   We were to get back to
our front line as best we could, every man for himself.
We were then about 40 yards from the enemy wire, our
only cover the mustard flowers, and being sniped at
whenever we moved.   Some decided to wait until dark
before going in, but as it was still early morning I
decided to attempt it at once, taking the few men of my
company with me.   It took us about two hours to get
back, crawling along ditches, stopping to bandage up
wounded, rushing over short open spaces, and slithering

carefully through the long grass. Several were hit during these movements, but at last we slipped quickly over our parapet and heaved a big sigh of relief.''

It was not until eight o'clock in the evening that the few survivors of '' A '' and '' D '' Companies who had reached the enemy line were able to make their way back. At that hour Lieutenant Parker came in with four men of '' D '' and a few minutes later Sergeant Brightman made his appearance with nine more as well as half a score of wounded whom he had picked up on the way. Now that darkness had fallen, the stretcher bearers moved about '' No Man's Land '' and brought in many more. Then at 9.15 p.m. came a message from the 24th Brigade that the 58th was to become the divisional reserve; on relief by the 1st Worcestershires the battalion was to retire to the assembly trenches south of Rouge de Bout. This move began about 2.45 a.m. on the 10th and was carried out without loss, and from thence the battalion made its way to Laventie.

The account of this battle would not be complete without mention of a certain gunner officer, believed to have been a Major Tudor, whose efforts during the attack were of great assistance to the battalion. He was observing for a battery of 8-inch howitzers, and used one of the line of trees along the front line as his O.P. He remained in this tree throughout the action, directing his battery, regardless of neighbouring trees being blown down. He certainly saved the lives of Lieutenant O. K. Parker and his men, for, having seen them, when a second bombardment was ordered he managed with great skill to drop his shells at a safe distance on either side of them.

The casualties in the battalion had been severe. Before the action the strength of the 58th had been 20 officers and 867 other ranks; this had been reduced by nearly 50 per cent. The total casualties were 426. The killed numbered 67, of which four were officers, namely, Captain G. Ward-Hunt and Second-Lieutenants Eden, Mason and Ryan, but this figure does not include a "missing" list of three officers (Second-Lieutenants Blacker, Randall and Viney) and 154 other ranks, a great many of whom, including all three officers, were subsequently reported killed. Of wounded there were five officers (Captain H. W. Jackson and Lieutenants Middleton and Beresford, and Second-Lieutenants Eldridge and Peake), and 154 other ranks. The only consolation—if consolation it could be—was that matters might have been worse, and bad as the figures were they were beaten by those of the 1st Battalion.

One might imagine that, for a week or so after a shambles like that, a battalion would sit licking its wounds and thinking deeply. That was not the way in the 58th, for on the 11th—that is the day after the battalion got out of the mess—there is the casual entry in the war diary, "Concert held in evening." There were messages of congratulation earlier from both division and brigade. Billets till May 19th, and then the war diary makes a solemn statement, "Battalion had a bath." On the 20th, the 58th went back to trench life, being amalgamated for the moment with the 5th Black Watch to make a composite battalion. The old "in and out" life was now resumed and the end of May found the battalion doing a normal spell of trench work.

The British attack on May 9th had led to a terrible butcher's bill. The 1st Division lost nearly 4,000 men; the losses of the 8th Division were some 500 more. Nevertheless, although the French attacks to the south had also fallen short of the success anticipated, some ground had been gained and the British commander-in-chief determined to renew his efforts to assist his allies, though on a less ambitious scale. This led to the almost equally bloody battle of Festubert, and the curtain was not rung down till May 25th. With this second and later phases of the fighting, we have, however, nothing to do, for the current of fighting ebbed away from where both the 1st and 2nd Battalions of the Northamptonshire Regiment found themselves after May 9th. The disastrous set-back in the battle of Aubers Ridge was due chiefly to an exaggerated confidence in the power of artillery against entrenchments and wire; and, secondly, to a lamentable underestimate of the power of breastworks to withstand bombardment. In the third place, the machine-gun loopholes at the base of the breastwork came as a most unwelcome surprise. Fourthly, lastly, and perhaps chiefly, was the lack of the element of surprise : the Germans knew of what was coming and were prepared to meet it. As a result, the two regular battalions of the Northamptonshire Regiment were terribly mauled.

CHAPTER VII.

1ST AND 2ND BATTALIONS—THE BATTLE OF LOOS AND THE END OF 1915.

IN spite of the comparative failures of Neuve Chapelle, Aubers Ridge and the French attacks on Vimy Ridge, General Joffre was still determined to make a further effort in the autumn to effect a break-through. He proposed to renew the attempts on the Arras front to take the Vimy Ridge while the British fought on the left of the French X Army. The main effort was, however, to be elsewhere, namely, in Champagne, east of Rheims. This necessitated the extension of the British front right and left in order to set free French troops to join in the main Champagne enterprise, and the remainder of the summer was occupied chiefly in these changes. The British were able to take over a greater extent of front owing to the arrival of divisions from the New Armies, or Kitchener's Armies as they were then called. The reinforcement thus conferred will be understood when it is stated that the four divisions and one cavalry division which had fought at Mons had in eleven months increased to twenty-eight divisions and five divisions of cavalry. The British were now disposed in three armies, and we are concerned chiefly with the First Army, which found itself facing the open plain of Loos.

During the summer vast preparations were taking place on the battle front. Guns, trench mortars and military stores had accumulated in enormous quantities. The one fly in the ointment was that, owing to the controversy between the " Easterners " and the " Westerners," a compromise had been arrived at which led to the Dardanelles Expedition, and, incidentally, the side-tracking of three New Army divisions to that theatre. Nevertheless, it was hoped that the enormous supply of artillery and ammunition now available would enable a breach to be blown in the German line, through which infantry could be poured in to the assault. A leaf was to be taken from the German book, by the British at any rate, for it was decided to employ gas. The general plan of this autumn campaign was, therefore, that General Joffre should make his great effort in Champagne; General Foch was once more to storm the Vimy Ridge; while the British First Army was to attack between La Bassée and Lens. Farther north still there was to be a secondary attack by the British north of the La Bassée Canal, and beyond that again a demonstration opposite Armentières.

In the great Battle of Loos four battalions of the Northamptonshires were destined to take part, for, in addition to the two regular battalions of the regiment, the 5th and 7th Battalions of the New Armies were here to receive their baptism of fire.

To go back for the moment to Aubers Ridge, the week that followed the terrible disaster of May 9th was spent by the 1st Battalion in reorganizing at Oblinghem and Bethune. Then came two months of comparative quiet, during which a succession of drafts brought the battalion nearly up to their original strength. The battalion did not remain out of the line during this period. They were moved up to Gorrebridge on May 16th, when the offensive was resumed at Festubert, but were not used in that engagement. Afterwards they did several tours of duty in the trenches south of the La Bassée Canal, but on the whole it was an uneventful period, the total casualties in two months barely reaching a score.

Meanwhile the depleted ranks of the battalion were refilled, a certain percentage of the drafts consisting of Regular soldiers who had been wounded in 1914. The subalterns who came out at this time were almost all young officers whose military experience dated from the beginning of the war, Second-Lieutenant A. W. Tuckey, formerly regimental sergeant-major of the 3rd Battalion, being an exception. There were, however, also a certain numbers of officers of the 1st Battalion, amongst whom may be mentioned Captain A. Moutray Read, who rejoined from the R.F.C.; Captain C. G. Buckle, from West Africa; and Lieutenant Jervois, who had been wounded during the advance to the Aisne. Captain E. L. Hughes also rejoined the battalion, but left it in August to take a staff appointment. Major G. A. Royston-Pigott, of the 58th, who had hitherto been acting as adjutant to the 3rd Battalion, joined the 48th in May, and assumed command when Major Dobbin was invalided home on July 21st.

At the time when Major Royston-Pigott became commanding officer, the battalion was holding the line east of Vermelles. The Higher Command at this period was anticipating a German offensive against our front, and fatigue parties were continually employed in constructing a second line of defence behind the forward system of trenches. But a month or so later all this was changed, and the energies of the Northamptonshires were devoted to the more dangerous task of sapping forward from our front line to form a new advanced trench for a British offensive movement. This work naturally resulted in some casualties, as the German snipers were active every night. During the last week of August Captain Buckle was wounded and Second-Lieutenant A. T. L. Neish killed while supervising the work at the sapheads, and there were about 20 other casualties in addition. Captain Buckle was awarded the Military Cross for the good work which he had done while with the battalion. This officer, in the later years of the war, won distinction as commanding officer of the 58th; he died gloriously in action during the great German offensive of 1918. The only other officer casualties which had been sustained since May 9th were Second-Lieutenant H. J.

Hambleton, attached from the Indian Army, who was wounded by a shell splinter on July 28th at Noyelles-Lez-Vermelles, and Captain A. M. Henniker, who received a slight wound on August 11th.

On September 7th the Northamptonshires left the line and went back to Burbure, near Allouagne, for a period of rest and training before participating in the big offensive that was about to take place. The arrival of another new draft at last brought the battalion up to full strength again, and after a fortnight or so at Burbure the Northamptonshires marched back towards the line, and spent the night of September 23rd in the railway cutting near Noeux-les-Mines.

The author of this history of the Northamptonshire Regiment has always contended that it is impossible to compile an intelligible record from official documents alone. The reason for this is not difficult to understand. War diaries and narratives, written in the field, are for the eyes of superiors familiar with the main topographical features of the area in question, and there is therefore obviously no need for the compiler of the diary or narrative to enter into a lengthy description of such features. When, however, a history is being written, which may be read by the relatives and descendants of those who actually took part in the operations described, the case is quite different. Any peculiarities of terrain must be noted and described; and the battlefield of Loos, being somewhat abnormal, deserves a brief survey.

To begin with, it is a purely mining district, one of the most important in France, and the terrain, so far from resembling a conventional battlefield, consists of undulating country covered with mass upon mass of chimney stacks, mine shafts, huge dumps and towering structures of machinery. The miners' villages, locally termed *corons,* group themselves about the pit-heads and form two long lines of almost continuous brick and mortar, separated by a shallow valley, normally under cultivation, but—at the time of the Battle of

Loos—lying fallow and deserted, varying in width from a few hundred yards to a couple of miles or so. In the centre of this valley is Loos, a village of some two thousand inhabitants. The place was conspicuous for miles around by the huge double shaft, the famous Pylons which rose nearly 300 feet above the surface of the plain. The two opposing lines of trenches ran roughly north and south parallel to the Lens—La Bassée road, and well up the western slopes of the valley, so that Loos lay about a mile behind the German trenches. The trench systems on either side had by this date grown into a maze of front, support, reserve and communication trenches; and as the soil was chalk the line of each trench showed up conspicuously through the green overgrowth of weeds.

In contrast to the white trench lines were two enormous black masses in the German part of the field. These were embankments, or dumps, formed by the accumulated deposit from the mines, and were known as the Double Crassier—the northern one, while the southern was called the Puits XVI Embankment. These two masses, which had become practically permanent features of the battle area, had been transformed by the enemy into exceedingly strong positions, mined, entrenched and fortified by every known means. It is worth noting that opposite the extremity of the Puits XVI embankment the Allied armies met, the right of the British line resting upon the left of the French X Army.

In order to attain the objects laid down, a four days' bombardment of the enemy's position was to be undertaken, to be immediately followed by an assault upon the fifth day. The actual dates were at first not specified, but were referred to as days V, W, X and Y for the bombardment, and Z—the day of days—for the actual assault. During the afternoon of September 20th the message was circulated, " To-morrow is day V," and accordingly, on the morning of the 21st, a roar from the artillery proclaimed that the Battle of Loos had begun. During those four days of ceaseless bombardment the enemy made very little reply, except at certain points, for his policy was not to waste his fire by distribution, but to concentrate it on certain definite localities. All through the hours of daylight the German trenches were subjected to a merciless rain of projectiles, and even at night one gun from each British battery fired steadily throughout the hours of darkness—not now on the enemy's positions, but on his billets and on certain places through which his reinforcements must pass on their way to the firing line. Then during the night of the 24th and 25th infantry patrols left the trenches to explore the conditions of the enemy's wire. The attack was to be delivered at 6.30 a.m. on the morrow.

Few people are able to get a better view of a battle— or at any rate the preliminary stages of it—than a gunner officer acting as forward observation officer, and the following description, consisting of extracts from an account of September 25th, will bring home to readers what the first moments of the Battle of Loos were like : " At forty minutes past Zero, or 6.30 a.m., every battery lifts its fire from the front line to the second, and still the furious fire continues. The morning dawned grey and dull. From the observing post it was hardly possible to see farther than the front line trenches at half past five, and until the moment of the assault the visibility did not greatly increase. I felt as though I were in a box waiting for the actors to come upon a stage before which the curtain had risen punctually. There was no sign of battle, no movement that the eye could detect over the whole of the wide prospect before us. And then, suddenly, came forty minutes past Zero, bringing with it a scene that could never be forgotten. From the whole length of our front trenches, as far as the eye could reach, rose, vertically, at first, a grey cloud of smoke and gas, that, impelled by a gentle wind, spread slowly towards the enemy's trenches, very soon enveloping the whole of our range of vision in its opaque veil. It was now 6.30 a.m. The infantry left their trenches and vanished into the smoke. All we could see were the columns scaling the ladders and starting to double across the open. Some seemed to trip as they ran, and fell in various attitudes from which they did not trouble to rise. At first we thought that our wire had not been thoroughly cut, and that these men had fallen over some unseen strands. But we soon realized the truth, the while that the roar of rifle fire from the enemy's side grew ever more menacing."

From this vivid pen-picture of the opening phase of the battle we can now turn to the share in it of the 1st Battalion Northamptonshire Regiment. The 1st Division, which was now under the command of Major-General Holland, was to attack the enemy's trenches north of Loos, its objectives being the chalk pit just west of the Lens—La Bassée road, the group of pithead buildings known as Puits 14 Bis a little farther south, and the Bois Hugo, which lay farther to the east. The 60th Rifles and the Loyal North Lancashires were to be leading battalions of the 2nd Brigade this time, with the Royal Sussex in support and the 48th (less "A" Company, which was detailed for work with the Royal Engineers) in reserve. At 9.30 p.m. on the 24th the Northamptonshires left the railway cutting and marched up to their battle positions in the old front and support lines, the 60th Rifles being ahead of them in the new advanced trenches. The 60th were the right-hand battalion of the 1st Division, the 46th Brigade of the 15th (New Army) Division being on their right flank.

It was 2 a.m. before the Northamptonshires were in position. About four hours later the bombardment, which had already been in progress for several days, became more intense, and at the same moment the gas, which had been stored in cylinders in the advanced trenches, was released. Possibly the wind veered slightly; at all events, for some reason or other, a great deal of the gas drifted over our own lines, incapacitating not a few of " A " Company and two whole companies of the 60th. At 6.30 a.m. the assaulting battalions left their trenches, but little headway was made on the 2nd Brigade front, as the gas had collected in the slight depression that lay between our position and that of the enemy. After an hour or more the 60th and Loyal North Lancashires were ordered back to the front line to reorganize. A second assault was then attempted, the Royal Sussex attacking on the left and the 48th on the right. The attack was carried out with great dash in the face of a deadly rifle and machine-gun fire. The 48th advanced as far as the German wire entanglements, but, as these were not cut, it was impossible to force a way through. The Northamptonshires were compelled to lie down in the open, where for some hours they suffered considerable losses from the enemy's fire.

On the left the Royal Sussex had met with no better success, but beyond them the 1st Brigade had stormed the German lines, while on the right of the 1st Division, the 15th Division had carried all before it. Thus the German troops holding the trenches immediately in front of the 2nd Brigade found themselves threatened from either flank. They therefore determined to surrender, and, flinging down their weapons, they emerged from their trenches, holding up their hands. Major Pigott thereupon ordered them in German to form fours and come towards our lines. The enemy, who numbered about 300, did so, and were at once sent back as prisoners.

Thus the way had been cleared for a further advance, but at a heavy cost. Captain Moutray Read and Second-Lieutenant Tuckey were killed in this action; while Second-Lieutenants A. H. G. Clarke, C. F. T. East and T. R. Price were wounded. Lieutenant G. H. D. Metcalfe, Lieutenant J. L. Elston and Second-Lieutenant C. Y. Kerpen were gassed. The casualties in the ranks were proportionately heavy.

There were many deeds of gallantry and devotion performed by the officers of the 48th during the war, but to Captain Moutray Read alone fell the supreme honour of winning the Victoria Cross, although he did not live to wear the token of his bravery. His was a fine action. Although critically gassed, he went out to rally a party of sixty men of different units who were returning in disorder owing to the drift back of our own gas. Under his command they went back to the firing line. Utterly regardless of danger, he moved freely about, encouraging his men in the face of ·a withering fire. He had gone into the battle with a soldierly elation. " I remember," writes a non-commissioned officer, describing the last moments before the attack, " I remember I found myself along-side Captain Read, and I shall never forget how eagerly he was awaiting the moment of assault so that he could ' get his own back,' as he put it." An easy target for the enemy snipers, Captain Read fell mortally wounded, and the Army thereby lost one of its finest athletes. He had established a record by winning the Navy and Army heavy-weight champion-ship three times. Eight times in succession he was heavy-weight champion of India, and twice successful in the middle-weights. For a short time he had served in the Royal Flying Corps, but had rejoined the 48th owing to a shortage of officers. Thus fell a gallant sportsman, and his death was one which every soldier can envy.

Immediately after the surrender of the Germans garrisoning the front line trenches, the battalion reformed and pressed on to its objectives, which were occupied without serious opposition by about 6 p.m. The battalion then entrenched near the Bois Hugo, the 10th Gloucestershires, of the 1st Brigade, being on their right, and the 60th Rifles coming up about two hours later on the left. "A" and " B " Companies held the front line, " C " and " D " being in support. Battalion headquarters were at Puits 14 Bis.

K

Here the battalion remained during the night. The men suffered considerable discomfort, as no rations could be brought up, and it was raining heavily.

During the day the 15th Division had achieved remarkable success. It had over-run Loos and pushed on over Hill 70, east of that town, but, by so doing, had become isolated, so that although by noon the prospects of a break-through had seemed bright, the fortunes of the day changed. No British reserves were immediately available, and the Germans, on the other hand, were able to bring up fresh troops and to counter-attack with effect.

So far as the 1st Northamptonshires were concerned, their share in the battle was drawing to a close for the present. Except for a little shelling, the enemy did nothing until about 5.30 a.m. on the 26th, when about 200 Germans attacked the position of the 48th. The enemy were mown down by our machine guns, which did very good work under the command of Lieutenant J. E. M. Pierson. Shortly after this, the Northamptonshires were relieved by a battalion of the 21st Division. Some casualties occurred as the 48th withdrew, as the enemy at once opened fire with rifles and machine guns. Second-Lieutenant W. B. Stanfield was mortally wounded at this time. For the remainder of the day the battalion stayed in what had been the British front line. Rations, water, and ammunition were brought up from the rear. At 8 p.m. the 48th were ordered forward to the ridge north-west of Loos, as the 21st Division had been driven back from the Bois Hugo. Next day the battalion again moved back to the former British front line, where some casualties were sustained from the enemy's artillery fire. On September 28th the 48th went out of the line to Mazingarbe for the day, to reorganize.

The total losses incurred by the Northamptonshires during these operations were 10 officers and 362 other ranks. Apart from the officer casualties sustained in action, the battalion at this time lost the services of

Lieutenant S. H. Lewis, of the Royal West Kent Regiment, who was accidentally wounded. This officer had served with the 48th ever since the end of the Battle of Ypres.

By the evening of September 27th all hopes of a speedy and decisive success were gone. No break-through had been achieved, and General Foch's attack also had been checked. Still, the vigour with which the Germans counter-attacked at various places showed the importance they attached to the localities wrested from them. Particularly fierce were their assaults against the Hohenzollern Redoubt, which they ulti-mately regained after a violent attack. As for the 1st Northamptonshire Regiment, on the evening of the 28th the battalion, the fighting strength of which had been reduced to 8 officers and 360 men, was sent up to the village of Loos to relieve the cavalry who were garrisoning the place. Here the Northamptonshires remained for three days. The Germans, who were now making a determined effort to regain the ground that they had lost, shelled the village heavily during this period, and some casualties were incurred. At 11 p.m. on October 1st the 2nd Brigade was relieved by French troops. An unfortunate incident took place during this relief; a shell exploded in the cellar which constituted brigade headquarters, killing the French general and his staff officer, and our brigade-major. The brigadier, General Pollard, was lucky enough to escape with a severe shaking.

The Northamptonshires now spent some days at Noeux-les-Mines, where they were reinforced by a draft of 198 men and 9 officers, among whom was Major H. R. H. Drew, who assumed command with the acting rank of lieutenant-colonel. On October 7th the battalion moved up to the trenches again and occupied the old German front line near Hulluch. A big counter-attack was made by the enemy on the following day, but it was repelled without the battalion being brought into action.

K I

After this repulse the Germans made no more big counter-attacks. They had won back important observation posts. These Sir John French was anxious to recover, and he decided to bring up the 46th Division for a fresh attack on the Hohenzollern Redoubt, while simultaneously the 12th and 1st Divisions should attack the quarries at Hulluch. Accordingly the 1st Northamptonshires were busy preparing for the latter offensive, which had been arranged for October 13th. Gas cylinders had to be carried up to the new assembly trenches, and much other work of a similar nature had to be done. During this time the battalion lost the services of the adjutant, Captain G. St. G. Robinson, who was invalided home with fever, his place being taken by Lieutenant J. Clark, who had just rejoined.

The first objective of the 1st Division in the proposed attack was the village of Hulluch. The 1st Brigade was to lead the attack, and, when it had taken the German first line, "A" Company of the Northamptonshires and "A" Company of the Royal Sussex were to follow up its success at once. The remainder of the 2nd Brigade was to be in support; the 3rd Brigade was to make a demonstration on the right. Accordingly, at about 1 a.m. on October 13th, the battalion moved up to the new assembly trenches. Twelve hours later the bombardment of the German trenches, which had been proceeding for some time, became intense; the gas was released, and, under cover of a smoke cloud, the 1st Brigade advanced against the enemy's lines. A report came back that the Black Watch had taken the front line, and "A" Company of the 48th left the support trench in which they had assembled, and advanced across the open to follow up the attack. They were now under the command of Lieutenant E. L. Purdy, Captain Jervois having been hit in the arm just before the advance commenced.

Unfortunately, the information sent back about the success of the 1st Brigade's attack was wholly inaccurate. The German wire had hardly been touched;

little or no effect had been produced by our gas. Consequently the Black Watch, who were attacking in our immediate front, had been unable to take the enemy's front line, and, even as " A" Company left their trenches, the broken remnants of the attacking troops were retiring to their own lines. Thus Lieutenant Purdy and his men were at once met by a destructive fire from the German position; Purdy himself was wounded in the shoulder, and nearly 60 of his men were shot down before they even reached our own front line. What remained of " A " Company scrambled down into our front line trench into comparative safety.

Meanwhile the German counter-bombardment had commenced, three shells landing directly in the trench occupied by " B " Company, killing or burying a dozen men. As the afternoon wore on, fresh units were moved up the communication trenches, and the front and support lines became gravely overcrowded. " C " and " A " Companies were now hopelessly mixed up with the Black Watch and the 10th Gloucesters in the front line. It was not until nightfall that any kind of reorganization became possible, and even then there was still much confusion. At 3.30 a.m. on October 14th, orders arrived for a fresh attack. The Northamptonshires were to lead the way and the enemy's line was to be penetrated at all costs. It was rumoured, rightly or wrongly, that this very emphatic order was due to the fact that the false report of success at midday had already been sent back to the Higher Command, and that as the German front line had been reported to be captured, captured it must be, whatever the casualties incurred by the units engaged. There was much delay in forming up for the attack, which had been ordered for 4 a.m. This was probably due to the confusion which still existed among units. It was well after 5 a.m. before the attacking force was assembled in position.

When the day broke, it was seen that a dense mist

shrouded the ground to the front. Reconnoitring patrols which had been sent out reported that the enemy's wire was virtually intact; none the less, at about 5.40 a.m. the leading companies of the 48th left their trenches and advanced through the mist towards the German lines. Hardly had they crossed the parapet when an order arrived cancelling the attack. Those who had left the trenches were recalled at once, and withdrew to shelter, having suffered very trifling casualties; two men had been killed and a few more wounded. The remainder of the day was spent in the overcrowded trenches, against which the shell fire of the enemy was from time to time directed. That evening the brigade was relieved by the 47th Division and went back to Noeux-les-Mines. Here it entrained for Lillers, where it was to stay for a month to be refitted and trained.

Such was the part played by the 1st Northamptonshire Regiment in the Battle of Loos. The gallantry displayed by all ranks in the engagement of September 25th showed that the fine fighting spirit of the old 48th still animated the battalion, and that it was as capable as ever of loyal and devoted service.

On the whole the Battle of Loos was a failure. The attack on October 13th was only partially successful, although it should be added that the bulk of the Hohenzollern Redoubt was recovered and retained. The total gain of ground was hardly worth the casualties, which amounted to between fifty and sixty thousand. On the other hand could be set the fact that the German losses were nearly as heavy. The enemy had lost 20 guns and over 3,000 prisoners. The performances of the 9th, 12th and 15th Divisions showed that the New Armies had made good and were likely to prove an important factor in the future. Finally, the moral effect of an attack—even of an attack which did not fulfil the high hopes founded on it— was not to be overlooked. A break-through had not been achieved, but another blow had been delivered.

Valuable experience had been gained, and the New Army soldier saw that man for man he was as good as any German.

Nearly nine months elapsed after the conclusion of the Battle of Loos before the 1st Northamptonshire Regiment was again engaged in operations of major importance. Except for two months spent in training and recuperation at Lillers, the battalion throughout this period was engaged in holding the line near Loos.

From this time forward a fresh change in the nature of the personnel of the battalion must be noted. Although the majority of the warrant officers and non-commissioned officers were Regular soldiers, still it was now exceptional to find one among the privates of a company. As against this it must be remembered that those who had joined the Army early in the war could not now be classed as recruits, and a fair percentage of the men in the ranks had seen more hard fighting in a few months than falls to the lot of the average " time-serving " soldier in a lifetime. As regards officers, from now onwards it may be said that as a general rule the companies were commanded by subalterns commissioned since the war, who were given the acting rank of captain. These acting captains were selected by the commanding officer with great care, and without any regard for seniority. Although inevitably a few mistakes were made in the selection of company commanders, on the whole it may be said that those who were promoted to the acting rank of captain amply realized the expectation of their commanding officer, and did extremely good work in the responsible position in which they had been placed.

On November 13th, the battalion, now once more under the command of Lieutenant-Colonel Dobbin, left Lillers and went into a section of the line north of Loos. Trench warfare had by this time become systematized. Better methods of drainage and the regular employment of working parties had made the trenches much more habitable than had been the filthy holes in which our men had crouched at Givenchy and Cuinchy during the previous winter. " Trench foot," which had then been common, was now comparatively rare; if a case occurred, a searching inquiry was at once instituted to ascertain whether all the prescribed precautions had been taken to avoid it. Reliefs were now quite regular; twelve days in the trenches alternated with six in billets.

The first two months in the trenches were not very eventful. There was a fair amount of shelling and a great deal of hard work. Much debris lay about which had been left there ever since the battle in September; some of the trenches were still littered with dead bodies; and frequently when a shell broke away part of the parapet it revealed the corpses of men who had been hurriedly buried beneath it. By methodical and steady work the Northamptonshires were able to hand over the trenches in January, 1916, in a much better condition than they had been when they first took them over.

There was very little actual fighting, although the casualties from the enemy's shell fire were much heavier than they had been in the same trenches during the summer months. On November 25th the Germans made a bombing attack on a sap held by the brigade bombers near " C " Company's front. Corporal Sharpe, of " C " Company, behaved with the greatest gallantry on this occasion, on his own initiative three times going out into the open to throw bombs at the attacking Germans, whom he finally dispersed.

Major Drew was invalided home on November 30th. On December 16th, Lieutenant-Colonel Dobbin received a staff appointment and left the battalion; he was subsequently awarded the D.S.O. for the excellent work which he had done while in command of the 48th. He was succeeded by Major H. K. Bethell, an officer from the 7th Hussars. The battalion spent Christmas Day in the trenches in front of Hulluch.

On the last day of 1915, Second-Lieutenant H. C. T. Neale was mortally wounded by a shell while he was inspecting gas helmets behind the support line. He died in hospital when the battalion was out of the line, and was given a military funeral at Noeux-les-Mines.

The 2nd Battalion did not share in the Battle of Loos, properly so called; but it took part in one of the subsidiary offensives to the north, the object of which in each case was twofold, namely, to secure definite tactical improvements in existing situations, while at the same time to " pin " the Germans and to prevent the transfer of reserves to the Loos sector. How this was carried out we shall soon see, but for the moment it is necessary to go back to the end of May, where we left the 58th getting its wind again after its experiences of the terrible 9th May.

Briefly the lot of the 2nd Battalion between that battle and the subsidiary operation in September was distinctly a quiet one. As one humorist puts it, "one would hardly have thought there was a war on." So hardened, indeed, had the British Army become from slaughterings like Ypres, Neuve Chapelle and Aubers Ridge, that periods when there was merely a steady drip of casualties—say a weekly bill of two or three killed and ten or twelve wounded—seemed really "quiet." This particular period with the 58th was just the normal routine of in and out of the trenches, and to some it may appear that it cannot possibly contain any "news value"—to use a Fleet Street barbarism. On the other hand, people reading this history fifty years hence may have no idea of what trenches were like and what they were for. In the next war they may be completely out of date. To the sons and grandsons of The Northamptonshire Regiment the very expression may convey no more than the words phalanx and *testudo*. A page or two may well be devoted to a description of what was such a marked feature of the Great War.

During the Battle of the Aisne each side dug in,

while trying to gain ground on its outer flank. Effort was foiled by counter-effort, and eventually each side reached the North Sea and could go no farther. The real commencement of trench warfare was therefore the close of the indecisive First Battle of Ypres, when the opposing outer flanks had fought themselves to a stand-still and when the various trench barriers had been successively joined up from the Swiss frontier to the ocean. War of movement and manœuvre had now become impossible, and, until some way out could be devised, each side began to improve its long furrows and to turn them from more or less temporary fire positions into regular field fortifications, where men could not only fight, but eat, sleep, live and have their being.

The so-called "trenches" on the Aisne were mere holes in the ground, subsequently joined together, but without any of the accessories which were soon found essential. A year later trenches had been drained (with considerable and uncomfortable exceptions); revetted; and boarded with floor boards. Shelters, rooms, cabins, "dug-outs" came into being, some reinforced with heavy concrete iron rods, which gave cover from weather and fire. Protection was afforded by obstacles, chiefly wire, of which veritable jungles were formed; trench mortars came into existence; machine guns multiplied; sniping became an important art; tele-phones connected the front line with headquarters, and —far more important—with supporting artillery; periscopes enabled people to see without being seen and thus to avoid the sudden death which was so unpleasant on the Aisne; "trench stores" of tools, etc., were an important item; there were horns for warning of gas attack; gongs ditto; blankets soaked in chemicals for the protection of dug-out doors against gas clouds. There were log books kept and handed over on relief; there were bombs and ammunition, rockets, pistols and Very lights. There were arrange-ments for cooking. There were arrangements for sanitation. But there were also rats in thousands and lice in trillions. There was a disease also called "trench feet," brought on by cold and impeded circulation and more deadly in the winter months than the Huns. To prevent it there were "gum boots, thigh," and whale oil and vaseline. In course of time the trench system became everywhere such a maze of fire support, reserve and communication trenches, that it became necessary to issue regular trench maps for each sector of the line in order that newcomers might be able to find their way about the labyrinth. A new unit, however, was always given a guide on entering the puzzle, just as a ship takes up a pilot for unknown waters. A large-scale plan of any sector resembles nothing so much as two spiders' webs, separated by a narrow space, the constructors of which used red and blue colouring material respectively. To distinguish the various trenches, they became named after the streets and places of the localities from which the units were drawn in the old country. The depot town was also much used. Some trenches, however, were named from more well-known thoroughfares, and there were Bond Streets and Park Lanes in ironic profusion. A happy touch, too, was Queer Street—with ominous suggestions. So much for the "trenches." These paragraphs will seem unnecessary to those who served in them—and there were hundreds of thousands to whom war and trench warfare are one and the same thing. But the information may be useful to a generation yet unborn, and may save its members from imagining that trenches were just shallow ditches which a battalion could dig in twenty minutes.

The war diary of the 2nd Battalion for June, 1915, opens with the laconic statement, "In trenches. Nothing to report." This is typical more or less of its experiences for almost four months onward, but it must be realized that " quietness " in war is a strictly relative term. It was quiet in the trenches in fine weather when the Huns were taking a day off, and it was almost halcyon in billets behind the line; but patrolling at night in No Man's Land could often be very disturbing indeed, and even on the finest and warmest day the German guns might open any moment. All that the expression "a quiet sector" really means is this: when you were in one it was really "odds on" that you finished the day alive; and this means a great deal in war.

One officer probably thought the expression "quiet" rather exaggerated. This was Lieutenant Phipps, who was wounded in the foot while working in the trenches on the 2nd. On the same day Captain Haldane returned from leave and assumed command of the battalion. The weather was now stoking up, and there is a note in the war diary to say that the trenches were "odouriforous"—which is diarese for "stank"—the reason being the number of dead unburied, or but partially so, in the neighbourhood. On June 6th the 58th made its way back to billets at La Bassée, and about a fortnight later the battalion paraded before the divisional general, who decorated the following with the ribbon of the Distinguished Conduct Medal, for conspicuous gallantry on May 9th: Sergeant Brightman; Privates Bull, Lapham and Goodman. Private Phillipson was similarly honoured for his conduct at Neuve Chapelle; and Company Quartermaster-Sergeant Asplin was prevented from receiving his ribbon owing to the fact that he was away wounded. Towards the end of the month the 2nd Battalion received a new commanding officer in Lieutenant-Colonel A. C. Buckle, who joined from the 1st South Staffordshire Regiment. The end of the month found the battalion up in the line.

July was a pleasant compound of leave, very fine weather, and peaceful Huns—tempered, however, by inspections, which had now set in with their usual severity. On the 6th the commander-in-chief presented Lieutenant O. K. Parker with the Military Cross for his gallant work on that day of days—May 9th. The quiet of this month was broken by a smart piece of work carried out by Second-Lieutenant Petley, assisted by Corporal Cooper and Privates Strudwick, Gibson, Hart and Robinson. It seems that this young officer had reconnoitred up an old sap towards some abandoned trenches of the enemy, and, like stout Cortez, had gazed "with a wild surmise" on derelict rifles. To return with his merry men was the next item on the programme, and between them these looters actually carted away a hundred muskets. It was a capital performance, which was deservedly commended by the brigadier. Beyond this little episode there was nothing else in July but the usual Box and Cox business and the usual trench routine.

Nor was there much difference in August. But there is one thing worth noting under date of 19th. In the division there had been several cases of sentries sleeping on their posts—a grave crime indeed in war and punishable with death. A battalion order was now issued to the effect that in each company everyone —except one section per platoon—should turn in immediately after breakfast, at dawn, and sleep solidly and shamelessly till noon. At night the whole company, be it remembered, was up; one half company being on sentry (in the proportion of one man standing to two sitting) and the remainder of the company digging or putting up wire.

The first three weeks of September were spent in billets. The weather was wet and cold, but there was more than a hint of warm work soon, for on the 10th there appeared a brigade order about an offensive which was to take place as part of the operations of the First Army. So far as the 8th Division was concerned it was about to try to kill two birds with one stone. In the first place it hoped to " pin " the Germans opposite it and to prevent them hurrying off reserves towards Loos; in the second place the offensive was directed to straightening out the position of the 8th Division, which bulged inwards in an awkward way, by drawing a cord, so to speak, across the loop.   In this operation the 25th Brigade was to do the actual assault; the 24th Brigade, in which was the 2nd Northamptonshire Regiment, was to be in support; while the 23rd Brigade was to form the divisional reserve.   The date fixed was September 25th, the same day as that on which the great push at Loos was to take place.

During the night of the 24th/25th the battalion was relieved in the trenches and assembled at Bois Grenier Post about 11 p.m.   At half-past four on the morning of the 25th the 25th Brigade advanced to the assault, and for two hours the 58th were waiting for eventualities.   About half-past six came a message for all bombing platoons to be sent up, and that of the 58th proceeded as ordered.   From that time onward for more than six hours the battalion was not called upon, and it was not until ten minutes to one that a message came to say that in view of an S.O.S. from the front line the 2nd Northamptonshires were to be prepared to move at a moment's notice.   Two companies were sent up shortly afterwards, under Captain Latham, but were not seriously engaged, for the assault of the leading brigade, which had been carried out with great dash, had succeeded in flattening out the bulge in the line, so that at 6 p.m. the battalion took over from the Lincolns a new front line from Dead Tree to the left end of the Bridoux salient.

In this subsidiary attack the 2nd Battalion had not been called upon for any supreme effort.   The casualties were few, and only one officer, Lieutenant J. A. Elliman, was wounded; and in the whole month of September the number of deaths in action was only three.   After a short time in the new line the battalion was relieved by the 1st Sherwood Foresters and went back to billets in Bois Grenier and the vicinity.   Here, on October 6th, Corporal Phillipson and Private Sleet were decorated with the Ribbon of the Russian Order of St. George.   An interesting exchange of correspondence took place in the middle of the month, when the 5th Battalion The Black Watch, who were leaving the brigade, wrote to the 2nd Northamptonshire Regiment, thanking that battalion for all the kindness shown while the two units were serving in the 24th Brigade, to which a suitable reply was sent by the Northamptonshires. The time of the 24th Brigade was now drawing to a close, for about the 18th it became part of the 23rd Division, the 58th going into billets at Fort Romper, the remainder of the month being spent in and out of trenches south of Armentières. The transfer of the 24th Brigade to a New Army division was in consequence of the policy of exchanging " old " brigades for " new " ones, with the idea of stiffening the new divisions with a leaven of experienced troops, and at the same time giving the new brigades thus relieved the advantage of working with a seasoned division. In this particular case the exchange—of the 24th for the 70th Brigade—although intended to be temporary, lasted until the middle of July, 1916.

The trenches here were of that distressing kind which did not take kindly to draining—in other words, there was water up to your knees in places. As a setoff, Armentières was a kind of Capua, for some reason undestroyed by the Hun, and there were still many of the amenities of civilization within it. During the month nothing in the way of fighting took place. On the 24th Lieutenant-Colonel Buckle went down sick, and his place was taken by Major Hayne, who had joined the battalion about a fortnight earlier. The same quiet discomfort lasted almost all through December until Christmas Day, when an artillery strafe was put down on the enemy, to which they replied with seasonable retaliation. Plum puddings sent out by the *Northampton Independent* gave a Christmassy touch to a rather cheerless day otherwise, and the end of the year found the 58th in billets at Jesus Farm, as divisional reserve.

CHAPTER VIII.

THE year 1915 had been one of disappointment to the Allies on the Western Front; the high hopes which had marked the early months of the year had not been fulfilled; while the complete failure of the Gallipoli expedition had come as an added blow. And the abortive efforts of the year which had just passed left the Allies in a position of some disadvantage, for they had spent the greater part of 1915 in France either in carrying out the vast preparatory measures for an attack in trench warfare or in actually attacking, and had therefore left themselves little time or energy for consolidating their defensive positions. The Germans on the other hand had been forced upon the defensive on a large portion of their front, and now, by the inevitable swing of the pendulum, found themselves able to prepare for a policy of attack. So much was this the case that the enemy considered it possible to deal France a knock-out blow. The story of the war in France during the year 1916 may be summarized by saying that, after some local experimental attacks along the line, the Germans made a terrific thrust at Verdun in the closing days of February. The struggle was long and bitter and by the middle of the summer the position of the French was serious. Pressure had at all costs to be taken off the fortress by a great effort in which French and British troops were to take part. The effort was the great series of battles of the Somme in which the 1st, 2nd, 5th, 6th and 7th Battalions of the Northamptonshire Regiment were engaged.

For the 1st Battalion the year 1916 opened mournfully, for on January 1st Second-Lieutenant Neale died of his wounds. During the night of the 11th/12th an excellent piece of work was carried out by a small patrol under Corporal Norman, of " D " Company. This non-commissioned officer took his men, under cover of darkness, over both our wire and that of the Germans, and stealthily approached a dug-out which had been previously marked down and drawn blank. This time, however, a light was seen coming from it, and the sound of voices could be heard. In dead silence Corporal Norman and his party collected round the entrance and then threw several bombs into the dug-out. The explosion was followed by screams and groans, and in the ensuing confusion the corporal and his men slipped away without casualties. For this piece of work the non-commissioned officer was complimented by the brigade commander.

In the middle of the month the battalion went back to billets at Lillers for a month's " rest "—which was the euphemism employed on the Western Front for a very strenuous programme of training for officers and men. The principal incident of interest during this time was the inspection of the 2nd Brigade by General Joffre. Towards the end of the month Captain J. C. O. Marriott, a young Regular officer who had done good work at Loos, became adjutant in place of Captain J. Clark, who now took over the command of " A " Company.

In February, Major Royston-Piggott received the D.S.O. for his gallant conduct during the September operations. Shortly afterwards this officer left the battalion to assume command of the 10th Worcestershire Regiment. Later in the year he led his new command into action on the Somme with his accustomed courage and skill, and finally met a soldier's death in circumstances which reflect the highest credit both upon himself and upon the regiment from which he came. Captain the Hon. D. P. Tollemache, an officer from the 7th Hussars, now joined the battalion, as second-in-command.

On February 15th the battalion returned to the line,

L

this time somewhat to the south of Loos. It remained in this area for four and a half months. The situation here was complicated by the existence of two large mine craters, named Hart's and Harrison's Craters. This section also included the Double Crassier, so curious a feature in the military landscape that, although it has already been referred to, it merits a more detailed description here.

The Double Crassier consisted of two enormous slag-heaps, running parallel with one another east and west at a point where the opposing trench lines ran north and south. These slag heaps were about 80 feet high, 1,500 yards long, and 30 yards broad at the top. They were some 70 yards from one another, a kind of valley lying between. At the time that the 48th first came to this part of the line, the enemy held all but 300 yards of the northern crassier, and all but 100 yards of the southern one. The British held the western ends of both crassiers. The situation was a curious one. Both sides had sapped along the tops of the crassiers until the sap-heads held by the English and Germans were barely thirty yards apart. Such close proximity resulted in mutual forbearance in normal times on the part of the bombers who held the sap-heads. On the southern side, the English trenches near the crassier were untenable during the day; the same thing applied to the German trenches on the northern side. While the 48th were on the Double Crassier they received a visit from some officers and men of the Grand Fleet: it is to be hoped that these naval visitors did not carry away the impression that it was a typical portion of the British front.

In general it may be said that there was more activity in the trenches south of Loos than in most parts of the line. Mining—not coal mining, of course—was continually in progress, patrols were regularly sent out into No Man's Land, and there were frequent bombing encounters at the various craters and sap-heads. As against this it must be noted that, while life in the front line was rather strenuous, the existence of large areas of ground covered with miners' cottages immediately in rear of the trenches made it possible to obtain very comfortable quarters, even when in support. A mining cottage—we are referring to coal mining here—has one great advantage over all other forms of residence in a much-shelled area; it invariably possesses a cellar.

April was a month full of incident. On the morning of the 5th Second-Lieutenant B. G. Marshall was killed by a rifle grenade near Hart's Crater. That same evening the Germans exploded a mine quite close to our lines, forming what was later known as the Seaforth Crater. The regiment then holding the front line failed to occupy this crater, and the enemy obtained complete possession of it. On April 8th, just after the Northamptonshires, had moved into the front line, our engineers exploded a camouflet near the crater, and in the ensuing bombardment Second-Lieutenant C. N. Crawford was killed by a fragment of shell. Captain F. G. S. Martin was wounded by a rifle grenade on the 10th. Next morning a party from " A " Company bombed Seaforth Crater, Private Neville subsequently receiving the Military Medal for a reconnaissance that he carried out on this occasion. He was the first man of the 48th to obtain this decoration.

On April 15th, while Captain Trefusis was paying " A " Company in the village of Les Brebis, a shell penetrated the roof of the house in which he was sitting, wounding him severely. Company Quartermaster-Sergeant Adams and two men were also wounded on this occasion. A fortnight later a raid was made upon the German front line near Puits 16. It was planned with considerable care and forethought, and carried out with remarkable dash and bravery; consequently it was a signal success. The artillery did their share of the work well, managing to cut the wire in front of the point selected for the raid without attracting the attention of the Germans unduly to that spot. At 8.30 p.m. the raiders, who numbered about 40 in all, left our front line. By

L I

8.50 p.m. they had assembled quietly in a sunken road near the enemy's wire, their position having previously been taped out by Major Tollemache and Captain A. E. Swell. The latter, a former non-commissioned officer of the 12th Lancers who had been gazetted to the 48th in the previous October, now took charge of the raiding party. For ten minutes our artillery played upon the enemy trenches, then lifted to form a barrage around the area selected for the raid. The moment the barrage lifted, Captain Swell and his party leapt up and dashed forward. They took the Germans completely by surprise, shot five or six of them, threw bombs into several dug-outs, and returned with a couple of prisoners. Our casualties in this well-managed affair were three men wounded by our own shrapnel, one of whom subsequently died. The only thing that marred the complete success of the raid was the fact that the prisoners were killed by one of our shells before they could be brought back to the British lines. Captain Swell received the Distinguished Service Order for his part in the raid, while Second-Lieutenant H. R. Phipps was awarded the Military Cross. On the following morning the Germans attacked the 16th (Irish) Division near Hulluch, and the gas cloud that the enemy released before the assault drifted across to the trenches held by the 48th, compelling them to put on their gas helmets for about an hour.

May was a less eventful month than April, but towards the end preparations were made for an offensive movement. This project was suddenly abandoned, no reason being given by the higher military authorities. Lieutenant A. W. Fricker, who had done good work in the raid on April 28th, was killed while supervising a wiring party about a month later.

Early in June, Major-General Holland handed over the 1st Division to Major-General E. P. Strickland, who remained in command until the Armistice. Like his predecessor, General Strickland had a fine fighting record behind him, and no one could have been more fitted to maintain the high reputation which the division had always possessed.

There were several more officer casualties in the 48th in June. Captain Attwater, a young officer of great promise, was killed by a trench mortar bomb on the 27th, Second-Lieutenant A. H. G. Clarke being slightly wounded at the same time. Second-Lieutenant Serjeant had been mortally wounded while wiring a week or so earlier. Second-Lieutenants N. T. B. McWha and G. B. Thompson were wounded during this same month.

Early in June the 48th found themselves close to the 58th, for the first time in the war. The 2nd Battalion were holding the line slightly to the south of the 1st, in the neighbourhood of Souchez. On the night of June 30th the Royal Sussex attempted a small attack on the Northern Crassier, while the 60th tried to capture a local salient, known as the Triangle, which lay to the north of it. The Northamptonshires were on the right of this area, and their only share in the operations was a demonstration to divert the attention of the Germans. Neither attack resulted in any permanent gain of ground.

During these days there was marked activity along the whole British front, preparatory to the great offensive on the Somme. When news arrived of the result of the opening attack on July 1st, there was much speculation as to whether the 1st Division would be employed in the subsequent operations. The matter was not long left in doubt. On July 5th surplus kit was dumped at Marles-les-Mines, and a day later the 48th entrained at Lillers and proceeded south towards the scene of the new offensive.

It will be remembered that after its share in the subsidiary operation to the north of the Battle of Loos, the 2nd Battalion at the end of 1915 were in billets at Jesus Farm, near Armentières. Here it remained—or rather in this neighbourhood, for there was, of course, the usual in-and-out of the trenches—for some seven weeks. On the whole it was a peaceful time, although such entries as "13th January. Quiet day. A few shells into Jock's Joy" and a note of "rather heavy shelling" on the 14th dispel any illusions as to a perfectly halcyon time. A notification was received that D.S.Os. had been awarded to Major Mowatt and Captain Haldane, while Captain Latham and Regimental Sergeant-Major Lee were among the recipients of the Military Cross, and the Distinguished Conduct Medal was conferred on Sergeant Clements, Lance-Corporal Hawkins and Privates Budworth and Toseland. There was not much activity during January, except a rather fruitless demonstration to make the Germans line their parapet, the intention being that they should then be mown down. On the whole the weather was an enemy more unpleasant than the Huns, and there is rather a significant account of how the whole battalion was employed on February 15th in an attempt to drain mud and water from the billets. Five days later the 58th left this sector, marching some dozen miles to Bleu, via Steenwerck and Le Vervier. The march was not without incident, for a German 'plane dropped three bombs on the column, but fortunately no casualties ensued. On the 21st the battalion moved on to a camp half a mile south-west of Sercus, where it remained for a week, the chief items of interest being heavy snow, long route marches and an unpleasant thaw.

A further move now took place, the battalion being railed down to the neighbourhood of Lens. This move was part of the operation of taking over the front of the French Tenth Army, due to the fact that the Germans had begun their terrific blow against Verdun. General Joffre wanted every French unit he could collect, and at his request Sir Douglas Haig had agreed to take over a portion of the French line. Such an arrangement was not without its drawbacks to the relieving troops, for, gallant allies though they were, it is no use evading the fact that on matters of sanitation the

French and ourselves do not see eye to eye. The 2nd Battalion had been soured by its experience at Bruay, where it had to hang about for three hours until billets had been arranged. Now on March 7th it moved to further billets in the Bois de Bovigny, and there is a rather tart entry in the war diary about the French huts being "very dirty," and the diarist adds gloomily that the snow hid more even than dirt. Next day the whole battalion girded up its loins for a real, old-fashioned, British general clean-up which sent the diarist to record, "filth appearing as snow melts." Taking over from the French was never a popular episode in the Great War.

Quite apart from the billets, the conditions in this sector were curious. The No Man's Land consisted of sticky mud to a depth of about two to three feet, and attack by a force of any strength was out of the question. As for the trenches taken over from the French, there was room in them for merely 166 men in the front line. The diarist frankly states, "there is no line at all." Company posts were, indeed, in some cases two hundred yards apart. Another curious feature of this sector was that some Saxon troops had been sent here for sixty days' "punishment." If this was for any lukewarmness over the war the result was not much different, for the Saxons practically refrained from firing a shot, and kept showing themselves ostentatiously from time to time, as if to emphasize the fact that they regarded themselves—for the time at least—as out of the war.

After some minor moves the 2nd Battalion found itself, in the last week of March, in trenches near Souchez, and shortly afterwards experienced some casualties. What was known as the Solferino Sap was heavily bombarded on April 2nd. Captain L. A. Haldane, D.S.O., was killed and Major Hayne was knocked out by the concussion of a shell which burst in the dug-out of battalion headquarters. After a few days in hospital he was, however, able to resume duty.

After some further " billets-and-trenches " the battalion marched back to Pernes and thence to billets at Reclinghem. The move to this latter place was carried out in very hot weather, and as an experiment the men were allowed to march " in French style," *i.e.*, " go as you please." The result was not a success. Very many men fell out. And there was much caustic comment from another battalion, marching in normal fashion, which was passed on the way. The next active spell was a period in the trenches in front of Augres, and during the stay in this sector visits were exchanged with the 1st Battalion, as related earlier in this chapter. June was a reasonably quiet month. The birthday honours list contained the name of Captain Carritt as having been awarded the Military Cross. In the middle of the month the battalion moved to a training area, and on June 30th the whole of the 24th Brigade was in hutments in Henencourt Wood.

CHAPTER IX.

THE SOMME, 1916.

THERE now followed four and a half months of almost continuous fighting, which began with a great Allied attack on July 1st, 1916. This series of battles, known under the general heading of " The Battles of the Somme, 1916," was of the nature of a vast tactical counterstroke and traces its origin to events some five months earlier. When General Joffre heard, at the end of February, of the great German thrust at Verdun he realized at once the significance of the attempt and exclaimed tersely " *C'est la bataille.*" He at once asked the British commander-in-chief, Sir Douglas Haig, to relieve the French X Army on the Arras front and pressed Lord Kitchener to hasten the despatch of the New Army divisions to France. Inasmuch however, as General Joffre's strategy aimed at attracting the German reserves into the actual battle area it suited him to fight decisively at Verdun as long as possible, but to be ready to strike back instantly when he should decide that Verdun was in positive peril or the defenders of that sector had reached the limits of human endurance. The great counterstroke was to take place north and south of the Somme, the attack in the former sector being the duty of British troops.

Towards the end of May the successes of the German Crown Prince's armies had brought about a position at Verdun full of menace to the French, and it was accordingly decided that the great counterstroke on the Somme should be launched on July 1st. The preliminary bombardment opened a week earlier, and so accurately had the French Higher Command diagnosed events that this initial stage coincided

exactly with the attainment by the Germans of their
furthest gain towards Verdun.

The German positions astride the Somme and Ancre
were strong by nature and had been made doubly
formidable by every device known to the military
engineer. Villages had become fortresses; two elaborate trench systems had been dug; the chalk country
lent itself admirably to the construction of deep dug-
outs; there was abundance of wire; there was a
collection of formidable redoubts at points of tactical
importance; and as the Germans had been practically
undisturbed on this line for nearly two years their local
knowledge stood them in good stead.

The fighting began on July 1st, and, confining ourselves to the operations of the British, a reverse was
experienced on the left and success was gained upon
the right. Sir Douglas Haig decided to continue the
operations on that flank. Divisions—amongst them the
8th—which had lost particularly heavily were replaced
by others from reserve, and the story can now be
narrowed down to the doings of the 2nd Battalion
Northamptonshire Regiment, of the 24th Brigade,
which now formed part, temporarily, of the 23rd
Division.

In the last chapter we left the 58th in Henencourt
Wood. It moved forward via Dernancourt to Fricourt,
where it arrived about 9.30 p.m. on June 6th, and
passed the night in part of what had been the support
line of the Germans. News had been circulated that
the division would go into action very shortly, and
on that day details were made known. The 23rd
Division was to attack at 8 a.m. on the 7th and
Contalmaison was to be taken and made good. In this
attack the 24th Brigade was to be on the right, the 68th
on the left and the 69th in reserve. The right wing
was strengthened by machine guns and Lewis guns,
and battalion commanders were warned to pay
particular attention to the necessity of searching cellars
and dug-outs in the village, when captured. The

artillery would maintain an intense bombardment from
7.20 a.m. till 8 a.m. At the latter hour the infantry of
the division would go "over the top" and the guns
would lift and put down a barrage in front of the enemy
supports till half-past nine.

Actually the share of the 24th Brigade may be said
to have started at 2 a.m. on the 7th. At that hour the
17th Division, on the right, made an attack, and it was
part of the arrangements that after this attack—if and
when successful—the 24th Brigade should relieve the
left flank of the 17th Division and then carry on as the
right wing of its own division, *i.e.*, the 23rd. Unfortunately, however, the attack failed, and the advance
of the 24th Brigade was in consequence somewhat
delayed.

Later, however, the situation cleared somewhat, and
at 8.12 a.m. orders were issued for the first line of the
24th Brigade, consisting of the 1st Worcestershire
Regiment and the 2nd East Lancashires, to move
forward while the 2nd Northamptonshire Regiment,
with a section of machine guns, was to move to Lozenge
Wood and Crucifix Trench, "C" and "D"
Companies to the wood and "A" and "B" to the
trench. A further instruction to "B" Company was
that it should continue its advance right up to Contalmaison and occupy the square in the village. It is not
easy to relate with absolute clarity what followed, for
there seems to have been some confusion from the start
and an account of a survivor states, "In going over the
top we were all mixed up anyhow." Rain was also
falling in sheets; the trenches were in an appalling
state; and congestion was quickly brought about by
dead and wounded. It is clear that "C" Company
moved up two approaches, christened Birch and Shelter
Alleys to support the Worcesters; and that "A"
Company made its way up a sunken road towards the
village. Both companies came under very heavy fire,
as also did "D," which was following "A" Company.
"B" and "C" Companies in particular were badly

knocked about and " on the right of us the Worcesters were getting mown down like flies." During this period Lieutenant Selby and Second-Lieutenant Jarvis were killed and Lieutenant-Colonel A. C. Buckle, Captain Parker and Second-Lieutenants Palmer and Ferguson were wounded.

" B " Company got as far as Peake Wood, just south-west of Contalmaison, but the situation here was complicated by the hurried retirement of some troops in front. In any case the enemy's artillery barrage was now so intense that a further advance was out of the question. Eventually the 58th was pushed back, in the retrograde movement, as far as Birch Alley, and here what was left of the battalion was reorganized and manned the parapet, under Captain Carritt. Some order was now brought out of the confusion, and the men were set to clean their rifles, which were in a dreadful condition from the chalky mud. Eventually the battalion dug itself in on a position assigned to it, and the night passed without further incident.

On the following day it was reported that Contalmaison—which had been won and lost on the 7th—had been evacuated by the Germans. The 58th and Worcesters were ordered to advance and occupy it, the advance of the former being led by the second-in-command, Captain Latham. It was soon clear that the operation would not be without opposition, for the Germans opened a particularly heavy machine-gun and rifle fire, in spite of which, however, the battalion managed to make its way to a little distance beyond Peake Wood. Casualties had been severe. Captain Carritt had been killed and Major Williams severely wounded. In all, the battalion, when it reached the vicinity of Peake Wood, was represented by but four subalterns and a score or so of other ranks. Contalmaison remained untaken during this day, and in the evening the battalion re-formed near Lonely Copse and Major C. G. Buckle came to take over command. July 9th was spent " resting " in the trenches, and on

the 10th the 24th Brigade was relieved about 2.30 p.m.
and marched back to billets at Bresle. About the
same time Contalmaison was at last taken by an attack
carried out by the 69th Brigade, on the left of the
division. At Bresle it happened that the 58th relieved
the 48th—an historic occurrence which evoked great
enthusiasm in both battalions.

On relief the 24th Brigade proceeded northward,
marching by easy stages to Longeau, where it
entrained, for Bethune, in record time. It will be
remembered that the 8th Division—to which the 24th
Brigade belonged—had been engaged in the earliest
phase of the Somme fighting. It had suffered terribly.
Some battalions lost every officer; the casualties in more
than one unit were 90 per cent. It was therefore
transferred to the I Corps of the First Army, and after
a short rest--and the inevitable training—it took over
the Cuinchy sector on the night of June 14th/15th,
and here the 24th Brigade rejoined and the 2nd
Northamptonshire Regiment was once more back in
its old division. On the last day of the month the
strength of the battalion was 33 officers and 778
other ranks. The casualties during July—practically
speaking, all at Contalmaison—had been over 300.

The 58th now found itself in an area which from an
early period of the war had been a cockpit of battle. It
had witnessed the sanguinary French attacks of 1914
around Vermelles, and later the Battle of Loos in its
many subsidiary operations. The " History of the
8th Division " describes how the front was a maze of
trenches, old and new, German, French and British;
trenches blown in and disused, or abandoned and
derelict; British fire trenches which had once been
German communication trenches; trenches ending in
saps twenty yards from the enemy lines; salients,
re-entrants and fortified mine-craters—all reeking of
death and stagnation. Any attempt to dig new lines
was gruesome in the extreme. Bodies were turned up
at almost every yard. In many places the parapet was

largely revetted with corpses, thinly concealed by rotting sandbags through which at night rats fled squealing from their ghoulish repasts. And here in this sector was the continual struggle of mine and counter-mine which had reared great crater mounds of gleaming chalk along the narrow No Man's Land. And here reigned day and night the nerve-racking expectation of being blown sky-high without warning. As a sector it was " unhealthy " in more ways than one.

August began quietly enough, but there are soon ominous references to activity on the part of enemy trench mortars and aerial darts. On the 8th the battalion took over the Quarries sector of trenches, and the war diary frankly records that these were "appallingly filthy and no work done for ages." Four days later there was a raid upon the 2nd West Yorks in the 23rd Brigade, and in the repercussion of this enterprise the 58th had eleven casualties. Then followed the usual routine of in and out and a period of general quiet. The Hohenzollern Redoubt sub-sector was occupied on the 23rd, and the war diarist writes with something almost approaching pleasure that " the line is exceptionally good and very clean."

During the night of the 24th/25th a raid was carried out on the German trenches. It consisted of two parties. One of them was composed of ten men under Second-Lieutenant Lane, but unfortunately the enemy was quite prepared for this pin-prick. Germans were lining the parapet, all ready, and they started shelling No Man's Land with great vim. In these circumstances a raid was out of the question, and the party had to return. Fortune was kinder to a similar party under Second-Lieutenant Lloyd, which got into the German lines and killed one officer and four other ranks. As, however, seven of the raiders were wounded, it was not possible to bring away a live Hun —which was always the main object of a raid. Next morning, however, a German was seen in No Man's

Land and promptly wounded by a sentry when he tried
to dash back to his own lines. He lay out until about
two o'clock until Lance-Corporals Lovell and Vickery
went out and retrieved the bird, which proved to be
from the 76th Reserve Regiment. For this piece of
work the two non-commissioned officers subsequently
received the Military Medal, as did also Sergeant
Talbot for good work in the raid itself. The two
officers concerned were awarded the Military Cross.

September was, generally speaking, a month of
continuous quiet and continuous fatigues. The non-
commissioned officers met their opposite numbers of the
1st Sherwood Foresters at football, defeating them
handsomely by 8—1. Company Sergeant-Major
Brightman received the Russian Medal of St. George,
1st Class, and the Military Medal, and on the same
occasion there were thirteen other recipients of the latter
distinction. On the 25th the battalion had to mourn
the loss of Captain E. B. L. Rushton, who was killed
by a stray bullet shortly after midnight and was buried
at Vermelles the following afternoon.

So the time passed, full of minor incident but without
event of special interest, until October 6th, when a
raid on a very large scale was carried out by troops of
the division, in which, however, the 58th was not
actively engaged. This proved to be the closing
incident of this period in line. The call of the Somme
was heard again. Next day came orders for relief. On
October 12th the 8th Division was relieved and commenced its move southwards to the Fourth Army and
to its second entry into the great battle. On the 19th,
the 25th and 24th Brigades went forward from reserve
positions from Bernafay and Trones Wood to relieve
two brigades of the 6th Division. It was a day of
dismal and incessant rain. The weather had broken
and the battlefield was a sea of mud. Tracks were for
the most part impracticable and the roads were deep in
slime and crowded with traffic. The new sector fronted
a long tongue of rising ground which covered the

village of le Transloy and was itself dominated by the still higher ground about Saillisel.

Here we are confronted with a difficulty in the order of the general narrative. It happened that both the 48th and 58th were involved in the tremendous series of battles known under the generic name of "The Somme, 1916." It is obviously impossible to describe the doings of the two battalions simultaneously—in parallel columns, so to speak, or by means of a graph. A choice must be made between the system of first taking one battalion right through the series and then going back for the other, and the system of relating the battles by "penny numbers" or, in other words, by interrupting the narrative every now and then so as to let the battalion whose story is in arrear get abreast of the other. Each system has something to be said for it and has also some obvious drawbacks; but on the whole the balance of advantage is probably with the second system mentioned above. We must therefore ring down the curtain for the moment on the 58th; and, on raising it again, the 48th is discovered entraining at Lillers on July 6th, as mentioned on page 149.

Shortly afterwards the 48th found itself passing through Albert, making its first acquaintance with the famous church and its famous figure of the overhanging Virgin. Albert was soon left behind, and the 48th made its way towards the front through a land which was almost invisible with battery after battery of heavy guns. The incessant firing of our guns; the crash of enemy shells; the continuous drone of aeroplanes; the constant stream of heavy ammunition columns, ambulance waggons and infantry transport; the processions of walking wounded, all told one tale. The younger men who had seen nothing of this kind before were eager for action, "but the older ones who had been through the whole thing before were a shade more thoughtful." It was during this march up to the line that the 48th met its sister battalion on July 10th, as has been told earlier in the narrative of the 58th, and at

11.30 p.m. that night the 1st Northamptonshire Regiment bivouacked in Becourt Wood, about two miles east of Albert and close behind the old British front line.

A new feature in the personnel of the officers at this time calls for comment. During the last few months in the Loos area, a number of young officers from Sandhurst had joined the battalion, and thus for the first time since the beginning of the war a considerable proportion of the subalterns were Regulars. They had received a more thorough grounding in the rudiments of military knowledge than it had been possible to give the Special Reserve officers who had joined after the commencement of the war, and, although they had but little previous experience of active service, these young officers did excellent work in the fighting that took place in the Somme area.

During the next three days numerous small parties of officers, non-commissioned officers and men were sent forward to get some idea of the general situation. At this date the advancing British troops had reached a position some two miles beyond the original German front line trenches, and preparations were being made for an attack upon the enemy's second main line. On the night of July 12th, Major Tollemache led a carrying party of 400 men, laden with wire, stakes, etc., up to the new front line, which was being held by the 1st Brigade. Some confusion was caused by a guide who led half his party astray, and about half a dozen casualties were incurred from German shell fire in the village of Contalmaison. On their return journey the carrying party brought back with them 70 wounded men, mostly Germans, who had been lying for some days in the cellars of the village château. Three days later the battalion moved up nearer to the firing line, and on the following evening it occupied a position north of Contalmaison, its right resting on the north-west corner of Mametz Wood. In front, just beyond the skyline, lay the German second main line, which

M

was to be attacked by the 3rd Brigade, who had hitherto
occupied the position now held by the 2nd Brigade.
That brigade advanced to the attack during the night of
the 16th/17th. Preceded by a terrific bombardment, the
assault was successful at the expense of a few casualties.
A considerable portion of the German second main line
was taken. It was during the counter-bombardment,
directed by the enemy against the Contalmaison
position, that the 1st Northamptonshire Regiment had
its first experience of gas shells.

On July 18th, the 48th sent several patrols out in front
of the newly-captured German trenches to reconnoitre
the enemy's new position. During the afternoon and
evening of the same day the German heavy artillery
shelled the line held by " B " and " D " Companies.
Although this bombardment was never intense, it was
extremely persistent; and, as the hastily-dug trenches
which the Northamptonshires occupied afforded but
little protection, a fair number of casualties were
incurred. Second-Lieutenant R. V. H. Knight, who
had joined the battalion only a few days previously,
was killed while leaving the trench to succour an
injured man. Twelve men were killed and twenty-five
wounded before the shelling ceased.

That night the Northamptonshires relieved a regiment
of the 3rd Brigade in the recently-captured trenches.
The position was in many respects a curious one. The
German main second line had consisted of two parallel
trenches, about 150 yards from each other. The original
front line was now the British support trench, while the
German support trench now constituted the British front
line. On the right flank of the 48th both trenches were
held by British troops. On the left flank both trenches
were held by the enemy, who were separated from the
48th by two barricades built across the trenches. About
500 yards north-west of the German barricades, the
high road from Bapaume to Albert, which runs from
north-east to south-west, crossed the trenches nearly at
right angles. On this main road, and to the left rear

of the 48th, was the strongly-fortified village of Pozières, which was in German hands. In front of the 48th, just beyond the crest of a rise, lay the village of Martinpuich, which is situated a little to the east of the main road. Between Martinpuich and the British front line the enemy had hurriedly constructed a defensive position to bar the farther advance of the British. This was known as the Switch Line.

The 48th had not taken over the captured German trenches merely to hold the ground already gained; their duty was to endeavour to capture a further portion of the enemy's position. Their first object was to obtain possession of a trench junction immediately behind the German barricades. This was a most important point, and it was determined to capture this trench junction by a surprise attack on the early morning of July 20th. Four storming parties were detailed, each consisting of ten picked men under a subaltern officer. Behind these were to follow consolidating parties, whose duty it would be to establish a block in the trench, fifty yards beyond each junction. There was to be no preliminary artillery bombardment, but supporting fire was to be furnished by the Stokes trench mortars.

At 2.30 a.m. the assaulting troops left their position and advanced towards their objectives. The enemy was on the alert, and met them with a deadly machine-gun fire, while the Stokes mortars did not prove as effective as had been hoped. On the right, Second-Lieutenant N. A. Chambers's party had some success, but Lieutenant M. A. R. Barthorp was killed as he leapt over the enemy's barricade. The four survivors of his party, after a gallant effort to maintain their ground, were forced back by the German bombers. Second-Lieutenant Chambers was then compelled to withdraw his men. In the German front line the assault was equally unsuccessful. Second-Lieutenant G. H. Gadsden, who led the attack upon the barricade, was wounded, and all his men became casualties. Second-

M I

Lieutenant F. C. Cockerill, who led up some men from the consolidating party in an attempt to support him, was hit by several fragments of a German bomb. On the extreme left, all the men of Lieutenant E. W. R. Jacques's party were shot down before they reached Pozières Trench. Their officer, who found himself alone on the German parapet, was obliged to take refuge in a shell hole and made his way back to his own trench with some difficulty. Meanwhile, Captain J. G. Clayton, with a mixed party from " A " and " D " Companies, had bombed his way up the German front line, but although he was able to rescue several wounded men, he was unable permanently to gain any ground. The total casualties in this attack amounted to 43.

The next two days were occupied in preparing for another attack, upon a larger scale. Parties from " A " and " D " Companies, together with some of the Loyal North Lancashires, dug an advanced line, known as Lancashire Trench, while another similar advanced line received the name of Sussex Trench. On the 22nd the orders for the new attack were issued. The advance in this part of the line was only part of a big combined movement by which it was hoped that Pozières would be captured. Shortly after midnight the attack began. The confusion that ensued at the commencement of it beggars description; hardly a unit arrived at its forming-up position in time. The trenches were dreadfully overcrowded; one company of the Royal Sussex was stumbling up and down the German second line in a futile effort to discover its assembly point long after the attack upon the right had been launched. No accurate and detailed account of all that took place on that night will ever be written.

Some of the 60th Rifles succeeded in reaching the Switch Line, though many of them were shot down by the German machine gunners, who were lying concealed in shell-holes in advance of the main position. When Captain Chisholm's company arrived at the

Switch Line, he found some parts of it held by the 60th and some still in the hands of the Germans. He at once took command of the British troops, and, detailing bombing parties to work to left and right, he succeeded in holding about 300 yards of the Switch Line, and began to consolidate his position. But before long his supply of bombs was exhausted, and having nothing with which to meet the persistent attacks of the German bombers on both his flanks he withdrew the mixed force under his command to Lancashire Trench. Captain Chisholm was afterwards awarded the Military Cross for his part in these operations. When day broke on July 23rd, it was seen that nothing had been achieved by the attack delivered during the preceding night. Among other casualties, Second-Lieutenant T. E. Bourdillon, who had been with the battalion only two days, was reported missing; it was subsequently discovered that he had been captured. During the day the German artillery shelled our front line heavily. Lieutenant E. D. Badcock was killed and Second-Lieutenants E. S. G. Robinson and H. C. Ramsay were wounded.

On the morning of the 24th, the 48th were relieved by the South Wales Borderers, and marched back to Albert. Their total casualties amounted to 8 officers and 260 other ranks, including many platoon sergeants. After a brief stay in Albert, the 48th went back to Franvillers, where Talavera Day was celebrated on July 28th. Then followed a fortnight's rest and training in Henencourt Wood—a period of preparation for as stern and terrible a test as ever the old 48th had faced in the Peninsular War.

The period of rest at Henencourt Wood ended on August 13th. On that day the 1st Northamptonshires, now refitted and strengthened by reinforcement drafts, marched out again towards the forward area, where the Battle of the Somme was still raging with undiminished fury. The night was spent at Maxse's Redoubt, just east of Albert, and on the 14th the battalion was moved off by platoons in the direction of Bazentin-le-Petit. German shells were falling rather frequently in the devastated area through which the advance was made, and four men were wounded before the battalion reached their destination. These were not the only casualties sustained, for Major Tollemache, who had gone ahead to reconnoitre the ground over which the battalion was about to operate, was hit by a fragment of shell. Fortunately his wound was not of a serious nature, but it was sufficient to incapacitate him during the next fortnight, when his presence with the battalion would have been of inestimable value.

The 48th spent the night of August 14th working to improve the trenches in the Bazentin area, which was situated a little over a mile due east of that portion of the German second main line that had been occupied by the battalion in July. Eight more casualties were incurred from shell fire. At 5 p.m. on August 15th the Northamptonshires moved up into the front line. The position into which the battalion was moved was situated on the southern slope of the ridge. On the right front this ridge was capped by the famous High Wood, the larger part of which was then in the enemy's possession. In the immediate front of the battalion, and some distance below the crest of the ridge, was a German trench, the capture of which was the task which had been allotted to the 2nd Brigade.

A few hours after the battalion had gone into the front line, two patrols were sent out to reconnoitre the position held by the enemy. Lieutenant C. Nye and Second-Lieutenant N. L. Giddy, who commanded these patrols, reported that the German line was not very strongly held, and that it would be possible to rush it by making a surprise attack without any previous artillery preparation. This advice was acted upon, and a detachment from " C " Company attacked the enemy's trench that same night. Unfortunately, it chanced that the enemy had a large working party out in front at the very hour selected for the surprise assault. As a result, the attempt failed. Second-Lieutenant Giddy was killed; Second-Lieutenant E. T. S. Syfret was mortally wounded; Lieutenant Nye and Second-Lieutenant Chambers were reported missing. The casualties among other ranks were not severe, one man being killed and two more wounded. Lieutenant Nye, however, made his way back to our lines on the morning of August 16th. He had spent the greater part of the previous night in a shell hole, and brought back information of great value concerning the dispositions of the enemy. As the Germans were now on the alert, the project of a surprise assault had necessarily to be abandoned, and arrangements were made for an attack upon a much larger scale in conjunction with the Royal Sussex, the advance to be preceded by an adequate artillery preparation. Lieutenant Nye, whose information had considerably facilitated the plans for this operation, eagerly volunteered to lead the attacking force—a gallant offer which cost him his life.

Shortly after 10 p.m. on August 16th the attack was launched. " D " Company, under Captain Swell, advanced on the extreme left; on their right was " C " Company, under Captain J. Clark; on the right of " C " were the Royal Sussex. The artillery barrage effectually kept down the enemy's fire from the trench in front, but from both flanks rifles and machine guns wrought havoc among the assaulting troops. On the left, the first wave of the attack, in their eagerness to close with the enemy, pressed forward into the barrage, and sustained several casualties from our own artillery, Lieutenant Jacques, who was leading the foremost platoon, being killed. The second wave, led by Second-Lieutenant Noakes, captured the enemy's trench, but their leader was mortally wounded by a machine gun firing from the left. Captain Swell, who had displayed his usual magnificent courage in leading his company forward, was shot through the head just as the trench was taken. " C " Company had also reached their objective, but not without sustaining heavy casualties. Lieutenant Nye had been killed and Second-Lieutenants B. H. Fergusson and H. R. Phipps wounded. Second-Lieutenant Chambers, who had been missing for twenty-four hours, was discovered after the trench had been taken. He had been seriously wounded on the preceding night, and died in hospital some days later.

The work of consolidating the captured German trench and of adapting it for defence was at once taken in hand, under the supervision of Captain Clark. But the enemy did not intend to relax their hold upon the position without a determined effort. At about 3 a.m. on the morning of August 17th they launched a strong counter-attack against the portion of the trench to the right of " C " Company, which was held by the Royal Sussex. They were successful in driving the Sussex men from their position, but their efforts to force their way into the part of the trench held by " C " Company were frustrated by the gallant resistance made by Captain Clark and his men. Captain Clark himself had already been wounded, but this did not prevent him from taking an active part in repelling the German counter-attack. Second-Lieutenant J. Lingham, a young officer who had only been with the battalion a few weeks, and who was superintending a working party when the counter-attack was made, also took a prominent part in keeping the enemy back. Both he and Captain Clark received the Military Cross for their exploits, and the trench that they helped save from recapture was later officially designated Clark's Trench, to commemorate the gallantry of the commander of " C " Company of the 1st Northamptonshire Regiment.

The daylight hours of August 17th were spent in continuing the work of consolidation. Both our men and the Germans had constructed barricades, by which the portion of Clark's Trench recaptured by the enemy from the Royal Sussex Regiment was separated from that held by the Northamptonshires. That evening "A" Company, under Captain Clayton, relieved

" C " and " D " Companies. Second-Lieutenant
C. E. Wilson, of " A," was killed shortly after the
relief had taken place. The total casualties since the
beginning of the attack on the night of August 16th
were about 150.

The enemy was not allowed to remain long in possession of that portion of the trench which he had
recaptured. A fresh attack was ordered for the
afternoon of August 18th. The 1st Loyal North
Lancashire Regiment was to move forward from the
former British front line against the enemy's front,
while " A " Company made a bombing attack down
Clark's Trench against their right flank. Two trench
mortars had been brought up to Clark's Trench to
assist this movement. At about 2.40 p.m. the attack
began. The fire of the trench mortars was well directed,
and the Germans holding the barricade that separated
their portion of the trench from ours abandoned their
position and fled for refuge into the shell holes in
rear of the trench. They were all killed, either by
our machine guns or by the artillery barrage that
preceded the advance of the Loyal North Lancashires.
" A " Company's bombers thereupon fought their way
down Clark's Trench until they joined hands with the
left company of the North Lancashires, who had
succeeded in reaching their objective. On the right
the attack was not so successful, but a considerable part
of Clark's Trench was regained from the enemy. The
casualties suffered by the 48th in this affair reached a
total of 44.

Next day, an effort was made to exploit the success
already gained. Patrols were sent forward by " A "
Company, and at 2 p.m. a line of posts was established
on the top of the ridge. Three companies from other
regiments were sent up to consolidate this new position
and to connect it with Clark's Trench by a communication trench afterwards known as Bethell's Sap. During
the night, however, a body of Germans, whose numbers
were estimated at about 50, advanced from High Wood

in rear of the position on the ridge and caused considerable confusion. Exactly what took place at this time will probably never be known. Captain Clayton, who, when last seen alive, was moving off in the direction of some men whom he supposed to belong to the Royal Sussex, was subsequently discovered dead. The presumption is that he approached a body of Germans whom he had mistaken for English soldiers, and that he was killed by them. Second-Lieutenant Lingham was wounded at this time, while 2 other ranks were killed and 12 wounded.

When day broke on the morning of August 20th, "A" Company was holding the advanced position on the ridge. Although this had now been put in a condition for defence, both flanks were exposed to attack, and the men of the company were in an extremely exhausted condition from their previous labours. At about 7 a.m. the Germans advanced in force against the position on the ridge, moving forward rapidly from shell hole to shell hole. The officer in command of "A" Company, considering his position to be untenable, ordered a retreat, and "A" Company withdrew down Bethell Sap. The officer concerned had on previous occasions given ample proof of his personal courage, and the worst that can be urged against him is an error of judgment. Lieutenant-Colonel Bethell at once ordered a counter-attack to be made to regain the lost position, and "A" and "B" Companies advanced against the Germans. The fight lasted all the morning, the battalion making several determined but unsuccessful efforts to recapture the post on top of the ridge. Second-Lieutenant C. S. Greenwood was killed during this part of the engagement, while Lieutenant F. H. Roper-Tyler and Second-Lieutenant Tappin were wounded. At 2.30 p.m. a final attempt was made, this time with some artillery support. After a hard fight, a post was established about 300 yards in advance of Clark's Trench, whence an excellent view could be obtained for artillery registration, but the original position occupied by " A " Company during the preceding night was not recaptured. During these attacks Second-Lieutenant E. R. C. Aylett displayed great courage and powers of leadership, and for his conduct he was subsequently awarded the Military Cross. About 140 casualties were incurred on this day.

During the following night the 48th were relieved by the 2nd Welsh, and marched back to Becourt Wood. In the past seven days the battalion had suffered heavily. Ten officers had been killed and seven wounded. Of other ranks 51 were killed, 60 missing, and 245 wounded, making a grand total of 374 casualties. Except on the terrible morning of May 9th, the battalion had never before sustained such losses during a similar period of time. But whereas on May 9th the lives of gallant men were thrown away to no good purpose, a concrete, definite and valuable gain of ground resulted from the fighting round Clark's Trench. It is impossible to conclude the account of this action more fitly than by quoting the Special Order of the Day issued on August 22nd by the general officer commanding the 2nd Brigade.

" On coming out of action, I desire to thank Lieutenant-Colonel H. K. Bethell, and the officers, non-commissioned officers and men of the 1st Northamptonshire Regiment, for their splendid and gallant conduct during the recent operations. No praise can be too high for the manner in which they kept in touch with the enemy and resisted all efforts on his part to drive in our line. The whole spirit of offensive and initiative displayed was magnificent throughout, and I admire it beyond words. I am proud to have such officers, non-commissioned officers and men in the brigade under my command."

After ten days in Becourt Wood and its neighbourhood, the 48th moved up once more to the front line on August 31st. A strong reinforcement draft had been received, consisting of men from the Norfolk

Yeomanry. This was the first large draft that had
come out to the 48th without having passed through
the 3rd (Special Reserve) Battalion of the Northamptonshires in England, although in the later stages of the
war drafts from other regiments became the rule rather
than the exception. Major Tollemache rejoined from
hospital on the day that the battalion again entered the
front line.

The trenches that the 1st Battalion now occupied
were a short distance inside High Wood, the
right flank resting on its eastern boundary. The
German trenches facing them were also in the wood,
some seventy yards farther north. Little worthy of
note took place during the two days that were spent in
this position. The artillery of both sides was somewhat
active, and in the early hours of September 2nd a party
of Germans made an ineffectual effort to throw bombs
into "B" Company's trench, and were repulsed by
rifle fire. Our snipers inflicted some loss upon the
enemy from an old German dug-out in front of "D"
Company's lines. It was about this time that the half-
dozen South African snipers, who rendered such
valuable service to the 2nd Brigade in the latter half of
the war, became attached to the 1st Northamptonshire
Regiment. As their commander was invariably
addressed by his followers as "Skipper," and by his
brother officers as "Sniper Bill," it may interest some
of his former comrades in the 48th to learn that his real
name was Second-Lieutenant Methven.

The battalion was relieved by the 1st Black Watch
on the evening of September 2nd, and marched back
to billets in Albert. Three days later the 48th moved
up to support trenches not far from Mametz Wood.
Here orders were received that, in the event of certain
operations now being undertaken by the 3rd Brigade
proving successful, the battalion would take part in an
attack upon the German trenches in High Wood. The
3rd Brigade did not achieve the success that had been
anticipated. but none the less the 48th were ordered to

move up again to High Wood on September 9th, to take part in a general attack upon the German position.

There was great congestion in the communication trenches leading up to the front line, and although " D " and " B " Companies, which were to make the attack, entered Elgin Trench (about 1,000 yards from the edge of the wood) at 12.30 p.m., they did not succeed in reaching the position allotted to them in the front line until 3 p.m. The progress of " C " and " A," the companies in support and reserve, was completely blocked for some hours, and they did not manage to struggle through to their positions until the attack was over.

The trenches from which " B " and " D " Companies were to attack were those which had previously been occupied by the battalion in High Wood. In front of " B " Company, which was on the right, lay a large crater formed by a mine that had been exploded prior to an unsuccessful attack made by the 1st Brigade on September 3rd. Another mine was to be exploded in the same place at the moment when " B " and " D " Companies left their trench to assault the German position. The first wave of the attack was to consist of two platoons of each company; the remaining four platoons were to constitute the second wave. If the enemy's trench was captured, " C " Company was to advance at once and form a line of posts in the shell holes immediately in the rear of it. This part of the plan could certainly not have been carried out, as at the moment of the assault " C " Company was still struggling up Elgin Trench.

After a very ineffectual trench mortar bombardment, the first wave went forward at 4.45 p.m. In spite of heavy rifle and machine-gun fire, the right-hand platoon of " B " Company, under Second-Lieutenant A. H. G. Clarke, succeeded in occupying the crater formed by the new mine, though several of our men were injured by the falling debris. Second-Lieutenant

Clarke's platoon was reinforced by the supporting platoon under Second-Lieutenant D. K. Cooper, which brought up a Lewis gun. The Germans at once made a vigorous counter-attack with bombs, put the Lewis gun out of action, and drove what was left of our two platoons from the crater. Second-Lieutenants Clarke and Cooper were both killed. The majority of the men in their platoons became casualties, and very few of them succeeded in regaining our lines.

Farther left, the attack met with no better success. This was partly due to the fact that the regiment on the left of " D " Company did not leave their trenches at the appointed time. The enemy in their immediate front were, in consequence, able to open a murderous enfilade fire upon the men of " D " Company, many of whom were shot down before they had crossed the parapet of their own trench. Those who did succeed in getting over unhurt found their advance greatly impeded by the undergrowth and fallen trees, and were only able to get forward about thirty yards. The survivors were then compelled to take refuge in shell holes from the deadly fire directed against their left flank. Second-Lieutenant N. G. Jackson, of "D" Company, was killed, and Second-Lieutenant H. G. Manning, who commanded the left platoon of " B " Company, was seriously wounded. The Germans, after the repulse of the attack, began to bomb their way down a sap that lay on the left of " D " Company, but Second-Lieutenant F. G. S. Martin, who had led the foremost of the assaulting platoons, succeeded in getting together a few men and forming a defensive flank, which kept the enemy in check. After sunset, the survivors of the attacking platoons made their way back to our lines. Second-Lieutenant Martin, with a small party of volunteers, again left the trench to bring in the wounded. The total casualties amounted to nearly 140, and, unhappily, a very large proportion of these were killed. These losses were not incurred in vain, as the action of the battalion was instrumental in helping the troops on their right, outside the wood, who occupied and held a portion of the enemy's trench.

On September 11th, the 48th were relieved by a London Territorial battalion, and marched back to the neighbourhood of Becourt Wood. After spending a night in the vicinity of Albert, the 1st Northampton-shires again moved up into the line on September 25th. During their absence from the forward area, the great offensive movement of September 15th had taken place, an offensive ever memorable for the fact that in it tanks were first employed in war. All High Wood was now in the hands of British troops, and fighting was in progress on the farther slope of the ridge, over a mile in advance of our former front line.

During this tour in the line the 48th was split up into companies, each of which was placed at the disposal of the commanding officer of some other battalion. Generally speaking, the companies spent their time carrying up stores to troops occupying recently captured portions of the enemy's line, and in improving the communication trenches leading from our old front line to the new positions. "C" Company, however, took part in a minor attack. That company was then under the command of the commanding officer of the 60th. They were occupying a portion of a double line of German trenches which was called the Flers Line, nearly a mile to the north-west of the village bearing that name. As had been the case near Pozières in July, each side was in possession of a part of both the front and the support line, the Germans being separated from the British by barricades. Just in rear of the British barricades, a communication trench joined the front and support lines, while beyond the German barricades a similar communication trench ran parallel to it. "C" Company was ordered to advance from the communication trench on the British side of the barricades and to capture the trench with which it ran parallel. Bombing parties were at the same time to assist the attack by fighting their way up the front and support lines towards the German barricades. This assault was to be made in conjunction with an attack delivered by the Loyal North Lancashires on the left.

The whole affair was very badly arranged. After a most inadequate artillery preparation, " C " Company left its trench at about 6.30 p.m. But no serious attempt was made to support it by bombing up the trenches, and in consequence " C " Company was attacking three sides of a rectangle from the fourth side. Such an attempt was hopeless from the outset. On the left of the company two officers and a number of men were shot down before they had advanced many yards. The right platoons could not reach their objective, and such officers and men as still survived took refuge in shell holes. After dark, the remains of " C " Company withdrew to their own trench. Second-Lieutenant E. Cole was killed and Second-Lieutenant R. W. Gates wounded in this attack, while the other casualties numbered about thirty. Fortunately, the North Lancashires were more successful on the left, and took and held a further portion of the enemy's line. On the evening of September 28th the 1st Northamptonshires were relieved, and took no further active part in the battle of the Somme, which still dragged on for many weary weeks. Many regiments in days to come will look back with pride to the part they played in that stupendous struggle, but none passed through a more terrible and searching ordeal than did the old 48th.

After a few days in the neighbourhood of Albert, the battalion went back to the rear for a well-earned rest. On October 3rd motor-buses conveyed all three infantry brigades of the 1st Division to the Abbeville area, some forty miles from the battle front. The Northamptonshires were billeted in the little village of Acheux-en-Vimeu, and here they spent a pleasant month in training and recuperation. On October 16th a service was held at Acheux-en-Vimeu to commemorate the officers, non-commissioned officers and men who gave their lives for their country in the battle of the Somme. On the same day, the officer who had commanded the 48th throughout those terrible months left the battalion. Lieutenant-Colonel Bethell had been appointed to the command of the 74th Brigade, and was about to take up his new duties. His farewell address to the battalion will never be forgotten by those who heard it. In him the 48th lost a commanding officer of magnetic personality and unrivalled powers of organization, to whose outstanding ability his subsequent successful career bears ample witness.

Lieutenant-Colonel Tollemache assumed command of the battalion on the promotion of Brigadier-General Bethell. The new commanding officer had been with the 48th as second-in-command since the previous February, and was known to all who had served under him in the Somme battle as an officer of remarkable intrepidity and coolness under fire.

When Captain J. C. O. Marriott gave up his position as adjutant to go as staff-captain to Brigadier-General Bethell, his place was filled by Captain McNaught. This officer, who was one of the few who served continuously with the 48th from August, 1914, until the Armistice, came out originally as transport-sergeant, and was promoted to commissioned rank in December, 1914. He acted as adjutant from November, 1916, till the end of the war, and was awarded the Military Cross for his services.

It seems well at this point to mention another officer whose service with the 48th throughout the war was virtually continuous—Captain Hofman, the quarter-master. In following the more eventful fortunes of the men in the line, one is apt to forget the more prosaic but not less important duties of those whose business it is to see that the fighting soldier is properly fed and clothed. We have the authority of Napoleon for saying that " an army moves on its stomach," and the duties of a quartermaster in war-time are more arduous

N

and less free from personal danger than some critics imagine. Seldom have the needs of a battalion in this respect been more efficiently cared for than by Captain Hofman and his trusty subordinate, Quartermaster-Sergeant Bull.

A word of praise in respect of the battalion transport would not be out of place here. This hard-working but often forgotten unit of the battalion, during the period under review had a very hard and trying time. Intermittently shelled and bombed by day and night while in their lines; leaving at dusk with rations, hot food, tea, ammunition, etc., for the troops in the front line, often held up for hours at a stretch by traffic jam, etc., in a gas-filled valley, pushing forward through a barrage of shells night after night put down expressly for the purpose of stopping them, their lot was by no means a pleasant one, and it was no uncommon thing for these men to arrive back at their lines at daybreak, after having spent the night under conditions which, to say the least, were not good for one's nerves. Transport animals, vehicles, etc., have to be looked after, even under the most adverse conditions, and by the time this work was done it was almost time to begin loading up again and preparing to face another night's adventurous journey to the front line. Throughout this period, and, indeed, throughout the war, these men carried on with splendid *esprit de corps,* their one thought being that if ordered up to the front line their one job remaining to be done in life was to get there.

The 48th were conveyed back to the Somme area at the end of October, and, after spending about three weeks in 'Albert, went up into the line near Eaucourt l'Abbaye on November 22nd. Although there was not much fighting during this period, the weather conditions were such that the ranks of the battalion were soon gravely depleted by sickness. On one occasion it took no less than twelve hours for a relief to be effected. Before long no attempt was made to hold entire sections of the water-logged trenches; detached posts, separated by intervals of about fifty yards, sufficed to hold the line, as the swampy condition of the ground precluded any serious attempt at an attack, either by the Germans or the British. Men who had grumbled at the conditions of the trenches in the Loos area during the previous winter, now looked back to them with regret as to a vanished paradise, while some old soldiers were even heard to say that the trenches occupied at Givenchy in the first winter of the war were comfortable, compared with those which they now held. Hence it will not surprise the reader to learn that although the total casualties from the enemy's fire during the six weeks spent in the forward area only amounted to 14 killed and 39 wounded, drafts totalling more than 500 men did not suffice to bring the battalion up to full strength.

The whole countryside was pitted with shell holes full of water—in fact, the whole area was water-logged and a filthy mass of mud and slush; the conditions were simply appalling. The forward posts in the Flers sector consisted of isolated shell holes, with which no communication was possible in the daytime and nothing could move before dusk, and then the question of relief and issue of rations was a perilous one, as the German front posts were similarly situated and one was almost as likely to wander into one of their posts as our own.

In the Eaucourt l'Abbaye sector the conditions were even worse. Although there was a trench system, the front communication trenches were in places thigh deep in water, mud and slush; dead bodies were lying in the bottom of the trenches, and as one waded through this awful filth one would step on or fall over a body half buried in the mud at the bottom and completely covered with water. Dead were lying or built in the parapet and all over the ground in front.

Frostbitten feet were very prevalent at this time, in spite of the whale oil issued for rubbing on the feet as a preventative, and in the course of a three-day tour in

N I

the line many men went down with the complaint, and many more who managed to stick the tour through went down on relief.

The issue of hot food of any description was a great problem; nothing, of course, could be cooked in the front line system, and of necessity had to be cooked at the transport line behind and carried up in food containers. These most excellent things when used under good travelling conditions, were found to be terribly heavy when they had to be carted up on a man's back under the conditions prevailing in the trenches near Eaucourt l'Abbaye, and it is no exaggeration to say that in many cases it took men three or four hours to reach the front line with them over the few hundred yards they had to carry them after being taken over from the transport men. It was a most exhausting and heart-breaking struggle, for the mud gripped one like a vice and many men became stuck and had to be pulled out. Attempts to carry rations over the top proved very little better, as the ground was absolutely pitted with water-logged shell holes, and a slip meant man and rations taking an involuntary bath and having to be pulled out, often with the loss of his load.

On one occasion a regiment marched up in gum boots to relieve the battalion, and arrived at battalion headquarters in a very exhausted condition owing to their long journey in gum boots, slipping and sliding over the mud. The relief of the front line then commenced, the men of the relieving battalion moving along the communication trenches. However, their troubles soon commenced, and man after man became stuck fast and had to be hauled out by comrades from the parapet, and as each man was hauled out his boots were left stuck in the mud. This relief took the whole of the night, not being completed until daybreak, and by that time some twenty or more men were in the dressing station minus their boots.

In order to complete the narrative of the year 1916

we must return once more to the maelstrom of the
Somme, into which, as we know, the 8th Division had
once more been drawn. It had come into line during
the night of October 19th/20th, and the 2nd
Northamptonshires had then renewed their acquaintance with the Somme battlefield. Great changes had
taken place in the three and a half months since
the 8th Division had left that area. The advance of
over a mile by the French and of two miles and more
on the British sector had been followed by six or seven
weeks of bitter and obstinate local fighting. During
these weeks the French, relieved of their anxieties at
Verdun, had gradually been strengthening their forces
on the Somme, while the British, heavily reinforced
from home and now utilizing an entirely new weapon
of war in the tank, were in fine fettle. It seemed, therefore, that if the weather would only hold that the Allied
push might yet break through into open country, but
as a matter of fact the weather broke—and broke
badly—so that it was impossible to exploit the situation
with the necessary rapidity.

The arrival of the 8th Division in line, accompanied
as it was by an all-too-short interval of better weather,
with bright days and frosty nights, coincided with the
preparations for a fresh attempt on October 23rd, in
which the British XIV Corps (4th and 8th Divisions)
was directed to attack upon the French left. The
motive of this operation was to prepare the way for an
attack on Le Transloy at a later date. The tactical
objective of the XIV Corps was, therefore, to advance
within assaulting distance of Le Transloy. The preliminary bombardment was already in progress when
the 8th Division came into line. The advance was to
take place on the 23rd, Zero hour being originally fixed
for 11.30 a.m. The 24th Brigade was on the left, and
its task was of a subsidiary nature, as will later be
seen.

When the 2nd Northamptonshire Regiment came up
into the line on the 19th, it was fortunate in meeting

the 5th Pioneer Battalion, the men of which gave immense and welcome assistance in bringing up rations. The following day was spent in repairing the trenches, a task which was continued on the 21st, and working parties were sent out to repair the road for the transport. So far all had been comparatively quiet, but during the afternoon the Germans got down to it with a steady bombardment. The 22nd was again fairly quiet, and in the evening the 58th moved up to relieve a battalion of the Sherwood Foresters. It was a typical Somme relief. Most of the guides lost their way—as well they might, considering that the country was blasted out of recognition and landmarks were hourly obliterated by shell fire—and it was nearly two o'clock on the morning of the 23rd before the relief was complete, and the 58th then took what rest they could, preparatory to the coming battle.

The position in which the battalion now found itself was in a small but pronounced bulge on the left of the line of the 8th Division. The task of the 24th Brigade was to straighten out that bulge, and this was to be carried out by the 2nd East Lancashire Regiment, which was nominally on the left—really to the left rear—of the 58th. This would be effected by the East Lancashires seizing a German trench to which the name Mild Trench had been given, an operation which would bring that battalion more or less in line with the 58th, the duty of the latter being to render what assistance it could in this forward movement.

The 23rd opened with a thick fog, and on this account it was decided to postpone Zero hour from 11.30 a.m. until half-past two in the afternoon. By that hour the fog had cleared and the attack started to time in much improved weather. With the operations of the 23rd Brigade on the right and of the 25th Brigade in the centre we are not for the moment concerned, and our attention may be fixed upon the operation of straightening out the salient on the left.

For the 58th the morning passed fairly quietly, but

later the enemy began to shell the communication trenches severely, as if he was suspicious that some forward movement was contemplated. The attack by the 2nd East Lancashire Regiment had narrowly escaped premature disaster, for information about the postponement of Zero did not reach battalion head-quarters until a few minutes before 11.30 a.m., and the attack was within an ace of being launched absolutely on its own. Having escaped this mischance, the East Lancashires went forward and captured Mild Trench with great dash and gallantry, the Lewis guns on the left of the 58th co-operating with great effect. The salient was now practically flattened out, and by 5.30 p.m. the general situation of the division was as follows : substantial success on both flanks, with a partial failure in the centre leaving an awkward gap. In the 58th Captain Mathewson, the medical officer, had been killed, and Second-Lieutenant Handsley wounded.

It was proposed to renew the attack by the 8th Division on the following day, but during the evening of the 23rd the weather again changed and rain fell steadily throughout the night as well as all day on the 24th, rendering any active operations impossible owing to the state of the ground, which became a quagmire. The 58th passed the day chiefly in trying to improve their position and in sniping a German strong point at the junction of Mild and Cloudy Trenches. "The snipers had a grand time," says the war diarist, glee-fully : " they claimed seventeen hits during the day." During the evening a patrol discovered that the strong point had been evacuated, and a working party was now sent out to join up with the East Lancashires. Nothing further of interest marks the share of the 58th in the Battle of Le Transloy, and, indeed, the battle itself fizzled out in mud. There was a final flicker from the Northamptonshires early on the morning of the 26th, when " at least sixty Huns were seen on their parapet." All available rifles and Lewis guns were at

once brought into action. Later German stretcher-
bearer parties were observed, and there were corpses in
the morning light. The 8th Division was now relieved
and marched back into the XIV Corps reserve area.
Rest and refitting was now the order, or, as the war
diarist curiously puts it for October 29th : " The
soldiery were given a chance to clean up during the day,
but rain prevented their feet being exposed to the sun
and air." There is something delightfully maiden-
auntish about this.

After a week's rest the division returned to the line,
going on this occasion to the right sector of the XIV
Corps, in front of Les Bœufs, the 58th suffering the
loss of two officers killed in Captain Trefusis and
Second-Lieutenant Rawlings. The effect of the weather
had made this Somme country the most God-forsaken
and miserable area in France, bar possibly the salient
at Ypres. The whole countryside was churned-up,
yeasty mass of mud as a result of the weather and of the
battle, which even yet had not petered out. Constant
rain was varied by spells of intensely cold weather and
some very heavy snowfalls. Everything was mud,
mud—and again mud. There was thin, liquid, watery
mud—mud like inferior gruel. There was a slightly
thicker mud—a porridgey kind of mud. But the bulk
of the mud was mud like simmering glue—in everything but the temperature, for it clung with icy chill.
Billets in the back area were camps of dirty, wet and
decrepit huts—gloomy archipelagos rising from mud
seas. The front " line " just beggars description. It
consisted of a mass of shell holes; of an ocean of mud;
of gulfs, inlets, lagoons and lakes of icy water.
Trenches scarcely existed, except for short lengths on
higher ground : of communication trenches there were
practically none; men had to do the best they could to
improve such shell holes " as were least full of water
and other more unpleasant relics of the battle."
Villages there were in profusion—on the map; but in
reality they were flattened brickwork. Looking back

on those days, it is hard to realize how human beings could have existed in such conditions. Mud, mud, nothing but mud. Mud that squelched; mud that gurgled; mud that gripped the ankles like a vice; mud that often wrenched the boots off a man's feet; mud that made movement a painful, dragging labour; thin mud, thick mud, never-ending, incredible mud. Mud that made reliefs a nightmare and ration-carrying like a scene from Dante's *Inferno*. A watcher from Mars might well have conceived that the earth was covered with a festering sore, and might have mistaken the million or so combatants for loathsome bacteria swarming in the oozy putrescence of the Somme.

The difficulty of rationing the front line under these conditions can be imagined. The 2nd Battalion, however, like the 1st, was fortunate in its quartermaster. Lieutenant R. Mayes (since promoted Major for his services), who served continuously with the 2nd Battalion throughout the war, was untiring in his zeal for his unit; assisted by Regimental Quartermaster-Sergeant Buck and a keen and efficient Transport Section, he did much to alleviate the prevalent discomfort.

During the night of November 17th/18th the 8th Division left this hell and crawled back to billets. Its *moral* and temper were at a low ebb. It had taken part in the fierce and unsuccessful attacks in July, and, with the sense of failure on it, had been sent to hold a sector which had been deliberately overstretched so that troops might be set free for the struggle on the Somme. Before it had time to find itself, it had been hurried back to take its share in the last and most trying portion of the advance. Fate had given the 8th Division no direct share in the victories, but had dealt out full measure of the bitterest and darkest hours of the Somme.

A rest, a clean up, training and games did wonders. The 58th responded quickly, and in December won the Divisional Football Cup by defeating the 23rd Machine

Gun Company, at St. Maulvis, by 3—2. Then came
the third Christmas in France. The war diarist records
no banqueting or joviality. He merely prints
CHRISTMAS DAY in block capitals, and then adds,
rather sourly, "There were no parades." The end of
the year found the 58th in harness again, for on
December 30th it marched out into divisional reserve
huts at Camp 107, near Billon Wood.

CHAPTER X.

THE year 1917 started in a way which distinguished it
from its predecessors and for a time held out hopes of
complete and early success.   The principle of universal
service had been adopted; adequate supplies of recruits
were thus provided for; and the number becoming
available at any given time could be accurately gauged.
This was an immense advantage in planning operations,
and further it put an end to the abominable system
whereby wounded and shattered men, who had voluntarily enlisted, were hurried out a second or third time
overseas in order that others whose patriotism and
courage were less pronounced might luxuriate in safe
and lucrative billets at home.   In the Government, too,
there had been an important change.   Early in
December, 1916, the Asquith administration had
collapsed and Mr. Lloyd George had become Prime
Minister; and there was much talk of a way of winning the war by a method speedier and less costly in life
than a war of exhaustion.   The year 1917 was above all
things to be the Year of Victory; and both in England
and France loans were floated and eagerly subscribed to
in the hope that within twelve months Germany would
be beaten to her knees.   These high hopes were, however, to be doomed to disappointment.

The beginning of 1917 found the 48th resting in the
vicinity of Albert.   Bell tents in a snow-covered field
near Bresle during the bitter weather of January would
not be generally considered the height of luxury, but
they were a welcome change from the rigours of the
front line.

On February 2nd the 48th left Bresle and marched to

Mericourt-sur-Somme, a village situated on the southern side of that river. The 1st Division was about to take over the front formerly held by the French, and advanced parties were sent up from the 48th to examine the line. Despite linguistic difficulties, the officers and men who spent a day among the troops of our allies found the experience an enjoyable one. On February 7th the 2nd Brigade relieved the French 108th Regiment of Infantry in the trenches opposite Barleux. The first few days spent in this part of the line were free from incident. Owing to the frosty weather, the trenches required little or no attention to make them habitable, and the enemy did not display much activity, although they had made a successful raid against the French a day or two before the British troops relieved them. When once the frost broke, the trenches soon became very muddy, and this involved a good deal of hard work for the 48th, but the enemy continued to be inactive. After patrols had been sent out, it was determined to attempt a raid upon the enemy's front line, and 4 officers and 80 men, under Capt. J. E. M. Pierson, went back to train for this purpose.

The raid took place early on the morning of March 6th. Two gaps had been made in the enemy's wire by our artillery. Through each of these gaps a party of about forty raiders was to make its way. A certain number in each party were detailed to protect the flanks of the remainder. The rest were to work inwards along the front line until they met.

At 3.30 a.m. our artillery opened an intense fire upon the German front line for two minutes, and then lifted to form a box barrage. Meanwhile the two raiding parties, which were lying out in front of our trenches, advanced towards the gaps in the wire. The right party were met by a shower of bombs from the Germans and found themselves unable to force their way through the gap. Second-Lieutenant E. P. Willoughby, who was leading the party, was wounded. Thereupon

Sergeant Forrester, though hit in the face and right eye, took command of the raiders and tried to rally them. Corporal Norman meanwhile advanced alone through the gap and bombed the enemy, receiving a severe wound in the face. The Germans then opened fire with a trench mortar, and the right party lost cohesion and retreated.

On the left, the raiding party commanded by Second-Lieutenant R. Leader reached the German parapet without opposition, and each group went to its allotted task. The officer detailed to clear the front line, Second-Lieutenant P. A. Heather, made his way to the right along the top of the trench, firing at the enemy below him as he went. He got nearly as far as the right gap in the wire, when, seeing the right party retreating, and having only two men left of his followers, he withdrew. The detachment guarding the left flank bombed two German dug-outs. Second-Lieutenant C. Renton left his men to go and ascertain what had become of the right-hand party, and was never seen again. Seeing that they were receiving no support from the right, the left party gradually withdrew, and the raid was over.

In addition to the officer casualties already mentioned, Second-Lieutenant E. E. Hurst, the scout officer, was wounded by a machine-gun bullet as he was assisting Captain Pierson to rally the retreating men of the right party. Second-Lieutenant Hurst had previously won the D.C.M. when acting as scout sergeant to the battalion, and had received his commission quite recently. The casualties among other ranks were 3 missing and 12 wounded. Captain Pierson was awarded the Military Cross for his conduct on this occasion, while Sergeant Forrester and Corporal Norman both received the D.C.M.

The raid described above had been undertaken partly in order to gain information about the expected retirement of the enemy to the Cambrai—St. Quentin line. When the German retreat actually did take place, about ten days later, the battalion was in billets at Chuignolles, some eight miles behind the line. On March 18th everybody was discussing rumours of the abandonment of the German trenches; so it was with a keen sense of expectancy that the 48th marched up to relieve the 2nd Royal Munster Fusiliers on the following day. The company commanders rode up in advance to ascertain what the situation was.

As yet, nobody knew how far back the enemy had gone, but the complete absence of any sounds of firing convinced the Northamptonshires that they must have left their original position. The excitement became intense when the 48th marched unopposed across No Man's Land and over the enemy's deserted trenches. Then they descended the slope to the Somme and crossed the river by the plank bridge which had been hurriedly constructed by the Royal Engineers to replace the one that the Germans had destroyed. Having relieved the Munsters just beyond Brie, a village on the eastern bank of the river, the 48th settled down for the night in the German main third line, one platoon, under Second-Lieutenant R. D. Martin, being sent forward to Mons-en-Chaussée, three miles farther east. Throughout the night, cavalry and cyclists pressed forward through the lines held by the battalion, to get in touch with the retreating enemy. On the morning of March 20th, " D " Company, now under the command of Captain F. G. S. Martin, occupied Mons-en-Chaussée, the platoon which first went there having been withdrawn. The 48th made no farther advance, but remained in front of Brie. Several officers went farther afield in order to see the condition of the country that lay behind the old German line. The sight of a landscape undevastated by shell fire made a pleasant change to those used to the desolation of the areas near the front line, but orchards full of destroyed trees, and villages in which incendiary fires still smouldered, bore witness to the ruthlessness of the enemy. Fortunately none of the 48th fell victims to any of the numerous "booby-traps" which had been left behind by the retreating Germans. The retirement of the enemy from their trenches in front of Barleux led to the discovery of a grave bearing the name of Second-Lieutenant Renton. As he had been buried near a German dressing station, it is probable that this officer died of wounds received during the raid of March 6th.

On March 21st the Northamptonshires were relieved by a battalion of the 59th Division, and recrossed the Somme. For the next fortnight they remained under canvas west of the river, helping the Royal Engineers to construct a more permanent bridge over the Somme, and repairing roads.

The 48th marched back to Chuignolles on April 7th, where they were joined five days later by Captain G. St. G. Robinson, who now became second-in-command of the battalion. Captain Clark, who had hitherto acted in this capacity, and whose long and honourable record of service in the firing line had entitled him to a less arduous post, afterwards assumed command of the Divisional Employment Company. Shortly before this the 48th had been deprived of the services of another officer who had done excellent work during the preceding two years. Captain Bourdillon, the medical officer, received promotion early in 1917, and left the battalion on February 16th. This officer had won the Military Cross on May 9th, 1915, and the D.S.O. during the Battle of the Somme. In each case the decoration had been awarded to him for his courageous disregard of his own personal safety while tending the wounded under fire.

The 48th did not remain much longer in the Somme area. After a month of training and recreation at Morcourt, they proceeded to Villers-Bretonneux, where they waited until arrangements were made for the conveyance of the 1st Division to the north to join the Second Army. The Northamptonshires entrained early on the morning of May 27th, and the afternoon of the same day found them at Bailleul. At this time the attack on Messines was being arranged, and for a fortnight the 1st Northamptonshires remained under canvas in a field between Fletre and Meteren, in readiness to move up to the scene of the new offensive, should their services be required. The 2nd Battalion was stationed close at hand; there were numerous meetings of old friends, and various athletic events were contested between representatives of the two battalions. Neither was employed in the operations near Messines.

On June 11th the battalion marched north to the neighbourhood of Cassel and went into billets among the scattered farm buildings that lie immediately south of the hill upon which the little town stands. On June 20th the march to the coast, which was the ultimate destination of the 48th, was continued. On one day the battalion travelled a few miles by train, but generally speaking the move was made by road. On the evening of June 23rd the 48th marched into a camp quite close to the seashore, and some three miles behind the trenches near Nieuport, the extreme left of the Allied line on the Western Front. The sector in which the 48th now found itself, and where it was to experience one of the greatest attacks in its long and eventful history, was quite different from any other in France. It was nothing but sand—flat as a rule, but with dunes rising some sixty feet above sea level, and thick clusters of rushes to break the monotony. Further inland the country was exceptionally flat and low-lying. Along the dunes there had sprung up at Nieuport and Lombartzyde little seaside resorts with red-tiled bungalows and bizarre houses with little gardens, snatched, as it were, from the surrounding sea of loose, powdery sand. The frontage of the sector now held by the 1st Division was about one mile in length. About half a mile in rear of the front line, and parallel with it, was the Yser Canal. The front-line system in front of the canal was usually held by two battalions. The left flank rested on the sea, while the right was bounded by a dyke known as the Geleide Creek, which joined the canal at right angles. The position itself faced roughly east, so that in case of attack the defenders would have to fight, throughout the morning at any rate, with the disadvantage of having the sun in their eyes. It was thought that the sand would tend to prevent the explosion of many of the enemy shells, but this proved to be a complete fallacy. The nature of the soil rendered the ordinary trenches out of the question, and breastworks—which showed up with terrible distinctness—took their place. Apart from this, it will be seen that the two battalions on the far side of the canal were in a dangerously isolated position. The Yser Canal was indeed crossed by three bridges, but these were but of a temporary nature and their exact position was, of course, known to an inch by the German artillery. At the mouth of the canal and on the near side of it lay Nieuport Bains, a small bathing resort. Nieuport itself was about two miles inland on the banks of the canal. In the distance Ostend could be faintly discerned. On the whole the position was one of very obvious danger and drawbacks, but so quiet had the sector been that it was considered distinctly " healthy," and was regarded as a suitable place to " try out " young officers and section commanders.

On July 4th the 48th and the 2nd Battalion of the 60th went into the front line, the 60th holding the left, so that the outer man of that battalion was the left-hand man of the whole great Western Front, the other flank of which rested on the Swiss Frontier. It so chanced— and a fortunate chance it proved to be—that a much larger percentage of officers and men was left out of the line than was usually the case. These details of the 48th numbered about 400, and remained on the near side of the canal, under Major Robinson. Captain McNaught had gone to England on leave, his place being taken by the assistant-adjutant, Second-

o

Lieutenant D. C. Chisholm, who had commanded " B " Company in the Battle of the Somme. Of the four company commanders two were not in the line, and the only other officers there, above the rank of subaltern, were Lieutenant-Colonel Tollemache, Captain E. R. C. Aylett, of " C " Company, and Captain Hayes, the medical officer. A fair proportion of the officers had never before been under fire, but, taken as a whole, not only was the battalion up to strength, but after a long period of rest and training it was thoroughly efficient and fully recovered from the fighting on the Somme and the hardships of the winter.

The expectation of a quiet and peaceful tour was not belied by the first couple of days in the line : in fact, July 6th was logged as "very quiet" and it seemed, what with the fine weather and a welcome whiff of the sea, as if the stay amongst the sandhills might prove to be an enjoyable change from the conditions of the interior of France. The spell was to a certain extent broken on the 7th, when there was a fair amount of shelling by the Germans—possibly with a view to ranging. The next night a successful enterprise on the part of the 48th put everyone in high spirits. The battalion scout officer, Second-Lieutenant McAnally, led a patrol towards the German lines. He and Sergeant Rivett, of " D " Company, cut a gap in the enemy's wire and a reconnoitring party went through. On the return of the party it was decided to wait to see if any Huns would emerge, and, surely enough, an officer appeared, followed by about twenty men. Second-Lieutenant McAnally shot the officer and bombs were thrown at the remainder, from whom " groans were heard." The raiders all returned safely, in spite of the inevitable rifle and machine-gun fire which followed. A further enterprise on the following night was, however, not so successful, for although the party under Lieutenant G. B. Thompson, did indeed gallantly penetrate into the German trenches and bombed several dug-outs, unfortunately no prisoners

were taken—and these were always wanted for identifi-
cation purposes—and the raiders had to retire with the
loss of one killed and one wounded.

Then came the tragedy; the *dies iræ dies illa;* and
July 10th was to take its place with May 9th as one of
the blackest days in the calendar of the 48th Regiment.

The day broke calm and sunny, and shortly after
dawn the German heavy artillery opened fire. At first
their attention was principally devoted to the reserve
line and the bridges over the canal. The various
accounts consulted differ as to the hour when the
tremendous German bombardment began, but it seems
that at 6.45 a.m. the Germans opened a very heavy
shelling with their 5˙9's. This lasted for exactly an
hour, when the barrage was put down on the support
line, and again, at 8.45 a.m., the fire was turned on to
what was—to the German artillery—the far side of the
canal. Throughout the morning the bombardment
increased in intensity. The din was appalling. Heavy
artillery, field guns and trench mortars united to swell
the tornado of fire. Those who watched the terrible
spectacle from points of comparative safety included
many who had been through the horrors of the Somme.
And all muttered that never before had they witnessed
a bombardment of such duration and intensity.

In the clear morning light the breastworks of the 48th
showed up clear and well defined. Under the torrent of
shells they soon collapsed. Before long they were
virtually obliterated. Such of the defenders as had
escaped death or serious wounds were compelled to
crouch in shell holes to shield themselves from the
inferno that raged against them. As has been
mentioned, many of the officers had never before been
under serious fire. The same was the case with the
men. But there is no record of any betrayal of the
traditions of the Regiment.

At a quarter to nine there was a pause of five minutes
in the bombardment, and then it was methodically
resumed, one hour being devoted to the support line,

O I

the south-west side of the Yser and the front line; after another pause of five minutes, the firing was again systematically renewed, although this time in a different sequence. This went on until five minutes to two, when a slightly longer lull—of from ten to fifteen minutes—took place. During the forenoon German aeroplanes flew over, quite undisturbed by our machines, dropping bombs on the reserve lines, but, luckily, casualties were few, as the details, under Major Robinson, and the transport, had been scattered among the sandhills. The front line was now completely isolated, for all telephone wires had been severed by the shell fire and the bridges over the Yser were in matchwood—two of them at any rate, and the third was approaching its end. The artillery of the 1st Division made heroic efforts to reply to the bombardment, but was quite outmatched, and during the day most of it was knocked out of action. Apparently no heavy artillery was available on our side, with disastrous results for the troops over the canal. In the lulls which occurred the men in the trenches were set to work digging out those who had been buried by masses of sand, and runners were sent to maintain touch between the companies, but these intervals were short, and soon "the whole thing commenced again and it seemed as if a shell were falling on every foot of ground. The earth was rocking; the smoke and sand were so dense that one could hardly see a yard in front. Hell was let loose with a vengeance. We were like a lot of stupid beings, as we were helpless to do anything but wait till the end."

From ten minutes past two until seven o'clock the bombardment went on without intermission, front line, supports and reserves being drenched under this torrent of fire. It is difficult to obtain any coherent account as to how the men endured the fearful ordeal during the twelve long hours it lasted. Survivors told how Lieutenant P. A. Heather, who commanded "D" Company, continued to go from post to post encouraging his men to stand fast, though he himself was badly wounded. No doubt there were many similar cases of heroism, but only too often those who could have borne witness to them perished. During the afternoon a physical exhaustion had set in. "Our heads were splitting and we were choked with fumes and sand. It was a tragedy. We knew our machine guns and Lewis guns must be the same. The only questions being asked now was, how much could our artillery help us and was any help coming across the river? Just as we were beginning to think that Fritz was not going to attack the bombardment recommenced. About 6 p.m. it eased up a little and the enemy were among us, appearing to come from the rear."

It was really nearer to seven o'clock when the German Marine Division—first-class troops—attacked the junction between the 60th and 48th. The attack was made in three waves, and when the British line was pierced the attackers turned outwards, splitting into two separate attacks in rear of the two battalions. If the Germans expected little or no resistance from enemies stunned to impotence by the awful bombardment to which they had been subjected, they were soon undeceived. As they surged forward across the wreck of the defences of the 48th, isolated groups of men who had survived the bombardment shot them down from shell holes. Captain Aylett, assisted by Second-Lieutenants R. C. Cowley and N. V. H. Coghill, offered a particularly effective resistance to the enemy. By his orders, the Lewis gunners of "C" Company had buttoned their tunics around two of their guns to shield them from the flying sand. Hence, when the enemy had crossed the point where our front line had been, he was able to direct a deadly enfilade fire against their advancing ranks. Such guns of the divisional artillery as still remained fit for action rained shrapnel upon the attackers and caused considerable execution.

But the odds were too heavy for the ultimate issue to be in doubt. On the left, the enemy had forced their way through the 60th, who still continued to fight on in a manner that was worthy of their regiment. Passing behind the Northamptonshires' lines, the Germans attacked their battalion headquarters from the rear. Indeed, the first intimation that the officers in the headquarters dug-out had of the launching of the attack was the appearance of several of the enemy at the mouth of the ventilating shaft. Bombs were hurled down this shaft and down the main entrance, several of the headquarters signallers being severely wounded. Lieutenant Chisholm at once began to destroy the more important documents in his possession, while Lieutenant-Colonel Tollemache at first declined to surrender, and wished to fight it out to a finish. Fortunately he broke his revolver, and was consequently unable to carry out his intention, for the position was hopeless, and no other course than surrender was open to the occupants of the dug-out. Describing this incident, an officer of the battalion writes: " In several English papers graphic accounts had been given of the manner in which the headquarters officers were killed while standing back to back firing their revolvers at the enemy. It may be said at once that these tales were untrue. The officers in question and the battalion to which they belonged have alike made for themselves too good a reputation for there to be any need to attempt to bolster it up by fiction."

After the capture of headquarters the enemy bombed the regimental aid post, several of its occupants being hit and the remainder surrendering. The same party took Captain Aylett's men in rear and turned a machine gun on them. After most of his followers had been killed and his two Lewis guns put out of action, Captain Aylett and the few survivors surrendered. Second-Lieutenant Cowley was badly wounded by a bomb before resistance ceased in this quarter. Elsewhere, too, the Germans gradually overpowered our resistance, but it was not until two hours after the attack was launched that weight of numbers finally prevailed.

With the exception of nine other ranks who succeeded in escaping by swimming the canal, every one of the Northamptonshires who was in the line on July 10th was killed or captured. The list of dead included Lieutenant Heather, and Second-Lieutenants G. H. Smith and J. H. S. Symons, while Lieutenant-Colonel Tollemache, Captain Aylett, Captain E. Hayes, and Second-Lieutenants Chisholm and McAnally were among those taken prisoner.

The Germans have often been censured, and rightly censured, for their callous inhumanity to British wounded and prisoners. It is only just to say that the conduct of the German Marine Division on this occasion shows that there were exceptions to this rule. The testimony of those who returned from captivity was that on July 10th the enemy treated their prisoners, wounded and unwounded, in a humane and generous manner.

It was long before any details of this disaster reached the remainder of the battalion, and for many weeks the relatives of those who were missing lingered in an agony of doubt as to what had happened to them. Most of those who escaped could give no lucid or coherent account of what had taken place. The most detailed information that was received for some time was the narrative of Sergeant Mansfield, the battalion scout sergeant, who escaped across the Geleide Creek and informed the battalion on the right of the Northampton-shires of the situation. The commanding officer of this battalion thereupon formed a defensive flank to check the farther advance of the enemy. Sergeant Mansfield received the D.C.M. for his services, and Sergeant Cope, a survivor of those who took part in the stand made by " C " Company, was awarded the Military Medal.

Such was the Nieuport disaster. The reasons why the two battalions involved in it obtained no adequate support from the British heavy artillery lie outside the scope of this history. It suffices here to say that the 48th and 60th, battered and hammered for over twelve hours by an artillery bombardment which would have

broken the *moral* of most troops, none the less offered
so stubborn and determined a resistance to the German
attack that it took one of the picked divisions of the
enemy's army two hours to overcome the survivors of
the 1,100 dauntless men that had held the front-line
system. The stand that the defenders made against
overwhelming odds evoked the warmest admiration
from all who witnessed it. A message sent to the
2nd Brigade on July 11th by the 1st Divisional
Commander, Major-General E. P. Strickland, voiced
the general opinion of the onlookers.

" I wish to express to you my feelings of deep
sympathy, in which I feel sure I am joined by the rest
of the division, in the losses which you sustained in
yesterday's fighting. There were no two finer fighting
regiments in the division than the 1st Northamptonshires and the 2nd King's Royal Rifles, and in an
extremely difficult situation they worthily upheld the
fine traditions of those regiments. They put up a fine
fight, and the enemy will doubtless have every reason
to remember their encounter with them."

After this disaster the 48th was moved from the sector
to rest and refit west of St. Pol.

We shall now leave the Northamptonshire Regiment
for the moment and give a rapid summary of the whole
situation on the Western Front from the opening of the
year. At the beginning of this chapter it was stated
that Mr. Lloyd George had become Prime Minister and
that he was anxious to secure victory without paying
the terrible price which had hitherto been demanded.
A feature of the new or Lloyd-Georgian system of
offensive was that the British Army was now placed at
the disposal of General Nivelle for the coming operations. That commander had therefore a double duty
to perform. He was at one and the same time the
commander-in-chief of the French armies and
generalissimo of the Allies in France. The arrangement was unmilitary and unfortunate and soon resulted
in friction, for when it was reported by the British that

the Germans were retiring from the whole of the old Somme battlefield, Nivelle, who was not in close touch with the happenings on the British front, discredited the report. The news was, however, true; the Germans were in retreat on the whole front between Arras and the Aisne; and had settled down upon what came to be known as the Hindenburg Line. As a result the enemy had now withdrawn from a considerable portion of that front from which Nivelle had intended to attack, and this circumstance naturally raised grave doubts as to the feasibility of that commander's plan. Further, not only had the Germans sensibly diminished their front—a fact which enabled them to increase their reserves—but they had exchanged the battered defences of the Somme for the strongest position yet constructed on the Western Front.

In spite of the altered circumstances the French Government decided not to interfere with General Nivelle. The spring campaign was to be opened by the British. The right of the new German line rested on Vimy Ridge and the British offensive was to take the form of an advance east of Arras and an attack upon Vimy Ridge a few miles north of that city. A striking success was achieved. The Canadians captured Vimy Ridge—one of the finest achievements of the war. Immediately to the south the Battle of Arras was the most successful which the British had fought on the Western Front since the Germans had stabilized their defences. But in spite of the high hopes raised by the success of the British spring offensive all ideas of a grand Allied strategical offensive had now broken down. Russia was in the initial throes of revolution and had become, in the stark military vernacular, "a wash-out." General Nivelle's great attack had been a costly failure. The offensive in Macedonia never started. In Palestine the advance from Egypt had been twice checked at Gaza. So far from these set-backs inducing co-operation amongst the Allies they seemed to have a divergent tendency,—and were it not that

America had entered the war on April 5th the general situation would have been by no means reassuring. Further, the war had taken on an aspect which if not entirely new was a development not quite expected. The real offensive on the part of Germany in 1917 was not upon land but upon the sea—or more strictly underneath the sea, for unrestricted submarine warfare had now been adopted by the German Government. Of all the Allied Powers none was so likely to suffer from this development as England, and the British operations in France were influenced to a marked degree by this new state of affairs. The chief base of operations for the German submarines was the Belgian coast, and, in the absence of any combined strategic objective, it was natural that in British eyes a new Flanders campaign should appear to be the course to be adopted. As a preliminary to such offensive it would be necessary to secure the Messines—Wytschaete Ridge, which dominated Ypres and the whole jumping-off line from which the offensive in Flanders could begin. For nearly a year and a half preparations had been going on with a view to the capture of the ridge. Engineering science had been called in to assist and nineteen enormous mines had been laid after prodigious tunnelling under the enemy's position. The total charges were nearly one million pounds. The mines were distributed over a front of eight miles. The largest was one of ninety-five thousand pounds of ammonal at a depth of one hundred and twenty-five feet, and there was one gallery seven hundred and twenty yards in length.

The Messines Ridge was duly blown sky high on June 7th. A notable gain in terrain had been made, and a pause of a few weeks now took place, the time being utilized by the Allies in making the elaborate preparations required for a further great offensive. Ypres could no longer be overlooked by the Germans from the south; but they dominated it in a measure from the east, north-east and north, and as the offensive was to be directed against this German ring it followed that the preparations for it could not be concealed. Thus the forces with which it was proposed to break out from the neighbourhood of Ypres and to gain the high ground still dominating the city had to carry out their arrangements in the latter part of July in full view of the enemy. Fully forewarned, the Germans had taken every step to meet the assault. They had by now realized that continuous trenches afforded poor protection against the terrific bombardments of the Allies, unless abundant underground cover could be provided, for which the waterlogged terrain of Flanders was unsuited. Accordingly they introduced what was almost a revolution in the tactics of defence, namely, the substitution of depth for breadth; that is to say, they held their ground by a series of rows of disjointed trenches and strong points, while scattered about were small concrete blockhouses with walls of great thickness each garrisoned by about twenty men with two or three machine guns. These were the famous " pill-boxes," now to be tested for the first time.

The strength of the British Army in combatant troops was now at its greatest. Sir Douglas Haig had sixty-four divisions and ten cavalry divisions under his orders and a mass of tanks, heavy artillery and aeroplanes. His plan was to make a great attack with his Fifth Army, which had been moved north for the purpose, supported on his left by a French army. The ultimate goal was to be the Passchendaele Ridge, from which it was hoped to be able to sweep with gun fire the plains beyond it towards Zeebrugge and Ostend, after which a combined naval and military attack, which had been secretly prepared in England, was to be made on the Belgian coast. In the initial attack the order of battle of the various divisions of the Fifth Army, working from right to left, was as follows :—24th, 30th, 8th, 15th, 55th, 39th, 51st, 38th and Guards Division, each corps—of which there were four—having two divisions in support. Zero day was to be July 31st.

The battle which then began was the Third Battle of Ypres, in which both the 48th and 58th were engaged, the share of the latter being the greater, as the 2nd Battalion took part in the opening phase, whereas the 1st Battalion did not come in until later. We propose, therefore, to go back now to the 58th, which we left on the Somme; follow its doings in pursuing the Germans to the Hindenburg Line in March and April; narrate its transfer north; and be with it, from the opening of the Third Battle of Ypres on July 31st, till the close of 1917. Having done that, we shall then take up the 48th, which was re-forming and refitting after the disaster at Nieuport, and tell its story for the latter half of that year. Then with both battalions, so to speak, under our hand, we can take a breath, have a look round, and then prepare a " lay-out " for the real year of victory, 1918, and the End of the War.

It will be remembered that at the end of 1916 the 24th Brigade was in shelters at Bronfray Farm, the remainder of the 8th Division being in line. Relief soon came, and on January 10th, 1917, the bulk of the division retired for a further fortnight's training in the vicinity of Belloy St. Leonard. As for the 58th, to follow its movements with more exactitude, it marched on the 10th to Sailly-le-Sec and bivouacked there for the night. The next day it moved to Mericourt, where it entrained for St. Airaines and marched thence to St. Maulvis. Further movements were an entrainment at Oisemont on the 22nd; a journey to Edgehill and thence by route march first to Camp 13, and then to Camp 17, near Sezanne. Towards the end of the month the division was in the line again, taking over the left of the XV Corps front, relieving the 40th Division. While the 8th Division had been at rest the XV Corps had side-stepped to the right, and the 24th Brigade, in the southern sub-sector, found itself with its right on Bouchavesnes. This point marked the junction of the British and French Armies; the 58th was in brigade reserve. There is now a mention in the war diary of carrying and working parties, but this was practically all that fell to the 58th during January. The month had been really peaceful, the bulk of it being taken up by training, gas helmet drill, bombing instruction, interior economy, inspections and church parades. A warlike note is sounded, however, by the entry on January 14th of the formation of a Battle Patrol Platoon, under Lieutenant Jarvis. The weather was exceptionally cold, a very keen frost setting in towards the end of January. Although the ground was so hard as to make digging difficult, all ranks preferred the cold to the never-ending struggle with the mud which had marked their previous period in the line.

February was also a peaceful month—more or less—with the usual in-and-out of the line, but there is a note in the war diary for the 21st hinting at " training for offensive operations." To cut a long story short, the British attacks north of the Ancre, and the losses inflicted, had convinced the Germans of the necessity of shortening their line. The Germans had been seriously shaken by the Somme fighting of 1916. In the neighbourhood of Beaumont Hamel the 63rd Division had made an important advance early in 1917. It had become increasingly evident that the German defence was weakening, and with the spring the conditions became relatively favourable for a withdrawal on their part, for the thaw which succeeded the period of exceptional frost had turned the old Somme battlefield into a quagmire once again, while exerting but little effect on the roads elsewhere. As a consequence, the Germans, if they chose to retire, could do so fairly quickly, whereas the Allies, in following up and being confronted first by the quagmire, must do so very slowly; and this takes no account of the artificial expedients which the Germans could employ to delay the pursuit still further. A withdrawal by the Germans on a wide scale had therefore been expected, and it had been definitely ascertained that they had been feverishly at work upon a new defensive line in rear.

This was the famous Hindenburg Line of history, which branched off from the original German defences near Arras, ran south-east for twelve miles to Quéant, and thence west of Cambrai in the direction of St. Quentin.   The immediate object appeared to be escape from the salient between Arras and Le Transloy, but it was also evident, from the preparations which the Germans were making on a grand scale, that they contemplated an evacuation on much wider lines.   The underlying motive of a withdrawal generally was to husband strength.   The move back to the Hindenburg system would cause a considerable diminution of the German front and a consequent increase in the number of German reserves.   It was clearly necessary for the Germans to take these measures.   They had lost very heavily on the Somme, and they knew perfectly well that the French were meditating a great offensive in the " Year of Victory."   There was, too, always the possibility of Russia even yet doing something big, and America might not always be too proud to fight.

During the night of February 23rd/24th the Germans began their first movement of retreat, although long before this date the British Higher Command, in spite of the incredulity of the French, had been convinced that a far greater withdrawal was in course of preparation.   It was, of course, obviously important that this retreat should be harried as much as possible and that the Germans should not be allowed to saunter back unmolested to another position according to plan. This is the explanation of the proposed offensive of the 8th Division.   The ten days in reserve were devoted to intensive preparation and rehearsals against a faithful reproduction of the German trench system.   The frost which then prevailed made the preparation of gun positions, various headquarters, etc., a matter of great difficulty.   But the thaw which came on February 20th, and brought rain with it, made matters ten times worse. So bad were the conditions that several men of the 4th Division were actually drowned during the relief of the 8th Division on February 21st. There were cases where officers and men had to be cut out of their nether garments and hauled by main force from their boots before they could be extracted from the mud. In these circumstances an attack was out of the question, and the date was put forward from February 27th to March 4th.

The objective was the possession of the German positions on the "hog's back" overlooking Bouchavesnes. The 8th Division detailed two brigades for the operation, the 25th on the right and the 24th on the left. In the latter brigade two battalions were in the front line of about 800 yards, namely, the 1st Worcestershire Regiment and 2nd Northampton-shire Regiment. Owing to the rain and mud it had not been possible to construct assembly trenches, and the two leading waves formed up on the front and support line posts. A feature of this attack was that chewing gum was issued to the troops, both to stop coughing during the preliminary wait and to give the men something to occupy their minds.

Zero hour had been fixed for 5.15 a.m., and shortly before that hour the barrage descended, lifting five minutes later. The assaulting troops carried Pallas Trench, their first objective, with little loss, and in strict accordance with schedule. A small section of German trench, opposite the junction of the two British brigades, had, however, been overlooked, and its garrison was causing some trouble to "C" Company, under Lieutenant Bird. The annoyance was, however, promptly dealt with by the Battle Patrol Platoon, under Lieutenant Jarvis, and twenty prisoners were bagged. Leaving Pallas Trench to be consolidated by the "moppers-up" the attacking troops continued their advance, and with similar success gained the second objective. So splendid was the dash and vigour of the attack—writes the historian of the 8th Division—that in one place where Pallas Support had been so destroyed by our artillery as to be no longer recognizable in the half light, part of "B" Company, under

Captain Fergusson, swept past it and on to the next German line. Here they killed several of the enemy, captured a machine gun, bombed a dug-out, and then, discovering their error, withdrew in good order to Pallas Support.

The enemy, however, fought with great bravery and determination. The key of the position was an arrangement of trenches known as " The Triangle," and here the victory was assured only by a sterling piece of co-operation between the 1st Worcestershire Regiment and the 58th. " C " Company of the latter had more than it could do to be able to hold all this important point, but the left company of the Worcestershires immediately extended its inner flank to co-operate in the defence. The attack of " C " Company was also materially assisted by an act of conspicuous gallantry performed by Lance-Corporal Rickard and Private Ette, of that company. These two rushed an enemy machine gun which was holding up the attack, putting the gun out of action and killing or capturing the gun team. Another act of great gallantry was performed by Private H. Bamford, of " B " Company. In the fight for the last strong point holding out in front of the 58th, Private Bamford, while working his Lewis gun, was struck in the face by a shell splinter and lost the sight of one eye. But he refused to leave his post, and, although half blinded and in great pain, worked his gun for two hours after he was hit, until he was wounded a second time.

The enemy was not yet done with. The Germans may have been retiring "according to plan," but they were determined to show their teeth while doing so. Five counter-attacks were launched by them across the open, and, although these were repulsed, the enemy also made several vigorous attempts to re-enter his last positions at points where German communication trenches led away from the last objective gained by us. These attempts were defeated, and Sergeant Parker, of " D " Company, distinguished himself by holding a post on the extreme left for half an hour single handed, until relieved by a party of the Sherwood Foresters.

At dusk the enemy at length, thoroughly beaten, gave up the struggle for the day. The attack had cost the 58th dear. The casualties were 242. In officers there were killed Captain Knight, Lieutenant Bird, and Lieutenant Palmer, while Second-Lieutenants Woodyat, Bishop, Jones and Frost were wounded. Shelling continued throughout the night, but at 3 a.m. the battalion was relieved by the 2nd Devons and returned to dug-outs at Asquith's Flats.

After a few days for rest and reorganization—at a place named " Aldershot "—the 58th relieved the 2nd Royal Berkshire Regiment in the Bouchavesnes north sector. The weather was now very bad, and much work had to be done in improving trenches and communications. Mud was again the enemy, and " working parties spent a good deal of their time digging each other out "—as the waggish war diarist neatly puts it. On March 12th, Lieutenant-Colonel Buckle, while walking round the front line, was wounded in the head by a sniper, but pluckily carried on with his duty. On this night patrols found the powerful German trench system unoccupied, and the whole Allied line, the French now alive to the situation, prepared to follow up and press the retreating enemy. On the 8th Division front patrols were out constantly and the line was pushed steadily forward, the division being on the Canal du Nord on the 18th. The 2nd Northamptonshire Regiment did its share of in-and-out of the line, the latter phase being occupied chiefly in road making and laying a pipe line. During the 28th and 29th patrols discovered that in the zone of the 8th Division the line Heudecourt—Sorel-le-Grand—Fins was strongly held by the enemy, and it was resolved to attack it without delay. This operation was successfully carried out by the 23rd and 25th Brigades on the 30th. The 2nd Northamptonshire Regiment, however, was getting ready for further fighting, the

P

war diary stating that " The battalion re-formed preparatory to offensive operations."

At the beginning of April the situation was that the Fourth and Fifth Armies, the latter on the left, were maintaining their pressure on the retreating Germans and the ground was cleared for the main British spring offensive opposite Arras and Vimy Ridge. This offensive has already been referred to earlier in this chapter, and here it is sufficient to say that, to assist it, the 8th Division, in common with the other divisions of the Fourth Army, kept steadily pushing ahead. On the 9th came the news of the successful launching by the Third and First Armies of their great Vimy— Arras offensive. Three successive systems of the German defences had been pierced. An unprecedented capture of ground, guns and prisoners had been made. But to secure the maximum of success it was essential that the Germans should be prevented from reinforcing the damaged sector of their front, and consequently the 8th Division, and its fellows, more than ever had to pin the Germans opposite them to their ground. The best way to ensure this was to get at grips with the enemy, and in this way Gouzeaucourt was captured on April 12th, and, nine days later, Gonnelieu fell.

It happened, however, that the 58th did not actively participate in either of these two operations. Its doings for the month of April may be briefly summed up as follows. The first week was spent in " standing-to " and in " side-stepping," or, in other words, in being prepared for the inevitable forward movement. On the 8th it was in brigade support and next day was spent in cleaning up : " foot baths were organized and feet washed." It was during the night of the 12th that Gouzeaucourt was taken ; three days later the 58th were back in billets at Sorel-le-Grand. Working parties and labour on roads were now the order of the day. On the 20th the 24th Brigade was inspected by the divisional commander, at which ceremony the D.S.O. was awarded to Lieutenant-Colonel C. G. Buckle and

the Military Cross to Lieutenant J. E. Jarvis and
Second-Lieutenant J. A. Preval. Second-Lieutenant
J. B. Oldfield, M.C., received a bar, and four
Distinguished Conduct Medals and seven Military
Medals were awarded to non-commissioned officers and
privates who had been recommended for these distinctions. During the evening of April 23rd the
battalion relieved the 2nd Devons and 2nd Middlesex
in the line before Villers-Guislains. Two days later,
under cover of the Battle Patrol Platoon, the battalion
moved forward and established a new line of posts. In
this operation an untoward incident occurred, Second-
Lieutenant B. J. F. Wylde and his platoon of " D "
Company becoming lost. They then bumped into an
enemy post, and in the scuffle which ensued the officer
and three of his men were missed. On the 27th the
battalion was relieved and went into brigade reserve.
The strength of the 58th at the end of the month was
33 officers and 896 other ranks, with a ration strength
of 707.

May was relatively a very quiet month, and for two
reasons. In the first place the Lloyd-George—Nivelle
offensive was a complete failure. The British armies
concerned had scored a splendid initial success at Vimy
and Arras, while farther south the Fifth and Fourth
Armies had kept the Germans engaged. But Nivelle
was late in starting his attack. The enemy were given
four days' notice in which to get things ready. The
French time-table broke down, and, although some
progress was made, the price which had to be paid was
terrible. All hope of a break-through was gone. This
reacted upon the sector where the 8th Division was
engaged, and operations there were slowed down by
another factor. The Germans were back on their
Hindenburg Line, and any attempt against it would
obviously be a very different proposition from driving
in German rear-guards. The Germans had made of
the Hindenburg Line an immensely strong position,
and here they intended to stop.

P I

Consequently there is not much to chronicle about the 58th in this month of May. The first of the month found the battalion at Vaucellette Farm, and in the evening it went into the line east of Villers-Guislains. The weather was now bright and warm. On the night of the 3rd a raid under Second-Lieutenant James was attempted against a German post, but it was " given away by the moon," with the result that the object was not achieved and the commander of the raid and two other ranks were wounded. Thereafter there were in-and-out and working parties, and on the 10th the battalion was in billets at Lieramont, whence it proceeded to Moislains. Here were training, football, "work as *per* programme," church parades and a battalion concert. On the 27th, in a musketry competition for the best section in the brigade, first place was taken by " A " Company section of the Battle Patrol Platoon. On the same day Second-Lieutenant Growse returned from leave and took over the duties of adjutant.

Meanwhile events were shaping themselves to bring about the transference of the 8th Division to another sector of the Western Front. The failure of the Nivelle offensive had been immediately followed by a startling loss of *moral* and discipline in the French Army. The outlook for the Allies was now gloomy, and the general situation, as already described on page 201, called for some immediate action. It was abundantly clear that until the French Army recovered its second wind it was upon the British that the main burden of supporting the Entente during the summer of 1917 must fall. Hence resulted the Third Battle of Ypres. In the struggle the British were severely handicapped; for with no similar offensive threatening elsewhere, all the German reserves could be diverted to the Flanders front.

This is, however, anticipating things slightly. We shall come to the battle in a moment. In it the 8th Division was destined to play a part. At the end of May it was ordered north and marched away across the old Somme battle-front. And thus it was that on June 6th the 58th found itself at Meteren in close proximity to the 48th and in gloriously warm weather. Germans or no Germans, the 48th must be put through it in both cricket and football, which events were quickly carried out with results distinctly favourable to the old " Steelbacks." The reader who desires to see how the narrative of the two battalions, in this chapter, intertwine, should refer to page 192, where these incidents are referred to. On that page the events are airily referred to as "various athletic events." The war diary man of the 58th, however, has entered "June 8. Beat 48th at football 4—0 " with a " that's that " air about it. Sterner things were now in store for the 58th. On the 14th it was in the line, " A," " B " and " D " Companies and battalion headquarters holding the front line from Menin Road (inclusive) to the Ypres—Roulers Road (exclusive), having relieved the 10th Liverpool Scottish. " C " Company had been left behind at L'Ecole de Filles " owing to the great strength of the battalion," but one platoon was employed as " mine garrison." "A" Company similarly provided a " crater jumping party," and " B " a " crater garrison "—curious terms which now appear in the war diary. Very soon the battalion was in brigade support, most of the personnel being in the cavalry barracks at Ypres, where they received a very heavy shelling on the 15th and 16th. For ten days from the 19th the 58th was in Dominion Camp, training, relieving the 2nd East Lancashires as brigade reserve in Ypres during the night of June 29th-30th.

Although the great battle of Ypres, 1917, did not open till July 31st, all that month was occupied, so to speak, in preliminaries for it. A break is now advisable in the narrative, so as to include all the battle in the one chapter which follows.

CHAPTER XI.

July-December, 1917—The Third Battle of Ypres.

In July the 8th Division had been withdrawn from the line for a period of intensive training with a view to the coming offensive. Accordingly, on July 6th the 2nd Northamptonshire Regiment found itself at Dominion Camp, whence it proceeded, chiefly by motor-bus, to Redinghem, where training went on for ten days. The work was hard and in every way intensive. Exercises in attack on trenches, specially flagged to represent the German system which would be the objective in the battle, were diligently and carefully practised. The ground over which the division was to attack was thoroughly reconnoitred by all commanders and staffs. The enemy's position, as well as the route to it and the method of advance to be practised over such route, were closely studied by all officers and non-commissioned officers with the aid of an exceptionally large scale map and a big raised model in which the features of the ground and the position of the German defences were faithfully reproduced.

After ten days spent in this way the division began to make its way back to the line, the 58th settling down by Ypres, where on the 22nd it " drew bombs, etc., for the approaching battle." The next day the battalion moved into the front line in the Zouave Wood sector, " C " Company remaining, however, at the Esplanade, Ypres. There was some smart shelling by the Germans during this day, and, in spite of a relief during the period, by the 29th the battalion had 1 officer and 14 other ranks killed; and 5 officers and 60 other ranks wounded. During July 30th the battalion put the final touches to its preparations and about 9 p.m. moved into its assembly trenches. The night was dark and cloudy, with a promise of rain, and the artillery on both sides was active. In the following order—" D," " A," " C," " B " Companies—the battalion moved to Kingsway and Kingsway Support, "via the south side of Piccadilly Circus, Oxford Street and Regent Street." The movement was carried out with difficulty owing to the mud and the damaged state of the communication trenches, but was completed by midnight. " A " and " D " Companies were now in Kingsway, with " B " and " C " in Kingsway Support. Battalion headquarters were situated in a big dug-out at Birr crossroads. On the right of the 58th was the 1st Battalion Worcestershire Regiment, and on the left the 2nd West Yorkshires.

Leaving the 58th to snatch an uneasy slumber till zero hour, let us take a general survey of the battle about to begin. The main burden of the great attack was to be borne by the Fifth Army. The front of its effort was some seven and a half miles in length, from the Zillebeke—Zandvoorde road to Boesinghe. In this advance the Fifth Army was to be assisted right and left. On the right the Second Army was to co-operate, but it was not to make any great advance, its share being chiefly to draw upon itself some of the enemy's artillery fire. On the left, the Fifth Army was to be protected from counter-attack by the advance of the French First Army. As for the Fifth Army, it consisted of four corps, their positions from north to south being XIV, XVIII, XIX, II. The last-named corps had three divisions in line, the 8th Division being on the left of the corps front. In the 8th Division two brigades were in front, the 24th being on the right, 23rd on left, and 25th in reserve.

The design of the attack was a methodical series of advances in three stages. There were three corresponding objectives, these being three successive German lines—Blue, Black and Green, exclusive of the German front line, which by the series of tactics then in vogue could only be lightly held. From the assembly area the first objective—the Blue Line—was distant about 1,250 yards; the Black Line some 800 to 900 yards farther on; and another 1,400 yards would lead to the third or Green Line. The left boundary for the division was the Ypres—Zonnebeke—Roulers railway, and its front, just before the flag fell, may be taken as being bounded by, and including, Zouave Wood on one flank and Railway Wood on the other. The area to be traversed included broken and wooded ground, and the task of the division must necessarily take the form of a frontal attack upon a strong and easily-defensible position. Particularly difficult would be the advance of the 24th Brigade, for between the German front line and the first objective—the Blue Line —lay two nasty obstacles in the shape of Bellewaarde Lake and Château Wood. As for the 2nd North-amptonshire Regiment, a certain definite sector of the Blue Line, with Wee Cottage as one of the flank boundaries, was assigned as the first objective of the battalion. " A " and " D " Companies were to attack in two waves, detailing one platoon from each company for mopping-up. Waves three and four were to be found by five platoons of " B " and " C " Companies, the remaining platoons being told off for mopping-up duties, an important task when various German lines had to be taken.

German patrols sent out during the night had been frustrated by energetic and active reconnoitring parties from " A " and " D " Companies, and from midnight till zero hour the night passed quietly enough, the artillery fire sinking to below normal. Zero hour was at 5.50 a.m., and a tremendous barrage was put down from artillery and machine guns. Under cover of this fire the troops left their assembly trenches and advanced under cover of the barrage, which crept forward at the rate of 100 yards in four minutes. The task of the 58th was a hard one, and, as the 8th Divisional History has it, " the hardest perhaps of the day." The battalion, however, went forward in fine style, and, in the words of the war diary : "The barrage came down with a tremendous roar, and the battalion, lying on the parapets of Kingsway and Kingsway Support, advanced under its cover. Perfect order prevailed, the battalion keeping its formation as if on the practice trenches back at Bomy." Casualties, however, had already begun, and Lieutenant G. H. D. Metcalfe and Second-Lieutenant C. J. Fisher were almost immediately wounded by shells.

The first wave, quickly followed by the second, passed over the weakly-held German front line with little opposition. And now came the difficulties of terrain already referred to. Nearly one half of the frontage of the battalion was covered by the obstacle of the Belle-waarde Lake. The greater part of the left of the battalion had to skirt the eastern edge of the lake, and then, having deployed on the northern edge of it, had to attack and capture Bellewaarde Ridge, which seemed to tower above. Then, south of the lake and in the path of the right of the battalion lay Château Wood, a mass of wire and fallen trees.

The companies of the 58th were, however, not to be denied. Flushed with their success in over-running the German front line, they carried out their task in an admirable manner. The country was extraordinarily difficult, for in addition to the obstacles already mentioned it should be stated that through Château Wood, parallel to the front of the attack, ran a ravine, full of water, which drained the high ground about Clapham Junction into the Bellewaarde Lake. Ploughing through the mud and water the four waves of the battalion, keeping in touch with the Worcester-shires, finally won clear of both lake and wood and began their deployment to the left. The advance was then resumed. By 5.30 a.m., Jacob Trench, immediately in front of the German Blue Line, was made good and duly mopped up. Number 12 Platoon also mopped up Château Wood and dug-outs in James Trench which ran along the northern edge of the wood. No. 6

Platoon performed a similar duty in a little wood east of the stream which drains into the lake, as well as other dug-outs and trenches. The commanding officer and adjutant now arrived, and communication by telephone was secured with brigade headquarters.

It was in this capture of Jacob Trench that Captain T. R. Colyer-Fergusson, commanding "B" Company, won the Victoria Cross. The difficulties of deploying and forming up were very great. The mass of the Bellewaarde Ridge loomed in front some 100 yards away, and the barrage was beginning to move forward To lose the barrage meant almost certain failure. Captain Colyer-Fergusson immediately grasped the situation. Right in front was an enemy strong post, well wired and occupied by a machine-gun crew which threatened to hold up any farther advance, unless at once dealt with. Hastily collecting some ten men, amongst whom were Sergeant W. G. Boulding and Private B. Ellis, his orderly, Captain Colyer-Fergusson pushed on under the barrage, and without further assistance gained a footing in Jacob Trench on the crest of the ridge. Almost at once a company of Germans was seen advancing in mass a bare hundred yards away. Captain Colyer-Fergusson and his picked men knocked out twenty or thirty of them with rifle fire, and the remainder put up their hands. The men of his own company were beginning to come up, when the German machine gun came into action. Leaving his company to hold the trench, and assisted by his orderly alone, Captain Colyer-Fergusson attacked and captured the gun. He then turned it on to another group of the enemy, killing a large number of them and driving the remainder into the hands of another British unit. Later, assisted only by Sergeant Boulding and Private Ellis, he attacked and captured a second machine gun. He had now been joined by the rest of his company, and had begun to consolidate his position, when, hearing that Colonel Buckle had arrived, he went to him to report.

Similar qualities of dash and leadership were exhibited by Second-Lieutenant Frost, of " C " Company, on the right. Encountering a German post of about fifty men, who were shooting down the Worcestershires, he rushed at them at the head of his men, killing a German officer and fourteen other ranks. Other Germans who were lurking in the large concrete shelters were blown up. One of these shelters apparently contained a store of bombs and Very lights, for a bomb thrown into it caused a great explosion, by which eight or nine Germans were killed.

Upon the left the 23rd Brigade had made equally good progress, and by this combination of successes the first objective was gained and the Blue Line made good. Lieutenant-Colonel Buckle now ordered " B " and " C " Companies to push forward a hundred to two hundred yards in front of Jacob Trench and to dig posts. While this operation was being carried out the battalion suffered a severe loss. Captain Colyer-Fergusson was shot through the head by a sniper and killed—a grievous loss not only to the Northamptonshire Regiment but to the Army. He had done magnificently, and the capture of Jacob Trench was largely due to his initiative and heroism. The Victoria Cross was awarded to him posthumously, and Sergeant Boulding and Private Ellis received the Distinguished Conduct Medal for their great gallantry on this occasion.

The 1st Sherwood Foresters now pushed through the 58th and the battalion moppers-up rejoined and assisted in the work of consolidation. Some seventy prisoners were sent back. About 6 a.m., " B " Company, under Second-Lieutenant Bondfield, went back to Railway Wood and for the rest of the day acted as stretcher bearers, under the A.D.M.S., the work being admirably performed.

The first stage had now been successfully accomplished all along the divisional front, and the capture of the Black Line was hardly less successful, although it was discounted by a partial failure on the right. As for the 58th, "A" Company, in Château Wood, suffered severely from machine-gun and shell fire.

About 10 a.m. the commanding officer ordered the company into the Blue Line, and two strong points were dug between the right of the Northamptonshires and the Worcestershires. It had been part of the original plan that when the 25th Brigade should have captured the farthest—or Green—German line, the 2nd Northamptonshire Regiment should then move forward and relieve the 2nd Middlesex. The Green Line, however, was destined to be untaken this day, and the 58th remained, therefore, in the Blue Line, being heavily shelled. The weather had been threatening all day, and about four o'clock rain came down heavily, so that the night was a most uncomfortable one. Word came that the 8th Division was to be relieved, and at 6 a.m. on the 1st the battalion was relieved by the 1st Cheshires and made its way in small parties to Halifax Camp.

This opening day of the great Third Battle of Ypres may be briefly summed up by saying that the Allied infantry experienced little difficulty at first, and only began to experience serious loss when advancing towards their second objectives. This was particularly the case on the right, where the two right-hand divisions of the Fifth Army were endeavouring to gain possession of all the commanding ground about and beyond Shrewsbury Forest and Sanctuary Wood to the south of the Menin Road. Here they failed to push forward more than a few hundred yards. Farther to the left, however, the assailants were successful at almost all points. St. Julien was captured, while the French stormed Bixschoote, which was actually beyond their programme. Even if the check on the right discounted the completeness of the victory, the battle had opened most encouragingly for the Allies. The Pilckem Ridge had been wrested from the enemy, and no longer could Ypres be overlooked from the north-east and north.

In prisoners the British alone had captured 6,100 and had taken 25 guns. The 8th Division had done its share. Nine commanding officers of infantry, including Lieutenant-Colonel C. G. Buckle, had become casualties. The total losses of the division in killed, wounded and missing were 160 officers and 3,000 other ranks. In the 2nd Battalion Northamptonshire Regiment 1 officer and 7 other ranks were killed, and 2 officers and 113 other ranks were wounded. The missing amounted to 35. To these figures must be added the casualties before the assault, namely, 5 officers (1 killed) and 74 casualties in other ranks.

After its relief by the 1st Cheshire Regiment (the battalion in another place is given as the 10th Cheshires) the 58th had a good wash and rest at Halifax Camp and then moved on to Steenvoorde. Here it remained nearly a fortnight, but it must not be imagined that this was purely a time of leisure. The division was not left long in doubt as to the nature of its next task. On August 2nd—when it had just left the line—a divisional order was issued to the effect that so soon as the remainder of the Black Line had been taken the 8th Division would co-operate in a general attack upon the Green Line—the "third objective," as will be remembered. Accordingly the succeeding days were spent in energetic attempts to reorganize the division and to restore it to a fit condition to take its part in an early renewal of the offensive. There was a good deal of "training as per programme." There were several route marches. But these were tempered by bathing parades, leave, and an occasional concert. They were also tempered by air raids and by bad weather.

The weather improved in the middle of the month, and it was decided to seize at once this opportunity of pushing on with the advance, the 8th Division returning to the line between August 12th and 14th. So far as the 8th Division was concerned, the front line was to be composed of the 23rd and 25th Brigades. Of the 24th Brigade two battalions were to be in divisional reserve and the other two to be " at call " of the front line, the 2nd Northamptonshire Regiment to be on Bellewaarde Ridge at the call of the general officer commanding 25th Brigade. Zero hour was to be at 4.45 a.m. on the 16th, and, accordingly, the 58th spent the previous day at Winnipeg Camp " bathing and cleaning-up generally."

At nine o'clock that night, the battalion, in the following order, headquarters, " A," " B," " C " and " D " Companies, moved up to the Little Gate of Ypres, where it arrived safely at 11 p.m. Here it remained for an hour and a half and then advanced by platoons, at 200 yards distance, to Bellewaarde Ridge. The platoons at once took up positions in the trenches and shell holes, and all was ready by 4.30 a.m.

Punctually at a quarter to five the barrage descended with violent intensity. The two front brigades at once advanced, and for a time all went well, but later a serious check on the right caused delay. There was also a check to the division on the left, with the result that the 8th Division found itself " in the air," having advanced a full 1,000 yards beyond the line held by this division. To remedy this the front of the division had to be brought back slightly and the rear of the division moved up. And it was this which led to the move forward of " C " and " D " Companies, under Captain C. E. Blake, from Bellewaarde Ridge to Jaffa Trench, which was practically part of the Black Line. This movement took place about 11 a.m., and Captain Blake and his two companies were ordered to get into touch with the 167th Brigade (of the 56th Division, on the right) and to find out the exact position of its forward troops. This task was duly carried out, and the companies of Captain Blake then continued to remain in Jaffa Trench.

A kind of lull now seems to have taken place. The initiative had to some extent passed to the enemy, although it was not until the afternoon that he made any further attack in force. About 2.45 p.m., however, the enemy were seen to be strongly reinforcing on the right. An hour later a strong attack was made all along the 25th Brigade front. The Germans made steady, if slow, progress. So menacing, indeed, did the situation become that even the personnel of brigade headquarters were put into the line.

The brigade commander now came in person to Captain Blake, about 4.45 p.m., and ordered up the two companies of the 58th to a line some 150 yards in front and marked by tapes. Immediately the Germans put a heavy barrage on these companies, but they moved forward with great steadiness and resolution. The fire was severe, both from artillery and machine guns, and Captain Blake was so severely wounded in the neck as to be incapacitated. Second-Lieutenant Frost, the officer commanding " C " Company, was also severely wounded in the head. Second-Lieutenant J. M. Bailey, although himself wounded in four places, immediately took command and conducted the advance with the greatest coolness and intrepidity. Under his leadership the two companies pushed on, drove back the enemy, and with remnants of Royal Irish Rifles, Royal Berkshires, Rifle Brigade and Lincolns, stabilized the line on the forward slopes of Westhoek Ridge. The arrival of these two companies had the further result of releasing the personnel of brigade headquarters for their proper duties, and also made it possible to fill up the gap between the right of the 25th Brigade and the adjoining 167th Brigade.

Meanwhile the remaining two companies of the battalion had moved forward to Jaffa Trench with little loss. The commanding officer, Major Latham, and Captain J. B. Oldfield went forward to reconnoitre, and almost at once Captain Oldfield fell dead with a bullet through the heart. The dead officer was a great loss to the battalion. He had come out with the battalion as a lance-corporal in 1914, had been through all the heavy fighting, including Neuve Chapelle and Aubers Ridge, and had won the Military Cross in January, 1917, gaining a bar to it at Moislains Ridge on March 4th. This gallant officer was buried at night on Westhoek Ridge.

During the night the battalions which had borne the main burden of the day's fighting were relieved, the 2nd Northamptonshire Regiment taking over half the front of the 25th Brigade, the order from left to right being " A," " C " and " D " Companies, with " B " Company in support in Jaffa Trench. Save for some sniping the night passed quietly, no counter-attacks developing. Infantry movement on the 17th was, indeed, confined on both sides to the collection of wounded. Artillery fire on the forward area was only slight, and the work of consolidation was carried on without interruption until the relief of the division on the night of August 18th/19th. The 2nd Northamptonshire Regiment was relieved by two companies of the 18th London Regiment and returned to Halifax Camp. It had gone into action with a fighting strength of 13 officers and 400 other ranks, losing 1 officer and 34 other ranks killed, and 3 officers and 92 other ranks wounded. The missing amounted to 3 other ranks.

The 8th Division was now transferred from the Fifth Army to the Second Army reserve, and moved back, chiefly by motor omnibuses, to the Caestre area. There is a note in the battalion war diary of " practised marching past "—a symptom probably of inspection fever prior to inspection of the division by Sir Douglas Haig on August 21st. About a week was spent in resting and training and in filling up with drafts. On August 23rd the division began its move south to the II Anzac Corps. The strain to which the British armies were subjected in the Ypres offensive did not permit the 8th Division being left long out of the line. On August 25th and 26th, therefore, the 24th Brigade was moved forward by bus to the Romarin area, and the end of the month found the 58th in Ploegsteert Wood—the " Plugstreet " of all time.

The sector here was " quiet "—that is to say, there

were no attacks made by either side, but there was quite
a fair amount of artillery fire and the German aeroplanes were enterprising and annoying. Quiet though
the new sector was by comparison with the scenes the
8th Division had just left, the absence of infantry action
did not mean that the enemy was left alone. Gas
attacks were carried out by a special company of Royal
Engineers, and the 2nd Northamptonshire Regiment
were inconvenienced to the extent of having to evacuate
a few posts and of suffering a shell-fire retaliation once
at midnight. It should be mentioned that the II Anzac
Corps had been taken out for transfer to the battle still
raging round Ypres, and that the front vacated by them
was taken over by the VIII Corps, which brought off
quite a useful demonstration on September 20th to help
in the further operations to the north. In this, however, the 2nd Northamptonshire Regiment were not
engaged, having been relieved by the 2nd Royal
Berkshire Regiment and the 2nd Lincolnshires a week
earlier. It is curious to see how the cadre of officers
was now largely composed of second-lieutenants, for of
twenty-six company officers, as shown in a list dated
September 13th, with the exception of one captain and
one lieutenant the whole lot were " one-pip " men. On
this day the battalion was gladdened by the news that
a V.C. had been awarded posthumously to Captain
Colyer-Fergusson, and the same *Gazette* mentioned the
award of the Military Cross to Captain Blake and
Second-Lieutenant Bailey, while Company Sergeant-
Major C. M. Underwood received the Distinguished
Conduct Medal. The remainder of the month passed
in the inevitable training, with a partiality for anti-
mustard gas and S.O.S signals. The latter caused a
slight mishap on the 19th, for Lieutenant-Colonel
Buckle was struck on the ankle by a signal, which,
instead of rising in the air, ran amok along the ground.
Although the accident was not serious the commanding
officer had to lie up for nearly a week. Parades and
training, of course, filled in most of these days at

Q

Romarin Camp, an interlude being a football match between the officers and sergeants, which the latter won to the tune of 4—o.

October opened with a minor disaster to a working party, the casualties being 4 killed and 3 wounded. On the 2nd medal ribbons were presented by Major-General Heneker, the divisional commander, to those who had been awarded distinctions. Then, on October 6th, the battalion went back into the line, relieving the 1st Worcestershires in the " Plugstreet" sector. The following day the company in support was shelled in its dug-outs, a Lewis-gun section being knocked out, with 3 killed and 4 wounded; while during the afternoon of the 11th a 4·2 shell penetrated battalion headquarters, but, although it duly exploded, no one was damaged. Relief for the battalion came on the 13th, when it was conveyed by light railway to Mene-gate Camp. Ten days later the 58th lost its commanding officer, Lieutenant-Colonel C. G. Buckle, who left to take up an appointment in England, his place being taken by Major S. G. Latham, M.C. In the brigade cross-country race on the 26th the battalion did exceedingly well, gaining first place by a large number of points and providing ten men out of the first twenty-two; and so back into the line again on the 29th, relieving the 2nd Royal Berkshire Regiment in support at Red Lodge.

During the latter days of October rumours had reached the division that it was to be sent to Italy under Lieutenant-General the Earl of Cavan, to form part of the British Army of Italy, afterwards commanded by General Sir Herbert Plumer. These rumours came to nothing, but early in November definite intimation was received that the division was to move to a much less attractive theatre. On November 6th a warning order was published stating that the 8th Division would shortly be relieved in the line by the 3rd Australian Division. The relief began with the arrival on the 9th of the Australian artillery, and on the following day the artillery of the 8th Division marched to Ypres. The interchange of infantry units followed, and the relief was completed by November 14th.

Accordingly, the battalion war diary for the month reveals considerable movement: the entries in sequence being Red Lodge: in the line: Romarin Camp: in the line: Warneton: Menegate Camp: Trois Fermes: Brandhoek Camp: Spree Farm: in the line: Outskirt Camp: Warrington Camp. The new front was in the Passchendaele sector, the village itself having been captured by the Canadians on November 6th. The 2nd Northamptonshire Regiment went up into the line on the 21st, and on relief two days later some men of " D " Company lost their way and found themselves in " D " Company's billets of the 48th, whose movements we shall shortly trace. This tour was by no means a bloodless one, having cost the battalion 15 killed and 48 wounded. The only other incidents of note in this month occurred before the battalion had trekked north. On November 3rd the 58th made its first acquaintance with the American Army, two subalterns being attached for instruction and were taken round the lines that night by the commanding officer and second-in-command. There are also during this period several references to " 48 hours' leave "—or even " rest "—at Calais.

Meanwhile, on November 20th, a warning order had been issued that the 8th Division would be relieved early in December and proceed to the Wizernes area, but before this relief took place there was to be another and more considerable local operation. In this, however, the 58th was not engaged, and the beginning of December found it at St. Martin-au-Laert. An unusually quiet spell was the result, and the war diarist was so gravelled for copy that he was forced to insert on the 10th that "the commanding officer dined with Lieutenant-Colonel Hill, commanding the East Lanca-shires " and there were " conferences re Xmas dinner." The division remained in the Wizernes area, resting and training, for a clear three weeks. Training facilities were good and a great deal of useful work was accomplished, of which lectures by specialists formed an important part. It was actually on Christmas Day—in traditional Christmas weather with snow and frost—that the move back to the line was commenced, the division returning once more to the Passchendaele sector, relieving the 14th Division in the very apex of the salient.

In this movement the 58th entrained at 11 a.m. at Wizernes, detraining at 3 p.m. at St. Jean, whence there was a march—in a snowstorm—to Junction Camp, when Christmas dinners were eaten. The following night the battalion went into the line in the left sub-sector of the North Passchendaele front. The ground was thickly covered with snow; the moon was shining brightly; and the relieving troops stood silhouetted boldly against the white background. As a result, the Germans anticipated an attack, S.O.S. signals went up from their front line, and the unfortunate 58th came in for a very nasty barrage and the inevitable rifle and machine-gun fire. Second-Lieutenant Martin was killed, as were 9 other ranks, and the wounded numbered 15, including Lieutenant Murray. These conditions made the carrying up of rations on subsequent nights a matter of great difficulty, but fortunately, when the battalion was relieved during the night of the 30th/31st it was very dark, and on December 31st, 1917, the 58th was resting at Warrington Camp.

And now to go back to the 48th. After the disaster at Nieuport in July, the strength of the battalion was about 400, all told. It was extremely fortunate that the second-in-command, the adjutant and three of the four company commanders had been out of the line when the disaster occurred. In these circumstances, the work of reconstructing the battalion was accomplished much more easily and rapidly than would otherwise have been the case. Another factor which enabled the 48th to recuperate fairly quickly was the large proportion of experienced and able officers sent to fill the gaps in the commissioned ranks. Among those who joined the battalion during the next few weeks were Captain A. C. Pickering, one of the original officers of the old 48th, who had gained the Military Cross for his services with the 5th Battalion; and Captain H. F. Pitcher, who had served almost continuously with the 48th during the first ten months of the war. Lieutenants H. C. Tetley and F. C. Papworth, both of whom had seen much service with the 58th, also came to the 1st Battalion shortly after Nieuport, while among the junior subalterns were several who had been promoted from the ranks of the old Regular Army, and who were experienced and capable leaders of men. Lieutenant-Colonel G. St. G. Robinson now assumed command of the battalion, a position which he retained until the Armistice. Major M. R. C. Backhouse, D.S.O., of the North Somerset Yeomanry, joined as second-in-command. After about a week spent in various villages near the coast, on July 19th the battalion arrived at St. Pol, a suburb of Dunkirk, where it encamped under canvas. Here the Northamptonshires received a big draft of non-commissioned officers and men, most of whom had been recruited in the Durham district. Talavera Day was celebrated by regimental sports, and afforded an opportunity of acquainting the Durham men with the glorious record of the old 48th.

In this history, the periods spent behind the line in training have generally been dealt with very briefly. While a few weeks' rest from the rigours of the front line was always very welcome to the weary troops, it was not often that such periods were marked by any events likely to be of interest to a person reading an account of them in later years. But August and September of 1917 form an exception to this general rule. The character of the training then undergone by the 48th, the circumstances under which it was carried out, and, above all, the remarkable nature of the projected operations for which it was a preparation, combine to make this period merit a fairly detailed

description. Le Clipon is a small hamlet situated on
the French coast between Gravelines and Dunkirk.
Prior to the war, some enterprising person had built a
casino there with the object of popularizing it as a seaside resort, but Le Clipon is not widely known among
the general public. Had the course of history been
but slightly altered, it might have been a name familiar
to Englishmen for all time. On July 30th the 1st
Northamptonshires left St. Pol and marched to Le
Clipon. There a large area, including the hamlet, the
casino, and a fair stretch of foreshore, had been fenced
in by barbed wire. Within this enclosure, most of
which was concealed from the view of the outside world
by sand dunes, the whole of the 1st Division was
concentrated. The purpose of this concentration was
not instantly disclosed in full, nor were the restrictions
which were enforced at once understood. The rank
and file of the battalion only gradually realized the
nature of the operations in which they were intended to
participate; veiled intimations, partial disclosures, and
a gradual increase in the strictness of the censorship
preceded the final announcement.

As mentioned earlier in this chapter, the Higher
Command had determined that the projected offensive
in the Ypres salient should be accompanied by a
landing in force upon that portion of the Belgian coast
which was in the hands of the enemy. The task of
making this landing had been entrusted to the 1st
Division, which had come to Le Clipon in order to be
trained for the attempt. It was at about this time that
an announcement appeared in the Press that, although
the general health of the British troops in France was
excellent, it had been necessary to segregate one division,
the troops comprising which were suffering from an
infectious disease. Under cover of this plea of infec-
tion, numerous precautions were taken to ensure that
no news of the projected landing leaked out. The wire
fence surrounding the camp was constantly patrolled
by sentries, to prevent the egress of any person. The

troops sometimes left the enclosure for the purpose of manœuvres, but they always moved in a body under the control of officers, and intercourse of any kind with persons living outside was strictly prohibited. The regimental transport, who remained outside throughout, deposited the necessary supplies in a specified enclosure on the margin of the camp, under the supervision of the sentries, whose orders were to prevent any conversation between the transport men and the fatigue parties detailed to remove the supplies thus deposited. In ordinary circumstances, the letters sent home by the non-commissioned officers and men had been censored only by their company officers, while the letters sent by the officers had practically not been censored at all. In Le Clipon, orders were issued to ensure that the preliminary censoring by the company officers should be much more thorough, the commanding officer of each unit was made responsible for the contents of the letters sent by his officers, and a special staff of censors was installed at divisional headquarters.

The part allotted to the 2nd Brigade in the projected operations was the duty of effecting a landing at Middelkerke, a seaside resort some five miles southwest of Ostend. The brigade was to embark at Dunkirk upon two monitors, between which was to be affixed an enormous raft. The landing was to take place in the early hours of the morning, under cover of a smoke barrage. It was intended that the two monitors, screened by the smoke, should come so close to the shore that it would be possible to step off from the raft on to the beach. The troops were then to disembark at the double, ascend the sea-wall which ran along that part of the coast, and occupy certain points situated a short distance inland. The task of each individual man was mapped out with meticulous care, and constant rehearsals made everyone thoroughly familiar with what he would have to do. In a field within the enclosure at Le Clipon the decks of the monitors were mapped out exactly, the measurements

being identical with those of the actual ships.   Baulks
of turf indicated the position of funnels, hatches
and other similar objects.   There was even a replica of
the trough which was to be installed for the benefit of
such men as might be troubled by *mal de mer* during
the voyage.   Embarkation and disembarkation from
this model monitor were practised again and again,
until every movement could be carried out with the
precision and regularity of a machine.

The ascent of the sea-wall was rehearsed in an even
more realistic manner.   Near the casino had been
erected a sloping surface of concrete, which purported
to be an exact replica of a portion of the sea-wall near
Middelkerke.   Up this men swarmed day after day in
full kit, gradually acquiring a dexterity and agility
almost simian in character.   Companies competed to
see which could get every man up in the shortest time,
and fearful were the objurgations that assailed those
unfortunates who spoilt the company record by persis-
tently failing to ascend the sloping surface.   Sometimes
a barbed wire entanglement was placed on the crest of
the slope; this had to be hacked through by the leading
men before the others could get up the "sea-wall."
The men to whom had been assigned the task of
carrying up Yukon packs laden with water and stores
wore boots supplied with special felt soles.   Further,
the continual study of large scale maps made every
officer familiar with the most minute details of the
streets of Middelkerke and of the country that lay
behind it.   Tapes were laid out among the dunes that
fringed the beach, to represent houses, and here the
later stages of the landing were practised.   So the work
of training went on, week after week, and speculation
was rife as to when the landing would be attempted.   It
could only be carried out on certain days, as a very
high tide was necessary.   On August 24th the postponement of the attempt was announced, but preparation for it still continued.   A few days later, naval
officers and men from the monitors that were to take

part in the projected operations paid a visit to the camp, and fraternized with their comrades of the land forces.

From the regularity with which German aircraft bombed the docks at Dunkirk on the nights when the tide was high, it would appear that the enemy had some idea of what was in the minds of the British Higher Command. Perhaps it was because of this that the landing was never attempted, though possibly another reason was that the offensive in the Ypres salient had not progressed as favourably as had been hoped. Whatever the cause, the prospect of the attempted landing became more and more distant as time went on. Gradually the nature of the training changed, restrictions on movement were relaxed, and long before it was definitely known that the scheme had been abandoned there was a general impression abroad that the landing would never be attempted. On October 12th the officers of the 1st Division were addressed by General Rawlinson. At the conclusion of his speech, the commander of the Fourth Army said : " You have for some time been known as the ' Hush ! hush ! Division.' Well, the hush is nearly over now." Ten days later the 48th left Clipon Camp behind them for good and all, and marched away in the direction of Ypres.

After leaving Le Clipon, the 1st Northamptonshires marched by easy stages to School Camp, which lay about a mile and a half west of Poperinghe. They arrived there on October 25th, moved into the town on November 6th, and proceeded by train to St. Jean on the following day. On November 9th they relieved the 60th in the front line, south-east of Poelcappelle. Major Forsyth Forrest was now second-in-command, Major Backhouse having been appointed to the command of another battalion.

The Third Battle of Ypres, which had been in progress since July 31st, was now nearing its conclusion. Weather conditions were making it impossible for the offensive to be continued. Although the 48th did not take a very prominent part in the concluding operations, yet this tour in the line was a severe test for the rank and file of the battalion, most of whom had never previously been under fire. They were at once brought into touch with the grim realities of war, stripped of the last vestige of glamour that so frequently obscures its real nature. Trench warfare, in the true sense of the word, had ceased to be possible in this part of the line. The troops holding the front line system were scattered about in isolated shell holes, which had been rendered more or less habitable, but which in many cases were filled with mud and water. Here and there were "pill-boxes," the ruined remains of houses strengthened by concrete. The front now occupied by the 48th had been fought over many times; continual shelling and heavy rainfall had combined to turn the whole of the surrounding country into a veritable quagmire, littered with decaying bodies and all the miscellaneous debris of a battlefield. Veterans who had served right through the war admitted that they had never seen anything to equal the squalid desolation of the Ypres salient at this stage of the battle.

For two days the 48th held a line of shell holes occupying a front of about 1,500 yards. The German artillery was very active, the casualties in the battalion amounting to 21 killed and the same number wounded. Second-Lieutenant Hopkins received a severe wound which resulted in the loss of an eye. Second-Lieutenant Irons, who had been company sergeant-major of "D" in the early days of the war, received a slight wound, but remained at duty. Second-Lieutenants M. W. Tipler and A. Moore led a party of forty volunteers against some pill-boxes occupied by the enemy, but the swampy condition of the ground made an advance impossible.

On November 11th the 1st Northamptonshires went back to Hill-top Farm, which is about three-quarters of a mile north of St. Jean. Here they were still under intermittent shell fire. About seventy men were admitted to hospital, suffering from the effects of their sojourn in the mud and water of the front line shell holes. Two days later the 48th returned to the front line, coming under very heavy shell fire as they stumbled along the duck-boards that lined the track. Next evening, a second attempt was made to capture the German pill-boxes. Two platoons, under Lieutenant A. E. Ward and Second-Lieutenant Myers, were employed in this attack. Again the nature of the ground made success impossible. Second-Lieutenant Myers was mortally wounded, and several other casualties were sustained. On November 15th the 1st Northamptonshires were again relieved, and the following day they went back to Dambre Camp, north of Vlamertinghe. Though this was some considerable distance behind the line, there was no respite from artillery fire; three men were wounded by a high velocity shell just as the battalion was marching into camp. Perhaps the existence of an ammunition dump in that vicinity attracted the attention of the German gunners; at all events, shells came over rather frequently.

When the 48th moved up into the front line again on November 21st, they occupied a line of shell holes somewhat to the right of their former position, and nearer Passchendaele. A German attack was anticipated, but although there was a fair amount of shelling the enemy made no offensive movement. On the 23rd the battalion went back to the area behind the fighting line for a rest. Its losses since the beginning of November had amounted to 26 killed, 65 wounded and 13 missing.

The next four months were spent in the northern half of the Ypres salient, periods in the line alternating with periods of rest. During this time comparatively few casualties were incurred, and, though the weather conditions were usually unfavourable, they were never quite so bad as they had been in November. A detailed account of the months spent in this part of the line would resolve itself into a monotonous record of uneventful days spent in shell holes and pill-boxes, sometimes under fire, but more often in comparative quiet. A great deal of work was done to strengthen the defensive system, and many hours were spent in constructing wire entanglements to protect the front line. It could not then be foreseen that most of this labour would be wasted, and that circumstances would compel our troops to abandon these carefully-prepared positions without a struggle a few months later.

CHAPTER XII.

RETREAT

TOWARDS the end of 1917 the outstanding feature was that success was apparently no nearer than at the opening of the much-trumpeted "Year of Victory." The extravagant anticipations voiced by the British Prime Minister had not been rounded off by fulfilment, partly from causes outside his control and partly from decisions on matters in which he was able to intervene. Russia had passed from collapse to defection, and the envoys who spoke in her name were actually engaged in peace negotiations. The Italian Army was defeated. In Macedonia there was practically a stalemate. Rumania was cut off from the Allies. Narrowing down the survey so as to include only England in the field, the view was hardly more reassuring. The financial situation was graver than ever it had been during the war; the submarine peril had reached a point that for some time justified serious alarm; the indecisive Battle of Jutland in 1916 had left the English rulers in such a state of uncertainty that, even eighteen months later, 300,000 men were locked up at home to guard against "a possible invasion"; the Germans were known to be transferring troops from the east to the west. There were, however, patches of blue in a sky which was otherwise heavily surcharged with clouds. British victories in Mesopotamia and Palestine, though to a certain extent of the nature of side-shows, were at any rate wearing down one of the allies of the Central Powers. And far above these in importance was the fact that American troops were now beginning to arrive, and even the German Supreme Command had been forced to envisage the possibility of the arrival of

450,000 soldiers from the United States before the following summer.

At the beginning of 1918, although in some respects things had altered to the advantage of the Allies, particularly in the influx of American troops, this was offset by the definite defection of Russia. As for the Allied armies, the Belgians were still quiescent; the French Army had been profoundly depressed after their failure on the Aisne—so much so that there had been open mutiny, and it was partly on this account that the British had been committed to the bloody struggle in Flanders in 1917. As for the British Army, the strenuous efforts of that year had left it at a low ebb as regards training and numbers, and this was accentuated by the fact that the British in January, 1918, took over, by extending its right, a sector of twenty-eight miles from the French. At the same time a change took place in the organization of the forces. Under instructions from home a reorganization of divisions from a twelve to a nine-battalion basis was completed in February. Apart from the reduction in fighting strength, the fighting efficiency of the units was to some extent affected. The general situation, therefore, was that Germany was now in a position of being able to force a decisive battle on French soil with her own resources, and in this theatre of war she had three enemies to reckon with—France, England and America. It was on this great battle royal that the fortunes, even the fate, of all the contestants in the tremendous struggle which had lasted for over three years would obviously depend. The decisive theatre was now clearly France. Other fronts sank to a subordination as marked as that of Russia. The war that counted in the eyes of the civilized world was that being waged between the North Sea and the Alps.

In dealing with this real Year of Victory—and all the more real because victory came after severe defeat—we shall first follow the fortunes of the 2nd Battalion. In the Passchendaele sector the conditions at the beginning

of the New Year were trying in the extreme. The
weather was fearful. Alternate periods of extreme cold
and sudden thaw, varied by heavy falls of snow and hail,
maintained a see-saw of intense discomfort, until on
January 15th a warmer spell was ushered in by a terrible
storm, the wind blowing with gale force and the rain
coming down in torrents. The 58th, however, seem to
have escaped the worst of these trials, owing to the fact
that they were for the first part of the month out of the
line in Warrington Camp. The New Year's Honours
announced that Captain (Acting Lieutenant-Colonel)
C. G. Buckle, D.S.O., M.C., had been appointed
brevet-major. On the 4th a move was made to Hasler
Camp, where the whole battalion was employed on
" foot-washing and putting up Nissen huts." About
this time Captain (Acting Major) S. G. Latham
received a bar to his Military Cross. Working parties
were the order of the day until the 9th, when the
battalion went up into the line in the Passchendaele
sector, the relief being "a very good one : no
casualties." This halcyon state of things was, however, interrupted next day, when " A " Company's
rations went sky-high owing to a shell which fell and
burst among the ration party. Relief came on the
11th, the battalion proceeding to Warrington Camp,
whence after about a week it moved to Eecke, with a
stay of one night at Hasler Camp. Then training was
resumed, special attention being devoted to " new
intensive digging" as well as shell-hole consolidation
and rapid wiring. This activity had not been
unnoticed by German airmen, and on the 30th an
enemy 'plane began to drop its eggs about, but fortunately there were no casualties. The opening of
February found the 58th still at Eecke, whence it
proceeded on the 3rd to Sunderland Camp, providing
working parties for what was called the Army Defence
Zone. On the 10th the battalion was at Junction Camp,
the 8th Division having now been about a fortnight in
corps reserve. A move to the line now followed, the

58th being "in" from the 19th till the night of the
22nd, when the division was relieved by the 29th
Division. The battalion went to California Camp,
finding the inevitable working parties. Then came a
three-days' tour again in the line early in March in
the Wattou area, followed by an inspection and more
training. On the 13th the battalion was in the Lumbres
area at Boisdinghem aerodrome. A big training programme had been drawn up, but was never put into
practice. Before a fortnight had passed the division
was summoned south to the greatest episode of its
career in France. For the " Big Push "—or " March,
1918 "—had begun.

To go back for a moment to the beginning of the
year. From the German point of view the situation
was such as to warrant Ludendorff in believing that
there now existed a definite prospect of winning the
war, and under the influence of this hopeful outlook
the German Supreme Command decided in favour of a
decisive battle in the western theatre of war in the
spring of 1918. By the end of March forty-four divisions had been transferred to the west, and others had
been detailed to follow. The question which then
remained to be solved was on which of the two allies,
England or France, the blow should fall. The
British had borne the brunt of the fighting of 1917,
when the Battle of Ypres towered over all other events
in significance, whereas the French had made but
minor efforts after the fighting on the Aisne, and their
cautious strategy gave ground for the belief that the
loss of *moral* which had set in after that battle had not
been overcome. Nevertheless, the general opinion on
the German side appears to have been that a success
over the British would be more easily and certainly
obtainable. One voice, indeed, was raised in opposition, for the chief of staff of the Army Group of the
German Crown Prince considered that an attack
against the French forces would be better policy.
" England," he said, " with her dogged self-confi-

dence, is not likely to end the war on account of a partial defeat of her army. She will be more inclined for peace when the power of the French is broken by a heavy defeat.'' Ludendorff, however, held fast to the plan of directing the blow against the British, and on January 24th the German Supreme Command definitely adopted this view. In view of the growing strength of the American forces, it was imperative that the offensive decided upon should be undertaken at the first possible moment, and preparations were pushed forward including an intensive system of training. On March 10th Hindenburg sent out an order fixing the morning of March 21st for the attack.

The fateful March 21st, 1918, was ushered in with a thick white fog, and at dawn a bombardment of great intensity was opened against practically the whole front of the Fifth and Third Armies, the former being on the right of the British line and touching the French with its right flank. Favoured by the conditions of weather and with practically the whole of his striking force— carefully selected and for months specially trained for the shock offensive—the enemy gained ground nearly everywhere along the line, and on the 22nd renewed his attacks with consistent vehemence. It is important to remember that the 8th Division was many miles away when the first blow was struck, and, consequently, when the 2nd Northamptonshire Regiment was put into the fight the whole line was bending backward and its share was chiefly a conforming to a movement which was already in progress.

It was at six o'clock on the evening of the 21st that instructions were received for the 8th Division to entrain on the 22nd and 23rd. The detrainment of the various groups took place at Nesle, Chaulnes and Rosiéres during the night of the 22nd/23rd, the 58th being off the railway about 7 a.m. on the latter day : after a breakfast at Nesle the battalion moved by companies to Licourt, west of the Somme. Events had indeed been moving quickly. The 24th Brigade, while

R

en route, had received orders that on detraining it was to march to Athies, on the far side of the river. The 58th had sent forward a billeting party in advance during the night of the 22nd/23rd, and it had duly arrived at the village. Accommodation was secured, but, owing to the rapid advance of the Germans, the billeting party had to fight its way out, re-cross the river, and fix up accommodation at Licourt.

So fierce had been the thrust of the Germans that the commander of the Fifth Army had decided to withdraw to the western bank of the Somme, and the task of the 8th Division was to hold the river from a mile or so south of Béthencourt to Eterpigny on the north, sufficiently long for the exhausted troops in front to fall back across the river, after which the bridges were to be blown up. The position of the 24th Brigade was in the centre holding the section between Pargny Wood and St. Christ Bridge. Of the 24th Brigade the centre battalion was the 58th, which was disposed as follows : Left to right, " D," " B," " A " Companies in front line, with " C " Company (which did not arrive until 9 p.m.) in support. At about 1 p.m., before the 8th Division was completely in position, the first elements of the retiring infantry began to trickle across the bridges, the guns and transport having already crossed. The bridges were then blown up, but the destruction was by no means complete, and several of them were passable for infantry. Several attempts were made by the Germans to cross during the night, but these attempts were repulsed. Apparently no serious fighting took place in the sector held by the battalion.

March 24th was marked by something more serious. The right brigade of the division soon found its outer flank " in the air " and was forced to give ground. This, of course, reacted on the 24th Brigade in the centre, but the promptitude and dash of Lieutenant-Colonel Roberts, of the 1st Worcestershire Regiment, which was the right battalion of the brigade, relieved the situation. He counter-attacked and brought considerable relief to the 25th Brigade in its retirement by clearing the south-eastern end of Epénancourt. Touch, however, with the inner flank of the 25th Brigade was completely lost, and by 5 p.m., when infantry action on this front ceased for the day, the right flank of the 24th Brigade had been bent back considerably. Of the 58th, " B " and " A " Companies had become involved, and had to bend back in conformity with the Worcestershires. The night passed quietly.

Early in the morning of March 25th the Germans delivered a very determined assault against the right of the 24th Brigade and forced it back a considerable distance. " A " Company of the battalion held on until it was practically surrounded and had to fight its way out. A general retirement on this portion of the front now became necessary, and was carried out in an orderly manner, the brigade withdrawing to the railway embankment near Marchelepot, and later—about 9.30 p.m.—a further withdrawal was made to a line in front of Ablaincourt.

Possibly the reader may by this be wondering why the story is concerned almost entirely with retirement without fighting in nature or quantity to account for it. To answer this implied question it is well to remind the reader that only a very small sector of the great battle has been described. The 8th Division was put in when retirement was in progress, and although the pressure against it was severe the real hammer blows were to the north and south which brought about the retrograde movements to which the 8th Division had to conform. This was all the more important, seeing that the main thing was that no gap should occur in our line. It might bend back, but on no account must it break.

This process of retirement in sympathy with divisions north and south enabled the divisional commander to report at 6 a.m. on March 26th that on its new line the 8th Division had both flanks in touch with neighbouring divisions. The 24th Brigade was now on the

R I

right, with headquarters at Vermandovillers and the 2nd Northamptonshire Regiment as centre battalion of the brigade. Early in the morning the division was attacked in considerable force, but this attack was driven off with heavy loss. From the negative evidence of the war diary it would seem that the 58th was not seriously engaged. About 10 a.m. orders were received for a further retirement in a south-westerly direction, due, as before, to events north and south and outside our immediate purview. In this withdrawal the 58th reached the vicinity of Rosières, passing through the 24th Division in artillery formation of platoons. The enemy followed up, with the result that portions of the 24th Division "leap-frogged" through the battalion and held Méharicourt in strength. The 58th spent the night in hard digging and wiring so far as material permitted.

It was now urged that no further retirement should take place, for French troops were hurrying to the relief and it was essential that the new line should be held at all costs till then. The corps commander of the XIX Corps sent a message to all units calling upon them to make one more supreme effort to maintain to the last the magnificent fighting qualities and endurance already displayed. The test was not long postponed. About 8 a.m. on the morning of the 27th the blow came, a determined attack being delivered along the whole front of the 8th Division. It was pressed most severely on the 24th Brigade on the right. The units on the outer flank were driven in, and the right flank of the 58th was thereupon exposed, but the trouble was averted by a smart counter-attack carried out by a small party organized by Second-Lieutenant Macgregor and Sergeants Goosey and Tibble. On the left of the division further trouble had been brewing, but the situation was restored, and although fighting went on the line was held. Once again, however, retirements north and south of the division compelled a further withdrawal, which began about 8 a.m. on the 28th.

The battalion war diary mentions a very strong attack on the left of the division, and a " complicated withdrawal " and a change of direction to the new position near Caix. The Germans followed up vigorously, and, in order to occupy some high ground which was the destination of the battalion, it was necessary to pass through a machine-gun barrage. In the valley, which gave some cover, Lieutenant-Colonel Latham personally organized the battalion and led it in extended formation to its goal, the operation being most successfully carried out at the cost of only two wounded. By this time orders had been received for a still further withdrawal, to Moreuil, and later the march was resumed to Jumel, where the battalion lay down to rest at 3 a.m. in billets, exhausted after a day's hard fighting and a retirement of 16 miles.

During the night the units of the 8th Division were collected at Jumel, and for most of them, including the 58th, the following day, March 29th, was a day of rest. The battalion had been fighting and retiring for nearly a week without cessation, and, in common with other battalions, the 58th was thoroughly done and so utterly exhausted as to be unfit for a move. A day's complete rest made a great difference to the battalion, and it was able to move with the remainder of the brigade, and the 23rd Brigade, to hold the Avre river crossing at Castel, early next morning. The 58th spent all day in reserve, and then in the evening relieved the 4th Hussars and 16th Lancers north-east of Moreuil. The following day was March 31st, and another violent German attack took place, in which the 58th, who were in the support line, suffered rather severely. The attack was repulsed, and in the evening a patrol from the battalion captured 5 prisoners and a heavy machine gun. The night passed quietly enough, and a counter-attack made next day by the 2nd Cavalry Division eased the situation considerably, although there is a note in the war diary saying that the machine-gun fire from the left flank was very unpleasant. Things had now become much quieter—so quiet that in the afternoon Corporal Scrivener and Private Pepper took possession of two wandering cows, which, after being duly milked, were sent back to the battalion transport. Unfortunately, the animals had to be abandoned next day. It was during the same afternoon that the welcome news was received that the division would be relieved the same night by the 133rd French Division. By dawn on April 2nd the relief was completed, and by lorries and march route the 58th found itself that night behind Amiens and out of the battle at last.

The battle, indeed, was practically over, and the Germans, although they had made an immense gain of ground, were at the end of their tether. The Allied line was bent, and badly bent, but it still held. Amiens was saved, and the front crystallized at once into the locked warfare of the trenches. The casualties in the division had been very severe, the total figures being 4,943 of all ranks, and of this total the price paid by the 2nd Northamptonshire Regiment was as follows: Killed, 23, including Captain Piggott, Lieutenants C. G. Robertson and W. J. Norwood, and the chaplain, Rev. H. Lawson; wounded 122, and missing 159.

Although the 58th had suffered heavily in the fighting just related, there was for a time the chance that it might be hurried north to cope with another great German offensive. Indications reached British G.H.Q. that the storm centre was shifting rapidly from the Somme to the north. The blow fell on the Lys front on April 9th, where the fighting was most severe, and the 8th Division, with others, received orders to stand by in readiness to entrain for the danger area. The movement was, indeed, cancelled, but the 58th was soon to be called upon to take part in a final flare-up—brief but very violent, on the Somme.

At midnight on April 17th the division came under the III Corps, with a view to taking over a sector of the line. The sector in question was astride the highway immediately east of the village of Villers Bretonneux. The 58th went into the line during the night of April 19th/20th, and, on relief about 10 p.m. on the 23rd by the 2nd Middlesex Regiment, it marched back to the Bois de Blangy, where it became part of the divisional reserve.

It had been anticipated for some time that a strong local attack would be made by the Germans on Villers Bretonneux, with the high ground in the vicinity as being the key to another big offensive against Amiens. Information to this effect had been obtained on April 16th from a prisoner captured before Villers Bretonneux, and on April 22nd came more definite information of impending attack from a sergeant-major of the 4th Guards Division, who was taken prisoner during the morning by the 1st Sherwood Foresters. This information was confirmed from other sources, and measures were taken in the way of preparation. These did not, however, succeed in checking the development of the German plan, for on the following morning, April 24th, the attack opened and was carried out by no less than five German divisions in line. In this attack German tanks took part for the first time in the war.

As the 58th were in reserve we shall pass over the onrush of the Germans against the front line, and view the battle, so to speak, from the back area. Early in the morning the wood in which the battalion was posted was heavily shelled with high explosive and gas. Casualties were quickly suffered; Second-Lieutenant Howard was killed and several other ranks killed or wounded. With some difficulty the companies were got out of the Bois de Blangy, and they reorganized on some open ground south of the wood. It was clear from the roar of artillery and the sound of rifle and machine-gun fire that the village of Villers Bretonneux was being hotly assailed. It was now between 4 a.m. and 5 a.m., when a message was received ordering the battalion to take up its battle position in reserve. This was done, the 58th then being in touch with the 8th Londons on the right and with the 1st Worcestershire Regiment on the other flank. A section of Vickers guns was in support. The frontage occupied by the 58th was very extended, and it was therefore decided to have four companies in front line, with the demonstration platoon and battalion headquarters as reserve, some quarter of a mile in rear.

. The battalion was now being heavily shelled, and a fierce artillery fire was raining on Cachy. Wounded men trickling back from the front line brought the grave news that Villers Bretonneux had fallen. No call, however, was made upon the 58th, and except for sending out officers' patrols the battalion was not actually engaged. These patrols had been ordered to discover the situation east of Cachy, and found that the enemy were digging-in 800 yards east of that village, and that German tanks were firing on our advanced troops.

Beyond this, the 58th, from its position in reserve, had been able to glean little real knowledge of the happenings of the day. It will assist to the understanding of the story of Villers Bretonneux if the day's fighting is now briefly summarized. At 3.30 a.m. a tremendous bombardment descended upon the Allied front and support lines. Mixed gas and high explosive shells were poured out continuously over a wide area, large numbers of trench mortars supplementing the efforts of the German guns. In places the German guns were standing axle to axle. The guns were fired with the utmost possible speed, the gunners stripped naked to the waist and reliefs standing by. The bombardment lifted from our front line after about two and a quarter hours, but remained on our reserve positions —where the 58th was posted.

Dawn broke dim and misty, and the lack of visibility was increased by the fog from German smoke shells, which were put down all along the front about 6.30 a.m. The defenders were unable to see more than twenty yards ahead. Suddenly, at about seven o'clock, large and terrible apparitions were seen looming through the clinging wall of fog—German tanks. This was at the salient formed by the east and south sides of Villers Bretonneux. In spite of a gallant defence the defenders were overrun, and when the fog lifted during the morning it was found that Villers Bretonneux was in German hands.

It is outside our story to tell of the valiant counter-attacks made, or of the battle of British *versus* German tanks. Those who witnessed this epic engagement might well have exclaimed, as Goethe did at the close of the Battle of Valmy : " To-day something new has happened in the history of the world, and you and I can say that we were present at its birth." The first tanks to meet the enemy machines were either the light fast " whippets " or " female " tanks, each armed only with machine guns. These could do little harm to the heavily-armoured German machines, and certain of them were put out of action by the small calibre gun carried by their opponents. This first tank action in the history of the world bore a curious resemblance to the first engagement between the Grand Fleets of England and Germany. Just as at Jutland, so here at Villers Bretonneux, initial success was with the Germans. When, however, the British " male " tanks arrived upon the scene, heavier metal at once told, and all German tanks encountered were put out of action or driven to retreat. Jutland over again. And the whippets, too, did admirable service. Moving faster than an armed man can run, in the afternoon they caught two German battalions in the act of deploying, charged and utterly destroyed them and returned to our lines their sides splashed high with blood.

The loss of Villers Bretonneux was serious. In the hands of the Germans it was a spear-head aimed at Amiens, the retention of which by the Allies was of the very highest importance. Acquiescence in the German occupation of the village could not be thought of.   But in view of the large number of machine guns which the enemy had brought up, a counter-attack by daylight across the open slopes which led to our old lines would almost inevitably break down with the most terrible casualties.   It was therefore decided to wait until after sunset and to carry out the attempt under cover of a darkness relieved by moonlight.

At 9.15 p.m. Colonel Latham returned from Head-quarters, 8th Division, with orders to follow the 13th Australian Infantry Brigade's attack south of the Bois d'Aquenne, and when it got clear of the eastern edge of the wood to swing left and attack Villers Bretonneux in a north-easterly direction.   The 58th were relieved in the reserve line by the 8th Royal Berkshires (53rd Brigade), and formed up on taped lines by 10.15 p.m. By this time the enemy had put down a very heavy defensive barrage, generally on the line of the Cachy Switch.   The Battalion advanced in artillery formation with the commanding officer at its head.   The general slope of the ground and the fact that the wire of the Cachy Switch ran diagonally across the line of advance caused the 51st and 52nd Australian Battalions to veer to the right, and the 58th to move on to their left.   As a result the three battalions were soon intermingled. The wire of the Cachy Switch was a formidable obstacle, and while getting through it the 58th suffered many casualties from machine-gun fire from the Bois d'Aquenne and from the road leading from the wood to Villers Bretonneux.   Soon after clearing the Cachy Switch, Lieutenant-Colonel S. G. Latham was killed by a shell and the Adjutant wounded.

Major H. T. Fowler now took over command, and the 58th moved on in artillery formation of half companies, with the demonstration platoon following in line of sections to pick up stragglers.   So soon as the battalion had deployed it encountered our own wire, which was here difficult of passage, and as during this delay enemy machine-gun fire was coming from

the south-east corner of the Bois d'Aquenne and elsewhere, numerous casualties were suffered by the
battalion, as well as by the Australians, who had swung
too far to the north.

Luckily a gap was found in the wire, and the
companies filed through into the valley and deployed
again. Meanwhile the 13th Australian Brigade had
been faced with a heavy task. Its path lay across a stiff
northward falling slope, and troops moving over such
terrain almost unconsciously crowd in the direction of
the falling ground. Further, a belt of wire ran diagonally across its front, and severe machine-gun fire met
the attacking battalions immediately they started to
advance. But in spite of heavy casualties the
Australians were not to be denied, and, overcoming
all obstacles and dealing effectually with enemy posts,
pressed on until the leading troops entered Monument Wood, just south-east of Villers Bretonneux.
Here the brigade was "in the air," the brigades right
and left not having come up into line, and accordingly
the 13th Australian Brigade fell back a short distance
and dug in.

The course of the 58th would have taken them to
the centre of Villers Bretonneux, but the whole valley
was lit up by Very lights, and when within about 500
yards of the railway the battalion was met by fierce
machine-gun fire directed from that position down the
steep bare slope which formed a natural glacis in front
of it. The casualties were severe, and it was clear that
any attempt to push on would be useless. Accordingly
the battalion was withdrawn for a short distance, and
side-stepped to the right. Touch was now gained with
the left of the 13th Australian Brigade, whose doings
have been briefly related above. The Australians
reported that they were held up, and arrangements were
now made for the 58th to form a defensive flank to the
Australians. Both were just south of Villers Bretonneux, the Australians facing east and the 58th facing
north, looking into the village.

It was still dark, but dawn came shortly. The situation did not appear too reassuring, for Germans were seen still holding the eastern edge of the Bois d'Aquenne, through which the battalion and the 13th Australian Brigade had passed. However, one of our tanks now cruised along the wood and cleared out the enemy posts. The Germans bolted for safety, and as they raced towards Villers Bretonneux the 58th caught them with enfilade fire with a captured German machine-gun. This activity was apparently observed by the Germans in Monument Farm, who retaliated with an enfilade machine-gun fire upon the North-amptonshires' right.

Meanwhile, although the knowledge had not as yet reached the 58th, the village had been entered from the north-west. Some time during the forenoon the news filtered through. Consultation with the commanding officer of the 51st Australian Battalion now took place, and it was agreed that the Northamptonshires should push forward, swing right-handed and take up a position near the railway station. It was a difficult task, for 150 yards of open ground had to be traversed before cover could be reached. In these circumstances it was decided to do the job in one rush. The plan succeeded, for the Germans were caught napping and only the slower members of the battalion came under really serious fire, the casualties being just a dozen. Arrived at the cover, the companies were quickly reorganized, patrols being sent towards the village and the railway station. "D" Company, under Second-Lieutenant Handley, also moved forward in the direction of the station and pushed out a patrol to get in touch with an Australian post. This patrol was fired on, and it was realized that the east side of Villers Bretonneux was still held by Germans. However, "D" Company, under cover of the railway embankment, reached a position near the station. "C" Company followed, and then "B" and "A," the last two companies totalling a mere handful of men. The demonstration platoon was in reserve. Two patrols were now sent into Villers Bretonneux to assist in mopping-up.

About 6 p.m. the Germans opened a particularly heavy artillery fire, searching the whole area behind our front line. This bombardment lasted for an hour, and the 58th had several casualties, Lieutenant Sheehan and Second-Lieutenant Maclean being among the wounded. With darkness things quietened down, and hot soup and tea were sent up, both of which were much appreciated. During the night constant patrolling was kept up, and two platoons of "A" Company, which had been cut off, rejoined the battalion, the strength of which at the end of the day's fighting had sunk to 8 officers and 190 other ranks.

Though the front taken up on the close of the successful counter-attack had been made secure, Monument Wood and some ground to the south of it were still in German hands. It was arranged that a French division should deal with this menace at dawn on the following day, April 26th. The 58th watched the French infantry moving forward in artillery formation and then extending to attack. The attempt was, however, unsuccessful, owing to machine-gun fire from Monument Farm. "D" Company of the 58th now sent a patrol past the railway station to discover what was the situation east of the village. Here a weak post of Australians was found. A report was circulated that the French were to attack again, but the attempt was not made, although farther to the south the French did succeed in recapturing a certain amount of ground. During the day the 58th were withdrawn to behind Villers Bretonneux.

On the following morning, April 27th, orders were received that the 8th Division would be relieved that same evening by the 4th Australian Division. The relief duly took place, and on the 28th the battalion marched via Longueau to Camon, where it went into billets. In this Battle of Villers Bretonneux the 8th Division had suffered heavily, the casualties being

3,420. As for the 58th, although it had not been in the front line at the beginning, the losses were 15 killed, 19 missing, and 251 wounded. Three officers were killed—the commanding officer, Lieutenant-Colonel S. G. Latham; Captain G. B. Vernon, commanding " B " Company; and Second-Lieutenant A. L. Thomas, of " C " Company. The wounded officers were the adjutant, Captain H. Essame; Lieutenant W. K. Sheehan, the intelligence officer; Captain F. M. MacGregor, commanding " A " Company; and Second-Lieutenant Maclean, of " D " Company. For their gallant services the commanding officer received the posthumous award of the Distinguished Service Order and Second-Lieutenant S. E. Farbon gained a bar to his Military Cross. That decoration was awarded, according to the war diary, to Second-Lieutenant F. M. Macgregor [sic], who is doubtless the officer of the same initials given above. Corporal (Acting-Sergeant) E. Driver received the Distinguished Conduct Medal. The recapture of Villers Bretonneux was a brilliant piece of work, splendidly carried out. By it the last desperate thrust of the Germans towards Amiens was definitely foiled.

The death of Lieutenant-Colonel Latham was a great loss to the regiment. He joined the 3rd Battalion early in 1915 as a subaltern at the age of 43. He joined the 2nd Battalion on May 11th, 1915, and served continuously with that battalion until killed at Villers Bretonneux. In 1917 he refused the command of another battalion in order to remain with the 2nd Battalion. He was a born soldier and devoted to the regiment.

By the end of April the Great Push of the Germans had burnt itself out. The offensive on the Somme had been followed by a further effort on the Lys which had likewise died away. This latter series of battles had necessitated the intervention of French divisions from the south, and to replace these it was decided to send certain British divisions southward. These

British divisions, although reconstituted, could not yet be considered fit for further battle fighting for the present. It was therefore originally intended that they should be kept in reserve for a time, and when they went into the line the sector should be a quiet one. The 8th Division was one of those selected. At the beginning of May it was sent south to form part of the British IX Corps, attached to the French Sixth Army on the Aisne. By May 4th the units of the division were comfortably established in huts and villages in the neighbourhood of Fismes.

Within a few days instructions were received from the French authorities that the 8th Division was to go into the line to relieve a corresponding force of the French, and the orders were accompanied by assurances that the sector was an extremely quiet one and of great natural strength. At first the eulogies seemed justified. The new front, which consisted of some 10,000 yards in the Berry-au-Bac sector, was certainly the most peaceful the division had ever been in. The country-side was in marked contrast to the mud and blood and blasted woods and ruined villages of the Ypres salient and the Somme. Here all was peace. The landscape basked in blazing sunshine. Trim villages nestled in quiet hollows beside lazy streams. True there were the signs and remnants of the great French offensive of 1917—one of the bloodiest battles of the war, but the shell holes were now filled with grass and water plants. Near the gun emplacements in the reserve line grew lilies of the valley, forget-me-nots, larkspur and honey-suckle. The whole battle area had become a shrubbery, a vast garden fashioned by artillery. There was but little shelling, and such projectiles as fell did so with a tired and listless sound.

There were some suspicious people on the British side who had learnt a thing or two in the war, and who did not share the rosy optimism of the French. The listless " crump " every now and then seemed always to drop near a battery position and appeared uncommonly like ranging or the calibration of new guns. Further, it had happened before in the war that the Germans soon got to know when a sector was being held by troops of the Allies who were in need of a rest cure, and that sector might—and often did—become suddenly anything but peaceful. Representations of this kind were made to the French authorities, but the British view did not meet their approval.

The 2nd Northamptonshire Regiment found itself in support trenches from the 19th to the 23rd, and on the following day moved up to the front line near Juvincourt, " A " Company being in immediate support at von Kluck Dump. The sector occupied by the 8th Division formed a right-angled salient pushed out into the German positions. The right flank of the division rested on the Aisne itself at the village of Berry-au-Bac, and this sub-sector was held by the 25th Brigade. In the centre was the 24th Brigade with the 2nd Northamptonshire Regiment in line, the 1st Worcestershires in the main line of resistance, and the 1st Sherwood Foresters in reserve south of the Aisne. The 23rd Brigade held the left. The 8th Division occupied the centre of the IX Corps front, the 21st and 50th Divisions being on the right and left respectively, with the 25th Division in army reserve. The 2nd Northamptonshire Regiment was, therefore, in the exact centre, being in the front line of the centre brigade of the centre division of the corps.

It will be noticed that the position was in front of the natural obstacle formed by the Aisne, and such a choice was in direct opposition to recent experiences, especially that just gained on the Somme and Lys. The British divisional generals earnestly protested, pointing out that it would be suicidal to ignore recent lessons and asserting that there was grave danger that the troops north of the Aisne might be cut off. These representations fell, however, upon deaf ears. The French commander was unwilling to abandon French soil to the invaders, and directed that the positions north of the Aisne should consist of two lines. The first was the outpost line, some 1,000 to 1,500 yards in depth, with a battle zone—still north of the Aisne— immediately in rear. The outpost line was to fight to the last, and the battle zone was to be held at all costs. These orders necessitated the main infantry strength of the 8th Division and the bulk of the artillery being posted on the enemy's side of the river.

When the 58th took up its fatal position rumours were already in circulation to the effect that an attack on a large scale was possible, but nothing happened, and even as late as the 25th everything was quiet. The truth was that the Germans had been for long training for an immense effort, and had taken the most elaborate precautions for effecting a surprise. The noon reports of May 26th revealed, however, an inkling of the truth. Greatly increased movement was observed behind the enemy's lines, and there had been much noise and sounds of activity at night. Further, two prisoners captured by the French had given evidence that an attack was to be launched on the 27th. All doubt was now removed, and battle positions were taken up at six o'clock in the evening. Major Forster and Captain Lenton were sent back for duty in the details camp, in accordance with the system of having a nucleus for the re-formation of a battalion in the event of a heavy attack.

The German plan was a simple one. Effective bombardment was to begin immediately and the first object was to be a thorough gassing of the Allied position right down into the Aisne valley. In view of the impending attack, which it was known would open at 1 a.m., our artillery started to carry out counter-preparations and harassing fire. Not a shell, however, came from the enemy. The time crept on towards zero until only a few minutes were left. Suddenly, at 1 a.m. to the moment, a few German gas shells burst, and within a second hell was let loose. An officer of the 23rd Brigade has left on record a stirring narrative of those

S

awful hours of the early morning of May 27th, 1918, and the following extracts from it are quoted from the admirable "History of the 8th Division." He tells how a thousand guns roared out their iron hurricane. The night was rent with sheets of flame. The earth shuddered under the avalanche of missiles. Ever above the din shrieked the fierce crescendo of approaching shells; ear-splitting crashes as they burst. Inferno raged and whirled round the Bois de Buttes, where the headquarters of the 23rd Brigade were located. The dug-outs rocked, filled with the acrid fumes of cordite and the sickly-sweet tang of gas. Timbers started: earth showered from the roof: men rushed for shelter, seizing kits, weapons, gas masks, message pads, as they dived for safety. It was a descent into hell. Gas began to filter down. Gas masks were hurriedly donned and anti-gas precautions taken—the entrances closed with saturated blankets, braziers lighted on the stairs. In some cases the hours of bombardment were spent in these stinking, over-crowded holes, their entrances sealed up, and with charcoal braziers alight drying up the atmosphere—suffocation rendered more complete by the gas mask with clip on nostrils and gag in teeth.

It is practically impossible to give, from official records, a coherent narrative of what happened when the German bombardment lifted and the German infantry pressed forward to the attack. In the first place, as happened with such uncanny frequency in the case of a German attack, morning broke with a dense blanket of fog. In the second place all the papers and documents of the 24th Brigade, including the war diary, were lost in the disaster. Nevertheless, from information supplied by survivors, supplemented by the researches so ably carried out by the author of the "History of the 8th Division," it is possible to give some account of the happenings of the day.

It will be remembered that the 58th was in the centre of the position, and this turned out to be both an advantage and the reverse. It was an advantage in that the German effort was directed to nipping off the salient and therefore the flanks of the IX Corps were the most hotly attacked. This is shown by the fact that although the S.O.S. was sent out from the 23rd and 25th Brigades no such signal was necessary for the 24th and its front was apparently "not badly knocked about." This phrase is, of course, merely relative, as will be seen from the following narrative of a company sergeant-major of the Northamptonshires, who says: " Our company headquarters occupied an old German dug-out with two entrances, both facing the enemy, with the result that shells exploded right down the stairway, which by 3 a.m. was completely blocked up. I set parties to work to clear away the earth and wood, during which time twelve men were suffering from shell shock and five from gas. I had only five men left when the barrage lifted, which was about 5 a.m. Leaving the men to man the trench, or what was left of it, I made my way to the front line trench to see how the platoons had fared, but there was no trench, the ground had been flattened out. On my way back to my company headquarters I ran up against a German party consisting of 1 officer and about 40 men. Several shots were fired at me, but the officer told them to stop, and asked me in English where the remainder of my men were. I informed him that they were in a dug-out, suffering from gas and shell shock. He told me to direct him to it, and, on arrival, I noticed that the five men I had left to man the trench had been captured, but not without a fight, for two were dead, two wounded, and one a prisoner. The officer told me to go down the dug-out and fetch the men up, but when I informed him that they were unable to move he sent a party with me. After a lot of trouble we got them up the broken stairway into the open. I then asked the officer if I could go down another dug-out to see how my company officer had fared, so he sent another party with me, and with much difficulty (for the entrance had been blown in) we got down to his quarters. All the occupants were suffering from gas or shell shock. My company officer and a battery observation officer had shell shock badly. They were not aware of what was going on; in fact, my officer asked me when he was going to get relieved. I told him his relief had arrived, but belonging to the wrong party. With difficulty we got them out, and then the German officer detailed a party to take me behind their lines."

The disadvantage, as will be realized from the above narrative, lay in the fact that when the brigades right and left had been forced back the Germans swarmed in behind the Northamptonshires, and an especial disadvantage of trench warfare is that everything is staked upon the chance of the enemy appearing from the front : when the opposite happens the whole scheme of defence collapses. This is what overtook the 58th, and after a terrible four hours' bombardment, in which many were killed, more were wounded and still more were stupified by gas, the battalion was in no state to offer an effectual resistance in these new circumstances. It would appear that remnants of the battalion, attacked on two if not on three sides, were gradually driven back to the battle zone. Tanks, apparently, were not used on this front; but, as the light increased, enemy aeroplanes were observed flying low over our forward system and firing into the trenches. Lieutenant-Colonel C. G. Buckle, whose conduct and example had been an inspiration to the men, was killed outside his battalion headquarters; but the 58th fought on, and in the battle zone the enemy's attack was definitely checked, repeated attacks being beaten back by the 58th and the Worcestershires. The position here was very strong, and our troops might have held out indefinitely against a purely frontal assault. But the Germans were able to make their way round from the flank and rear, and the defenders were cut off and surrounded. Soon after nine o'clock the collected remnants of the brigade were holding a trench on the north-east side of Roucy. Its strength had been reduced to 3 officers and 68 other ranks. Of the 2nd Northamptonshire Regiment only two escaped—the adjutant (Captain Blake) and the regimental sergeant-major. The 58th had been blotted out.

When last seen, Colonel Buckle was standing in his shirt sleeves in front of his dug-out, revolver in hand and refusing to surrender, facing a horde of Germans. At four o'clock he was shot down. After the armistice his father, Major-General Buckle, visited the dug-out and found, pinned to the wall, Colonel Buckle's last order to his companies, written during the bombardment. By the son's grave were two of the dead Germans killed in this last struggle. In Colonel Buckle the 58th lost a gallant commander, whose death every soldier will envy. None died that day with more glory, yet many died and there was much glory.

During the day 4 officers and 76 other ranks of the battalion returned from a Lewis gun course and were " brigaded "—if the euphemism is allowed—and sent up under the officer commanding the 1st Worcestershire Regiment, while the details under Major Forster moved forward and took up a position between Ventelay and Bouvancourt. Desperate fighting continued for the next five days, by which the Germans created an immense dent in the Allied line between Soissons and Reims and the invaders once more looked down upon the waters of the Marne. The 8th Division had nearly 8,000 casualties; as for the 58th it was represented now merely by its transport, for stragglers and men from hospital were sent to help make up a composite battalion. The division gradually worked its way back to the vicinity of Abbeville, for reconstruction. The task of rebuilding the 58th was put in hand. On June 17th Lieutenant-Colonel S. S. Hayne joined and assumed command, and the following day Major Rowe, from the 2nd/7th Worcestershires, became second-in-command, and 12 officers joined, mostly from the Royal

Berkshire Regiment. On the 19th and 20th drafts of
600 other ranks flowed in, and another batch of 10
officers on the 22nd. As a battalion the 58th had now
—phœnix-like—risen from the ashes, but little, of
course, remained of its original constitution and
personnel. With characteristic *insouciance* this fact
was marked by a football match on the 29th, " Old
58th *v*. New 58th." Reading this, a thoughtful
foreigner will understand why the British Army is never
beaten. The end of June found the reconstituted 58th
" finding itself " and thinking of itself as the old
Steelbacks, in the neighbourhood of Fressenville.

CHAPTER XIII.

BATTLE OF THE LYS.

LEAVING the 2nd Battalion, we now take up the story of the 48th. In the closing paragraph of Chapter XI, the 1st Battalion was left in the Ypres Salient at the end of 1917, and the comparatively quiet period of the ensuing four months was there foreshadowed. Some incidents, however, merit relating. Thus, it was during this period that the heavy losses sustained by the British Army during the 1917 fighting made it necessary to reduce every infantry brigade to three battalions. The Loyal North Lancashires were the unit which left the 2nd Brigade. Although various Territorial battalions had from time to time been attached to the brigade, until now the four original regular units had never been separated from each other. Another innovation of a more pleasant nature was the introduction of the practice of permitting officers who had served for an exceptionally long time in the firing line to return to England for a month's leave and five months' home service. Captain J. E. M. Pierson, who had served continuously with the 48th since June, 1915, was one of the first to obtain this privilege. Towards the end of March, 1918, when the great German offensive was about to be launched against the Fifth Army in the St. Quentin area, the artillery of the enemy became rather more active. The 2nd Brigade at this time had three different commanders in one week. First Brigadier-General Kay was wounded, and then his successor, Lieutenant-Colonel Bellamy, of the 60th. Lieutenant-Colonel Robinson then assumed command of the 2nd Brigade for three days.

It was considered essential at this time to obtain some

clue as to the identity of the German troops facing
the 1st Division. On the night of March 21st/22nd,
Second-Lieutenant W. C. Furminger, of " D " Company, a young officer who had only recently joined
the battalion, led out a patrol of eight men, his intention
being to capture one of the enemy, if possible. It was
a clear, moonlight night, and the patrol moved forward
very cautiously until they came in sight of a German
" pill-box," about 2,000 yards north-west of Passchendaele. The original intention was to attack this " pill-
box," but, while preparations were being made to do
so, one of the enemy was seen to leave it and to walk
away in an easterly direction. The patrol thereupon
followed this man, who finally entered what appeared
to be another German post. Presently he came out
with two more of the enemy, and all three of them
stood in the moonlight talking to one another. This
was Second-Lieutenant Furminger's opportunity. A
careful examination of the enemy's wire revealed a weak
point in it, through which the patrol passed. Then,
when the officer gave the word, a sudden rush was
made at the small group of Germans, who promptly
fled. The patrol reached the post, and a bomb was
thrown into the shelter. One of the enemy hurriedly
emerged, holding his hands above his head. He was
instantly secured and hurried back towards the British
lines. Although a machine gun opened fire upon the
retreating patrol, none of them was hurt, and the
prisoner was brought safely back. For this exploit,
Second-Lieutenant Furminger received the Military
Cross.

The above incident occurred during the last tour in
the line that the battalion was destined to make in the
Ypres Salient. The great German offensive directed
against Amiens was now in progress, and the Higher
Command, who correctly anticipated another attempt
to break the British line in the neighbourhood of La
Bassée, resolved to move the 1st Division down to that
area. On April 4th, when the battalion was at rest

in Kempton Park, a camp near St. Julien, orders were received to be ready to move at ten minutes' notice. Next day the 1st Northamptonshires entrained at Boesinghe and proceeded south to Chocques, a station not far from Bethune.

It is impossible to conceive a more complete contrast than that between the Ypres Salient and the district in which the battalion now found itself. In Belgium, where the ground behind the British line had been the scene of three colossal battles, there was an enormous area of devastated country: villages situated six or eight miles behind the firing line were desolate and uninhabited. In the neighbourhood of Cuinchy, just south of La Bassée Canal, things were very different. Neither side had made any material advance since 1914. In consequence, civilian inhabitants were still to be found in Cambrin, about one mile from the front line, while at Le Quesnoy, not four miles from the German trenches, the villagers continued to live their ordinary lives, seemingly oblivious of the proximity of the enemy.

The 48th went into the front line east of Cuinchy on April 7th. Their left rested on the La Bassée Canal, beyond which the 55th Division was holding the line in front of Givenchy. At first, everything was very quiet, but the calm was not of long duration. As a matter of fact, the Germans were about to undertake another offensive. At first, the idea was that the attack was to be merely a diversion, but when it became clear that the " Big Push " on the Somme would not lead to complete victory, the offensive on the Lys was extended in scope, with the aim of forcing a final decision. A break-through was projected along the front Armentières—La Bassée Canal, with Hazebrouck as the first objective. The first sharp thrust was to be made against the sector held by the Portuguese—troops who had not yet been " tried out." It will be noticed that, as the La Bassée Canal was the southern boundary of this new offensive, the 48th were technically

outside the area; but, as will be seen, they were brought
into the inferno, and did sterling work.

April 9th was the day on which the Germans launched
their offensive against the Allied line north of the canal.
The preliminary bombardment began at 4.20 a.m.
Although the shelling south of the canal was not as
heavy as that directed against the trenches which were
about to be attacked, it was none the less of a very
severe character.   The morning was so misty that it
was impossible to see for any distance.   For some hours
the 48th remained on the alert, peering through the mist
to see whether the enemy were moving forward to
attack.   On the left, the Germans had fought their way
into Givenchy, but it was impossible for the Northamptonshires to ascertain what was happening there, as
the mist shrouded everything in an impenetrable cloud.
In the afternoon, the 55th Division counter-attacked
and drove the enemy back to his former position.   The
mist had now lifted, and " A " Company, who were
nearest to the canal, were able to bring an effective rifle
and Lewis-gun fire to bear upon the retreating
Germans, inflicting numerous casualties.   The losses
of the battalion during this day totalled 26, Second-
Lieutenant M. W. Tipler being among the wounded.

Although the enemy had gained little immediately
north of the canal, his success against the Portuguese
on the left of the 55th Division had turned the Givenchy
position into a dangerously-exposed salient.   The 48th
had therefore to consider the possibility of the Germans
obtaining possession of the ground north of the canal,
and the scheme of defence was reorganized so as to
provide for this contingency.   Nothing, however,
happened of a serious nature.   The battalion was
relieved on April 13th by the Royal Sussex, and went
back to Cambrin.   The few remaining civilians were
evacuated, and the village was put in a state of defence.

On April 18th, the enemy again attacked Givenchy,
which was now held by the 1st Brigade.   Cambrin was
heavily shelled, and the battalion stood to arms.

" D " Company was sent to the north bank to hold the bridge-head at Pont Fixe, a point where the canal had once been spanned by a permanent iron bridge. This structure was now in ruins, and on its western side a temporary pontoon bridge had been built. In full view of the enemy, Captain Martin led his company across the bridge and took up a defensive position on the far side. Here " D " Company maintained themselves for several days, in spite of a continual bombardment, which killed or wounded nearly 40 of them. Captain Martin was subsequently awarded the Military Cross.

Meanwhile, the enemy had succeeded in forcing their way through our defences north of Givenchy. Although the 1st Brigade checked their advance and drove them out of some of the trenches they had occupied, at the end of the day the Germans still held a piece of high ground north of the village, from which they overlooked much of the surrounding country. The task of recapturing this position was entrusted to the 48th.

Lieutenant-Colonel Robinson, together with Captain A. C. Pickering, of " A " Company, and Captain H. C. Tetley, of " C " Company, went forward to reconnoitre the enemy's position on April 19th. It consisted of two lines of trenches, having a frontage of about 450 yards. Behind these were several mine craters, joined to the trenches by saps; these craters lay between what had formerly been the British and German front lines. That night, " A " and " C " Companies crossed to the north side of the canal, where Lieutenant-Colonel Robinson had established his battle-headquarters. At 4.30 a.m. on April 20th, the two companies silently formed up along a pre-arranged line of deployment, " A " being on the left. A quarter of an hour later, just before day-break, the attack began. Preceded by an artillery barrage, the 1st Northampton-shires advanced resolutely through the battered remains of the village towards the enemy's trenches. In spite of a heavy machine-gun fire, they pressed steadily on, following the barrage closely and keeping their direction well. They reached the German trenches, and killed or captured such of the enemy as did not save themselves by flight. Twenty minutes after the attack had commenced, the German trenches were in our hands. But the enemy did not relax his grasp upon the position without a determined struggle, and shots were exchanged at close range all along the line, before the Germans finally withdrew. An attempt was made to bomb the 48th out of the trenches, German bombing parties attacking both flanks from the saps leading to the craters, but the Northamptonshires clung tenaciously to the ground that they had won, and repelled the enemy's bombers. The captured position was at once consolidated, two platoons of " B " Company being brought up to reinforce " A " and " C." No organized counter-attack was made by the enemy, although the trenches were rather heavily bombarded in the evening.

The attack had been admirably planned and executed, and the casualties had not been unduly heavy. " A " Company had Lieutenant F. C. Cockerill and Second-Lieutenant B. A. Hill wounded, and 40 other casualties. Captain Pickering was hit in the hand, but he gallantly refused to leave his company. In " C " Company, the casualties were somewhat more heavy. Lieutenant J. B. Pilkington was killed, and Second-Lieutenant J. Caldwell was reported missing. It was not until some time afterwards that it became known that the latter officer had been captured by the enemy. Second-Lieutenant F. H. Tucker was gassed, and the casualties among other ranks totalled 56. The German losses were undoubtedly very heavy, and, apart from those killed and wounded, 23 were taken prisoner.

In the congratulatory message sent by Brigadier-General Kelly to the 48th, the commander of the 2nd Brigade wrote : " There is no battalion better qualified than the 1st Northamptonshires to show the enemy what dash in attack and determination in holding on means." The Military Cross was awarded. to Captain Tetley and to Lieutenant R. D. Martin. The latter officer had rendered valuable services in the preliminary reconnaissance, and had also displayed great gallantry during the actual attack. Captain Pickering was given a bar to his Military Cross, while Sergeant A. Jelly, of " A " Company, received the D.C.M. Fifteen other ranks were awarded the Military Medal or bar. Among the recipients were one man of " B " Company and two of " D." No. 15 Platoon of the latter company had been detailed to act as carriers for the machine gun companies during the attack. This platoon, which suffered only 3 casualties, received a special message of thanks for its services.

After the successful counter-attack of April 20th there was little more serious fighting in the La Bassée area during the four months which the battalion spent there. The German attack had made a great dent in the Allied front, but had not broken it. For some time, however, the artillery on both sides displayed more than normal activity. Lieutenant H. C. Ramsay was killed by a shell on April 22nd. The total casualties for the month amounted to 205. May was an uneventful month. Only about 20 casualties were incurred. Two officers were wounded, Captain Hayes, the Battalion M.O., and Lieutenant A. P. White. June was quieter still. There were barely a dozen casualties in the line, but a large number of officers and men were temporarily incapacitated by an outbreak of a species of influenza fever. Captain B. C. Carey was awarded the Military Cross during this month. On July 1st, H.R.H. the Duke of Connaught inspected the 2nd Brigade near Bruay, and expressed his pleasure at the fine turn-out and soldierly bearing of all ranks. Talavera Day was celebrated at Noeux-les-Mines. On July 28th, Major Forsyth-Forrest left the battalion to assume command of the 1st Loyal North Lancashire Regiment, his place as second-in-command being filled by Major G. D. Gould, of the Durham Light Infantry.

On August 14th, the 48th lost the services of two of
its best officers.   Captain F. G. S. Martin was wounded
in the hand by a fragment of shell in Cambrin village,
while, on the same day, Captain Hofman left the
battalion to become A.D.C. to Major-General H. K.
Bethell, who now commanded the 66th Division.
Captain E. E. Hilbert now joined the 48th as Quartermaster.   A few days later, Second-Lieutenant Legg
was wounded.   On August 31st, the battalion, which
had just spent a week out of the line at Bours, entrained
at Dieval for Arras.   Its sojourn in the La Bassée
district had ended.   Though the latter part of its stay
had been uneventful, in the first month the 48th had
rendered services of lasting value to the British Empire.

CHAPTER XIV.

SHORT HISTORY OF THE SERVICE BATTALIONS AND FINAL PHASE OF THE WAR.

THE story of the war has now reached a point of intense interest. The tide had now begun to turn. Historians will probably agree in maintaining that never in the course of the world's history has there existed a period so fateful as that which began on March 21st and ended on November 11th of the year 1918. In that space of just eight months, the whole future not only of Europe but of the whole world hung in the balance, and there took place an ebb and flow of military success of an unprecedented kind. Within the space of just 235 days, England sustained the greatest defeat which had ever attended her arms, while Germany, on her part, experienced an overthrow so stupendous that its significance could scarcely be grasped at the time. Future generations will stand bewildered at the survey of the events of that *annus mirabilis,* and will speculate upon what must have been the experience of their fore-fathers whose life embraced that eight-month span of the history of the world.

Before, however, we follow the course of the flood which swept Germany away, it will be well if we use the brief period of slack water to look back and survey the scene once more. It is indeed only by having in our minds a précis, so to speak, of the four years' warfare that we shall be able to grasp the full signifi-cance of the narrative which is now to follow. Before half the year was completed, one battalion of the regiment was almost annihilated. Hardly had the year drawn to an end before the colours of another battalion of the Northamptonshire Regiment were borne in triumph by the waters of the Rhine. The happenings of the last few months of the war require, therefore, an adequate setting. It has been a commonplace throughout this volume that after a hard battle the battalion concerned has been withdrawn to " refit and reorganize." Some similar process is required in the narrative itself. Particularly is this the case for two reasons. So far, only the barest reference has been made to the course of the war in theatres other than France; but, without a fuller reference to them now, the last act of the long drama will not be understood. In the second place, it is now time to give some account, even if a brief one, of the heroic doings of the Service Battalions of the regiment. Admittedly, this volume is concerned chiefly with the 1st and 2nd Battalions. Nevertheless, the History would be poor and incomplete were it not at least to touch upon the magnificent services of the 5th, 6th and 7th Battalions. A brief sketch of the history of the 1st/4th Territorial Battalion is given in Chapter XVI.

To go back to 1914, the situation at the end of this year was briefly as follows : The grandiose German plan of bringing France to her knees within six weeks and then transferring the bulk of her forces in France to her eastern frontier to assist Austria in finishing off Russia had gone by the board. It collapsed utterly at the Battle of the Marne. The plan had been a daring one, and the German Great General Staff had staked everything—had put their shirt on it, so to speak. Ambitious though it was, it might yet have succeeded had it not been for one enormously important factor, over which the Germans had made a colossal miscalculation. They made up their minds that England would not intervene. The Germans persuaded themselves that England was played out; that the Irish question would tie her hands; and that labour unrest would contribute to restraining England. When the latter intervened, the whole outlook was changed. England, it was true, had a small army, but her navy assured her command of the sea. Germany could thus be blockaded. The whole British Empire was a huge reserve of man-power, and its resources in money and material were almost incalculable. If the Allies could hold their own until England " got into her stride," it seemed obvious that the Central Powers (that is, Germany and Austria) must be outmatched.

We can omit from our survey the immense response made by the Overseas Dominions and the question of resources, that is, money, munitions and supplies. What immediately concerns us here is the expansion of the army. When Lord Kitchener became Secretary of State for War on the outbreak of the great struggle, he at once grasped the need for immediate and immense expansion. There were really two methods of doing this : either to use the existing Territorial framework, or to create entirely new formations. Without going into the vexed question of whether Lord Kitchener was right or wrong, it can be mentioned simply that he adopted the latter system. He decided to raise new divisions. These divisions were to be created as armies (popularly termed " Kitchener " or " K " Armies), each of 100,000 men. The nucleus of the I New Army was at once commenced by forming the unit organization of six divisions and drafting into them the necessary personnel. Five armies in all were formed, of which one—" K. IV "—was used for draft-finding. Side by side with these " New " armies—and indeed in a sense competing with them for equipment and arms— were the Territorials, who were, of course, expanding too.

From the outset, Lord Kitchener, almost alone of those in high places, realized that the war would be one of years, not of months as some had complacently thought. An expansion by 500,000 men was arranged for, and on August 8th, 1914, Kitchener asked for 100,000 to start with. Within a fortnight he had obtained them, and Northampton was not behindhand in contributing her share. Indeed, the difficulty then was not to obtain recruits, but to deal with them as

T

they came.   The rush to enlist had begun on the very
morning of Tuesday, August 4th, when it was clear
that, even if England did not join in the war, she would
need to be ready.   On that day, when the officer in
charge of Great Scotland Yard, the chief recruiting
office in London, arrived at his office, he found a seeth-
ing mass of men waiting to be enrolled.   It took him
twenty minutes, with the help of twenty policemen, to
force his way in, and he was attesting men as hard as
he could during the whole of that day and for many
days to come.   And so it was all over Great Britain.
Men of all classes, married, single, childless, with
families, rich and poor, barristers, peers' sons, artists,
writers, schoolmasters, working men, parsons and
loafers swarmed into the recruiting offices.   And all
this time, the Territorial Force, nearly the whole of
which had individually volunteered for service overseas,
had been quickly raising recruits for itself, supple-
mentary to the recruits raised by these different methods.

These raw recruits had to be housed, fed, clothed,
armed, equipped, distributed into units, and taught
drill, discipline and the technical skill needed of
modern soldiers.   They had to be animated with *esprit
de corps* for their units.   It was a tremendous problem.
Accommodation was a great difficulty.   Millions of
suits of uniform, pairs of boots and other necessaries
were required at once, and could not, of course, be
immediately obtained.   The most serious material
deficiency for the training of the new armies was, however, the lack of guns, rifles, ammunition, and all other
ordnance stores.   Looking at these handicaps, there
were some of the Regular Army frankly dubious of the
success of these new formations.   Some prophesied the
absolute impossibility of these "untrained mobs"
taking the field for two years at least.   Long before
these two years had passed, these " mobs " had shown
themselves magnificent fighters against the best of the
German troops on the Western Front.

The response of Northampton to the call to arms is

to be found in the creation of the 2nd/4th and 3rd/4th Territorial Battalions—in addition, of course, to the mobilization and service overseas of the original 4th—which now became the 1st/4th Territorial Battalion—the first two named being used for training and draft-finding; and in the 5th, 6th, 7th, 8th and 9th Battalions. Of these, the 5th was a pioneer battalion, and the 8th and 9th were used for training and dispatching drafts. Later, there came the 1st and 2nd Garrison Battalions. We shall briefly relate the doings of such of the above battalions as fought overseas, placing their achievements in a frame, so to speak, made up of a précis of the war year by year.

The events of 1914 have been told in some detail earlier in this volume, and the fighting of the year may be said to have ended with the holding up of the first onrush of the German hordes. Unfortunately, the year was also remarkable for the entry into the war—on Germany's side—of Turkey. This was a serious blow, especially for England and Russia, and prolonged the war considerably. Turkey was not only in a position to attack Russia through the Caucasus, and Egypt by way of the Suez Canal, but, by blocking the Dardanelles, could put a stranglehold upon the passage of supplies to and from Russia, and by propaganda could stir up the Mohammedans in the British Empire. Russia appealed for help, and from February to December, 1915, desperate efforts were made to force the Dardanelles both by naval attack and by landings on the shores of Gallipoli. The result was a costly failure, only redeemed from disaster by a successful withdrawal. A Turkish attack on the Suez Canal in January and February, 1915, was, however, equally unsuccessful, and in Mesopotamia the British and Indian forces, which had been landed in 1914 at Basra to protect the oilfields, made considerable progress towards Baghdad. General Townshend, after the Battle of Ctesiphon in December, 1915, was forced to withdraw and was eventually surrounded at Kut-el-Amara, where in

T 1

April, 1916, on the failure of relief operations, he was forced to surrender.

On the Eastern Front in 1915, the Russians were driven back with terrible losses out of East Prussia, Poland, and Galicia, but eventually managed to dig themselves in and hold the Germans and Austrians up.

On the Western Front the Allies made several unsuccessful attempts to break through the German line, in the course of which the British fought the Battles of Neuve Chapelle, Festubert, and Loos, and, on the whole, the year 1915 was marked by a stalemate, neither side being able to gain very much.

The 5th Pioneer Battalion had been formed at Shorncliffe in September, 1914, and was attached to the 12th, one of the New Army divisions. For eight months, the battalion was strenuously engaged in battle training and engineering work round Aldershot. The last day of May, 1915, saw the battalion at the front in France, working at night in the vicinity of Ypres and resting during the day. Much digging and wiring of support and reserve lines was carried out, and the battalion had its first experience of gas. Prior to an attack, a platoon of " B " Company had distinguished itself by dragging a gun up to the first-line trench and making an emplacement for it. Next day, the gun was used with successful results against a nest of German machine guns. Lord French thought so highly of the incident, that he mentioned it in his despatches. During its stay in this shell-swept area, the battalion was very fortunate as regards casualties, having only 8 killed. Night after night, it had to cross the bridges over the canal, and it invariably happened, going and coming, that the battalion was just short of the bridges or had crossed them when the crossings were shelled. The feeling grew that the 5th was a " lucky " battalion. For the rest of the year, the battalion was employed round Armentières and Loos, where it lost 2 officers killed and 2 wounded, and 31 other ranks killed.

The 6th Battalion of the Northamptonshire Regiment had the splendid record of winning four V.Cs. in
the war. Raised in September, 1914, the command
was given to Colonel G. E. Ripley, a retired officer
of the regiment, who had seen much active service in
the South African War. The first period of training
was at Colchester, where the 6th were part of the 54th
Brigade of the 18th Division. Later, the battalion
moved to Salisbury Plain, whence it proceeded to
France, landing on July 26th, 1915. No great battle
came their way that year, and the winter was spent in
trenches at Suzanne and Fricourt. It was a trying
period, for the Germans had laid many mines, and the
men of the 6th were in constant danger of being blown
up without warning. Scarcely a week passed without
such an upheaval, and once five mines exploded within
a week. In addition, the Germans constantly bombarded the trenches of the 6th very heavily, to which
no reply could be made by our side, owing to a shortage
of ammunition. Shell fire, snipers' bullets, and mining
took almost daily toll of the battalion. In one mine
explosion, Lieutenant Lambert and three men were
killed, and five were wounded. One day in December,
the 6th were the victims of a new form of attack. They
were under a fierce fire for two hours, during which
the Germans threw over 2,000 shells, many being of the
tear-gas variety. Then the enemy raided portions of
the front line, capturing 20 of the battalion in a dug-out.
Later, a similar raid was carried out, but this time the
6th were not caught napping, but bombed and
bayoneted the Germans out. The first Christmas was
spent in the trenches near Fricourt.

The 7th Battalion was pre-eminently a battalion of
sportsmen. Most of its members enlisted as " pals,"
with the friendships formed on football and other
playing fields. A leading spirit in the formation of
the 7th was Edgar Mobbs, the Rugby international,
who within forty-eight hours rallied round him 400
friends and admirers, from which 250 were chosen to

form a company.   By the second week in September,
1914, the battalion was in being.   Training was carried
out at first at Shoreham and later at Woking, whence
the battalion proceeded to France at the end of
August, 1915, under the command of Lieutenant-
Colonel Parkin, a former officer of the regiment, as one
of the units of the 24th Division.

Its baptism of fire was not long delayed, and the
word " baptism " has perhaps too slender a significance
—total immersion would be better, for the 7th was to be
tried by a test of extraordinary severity.   The year
1915 was characterized by desperate attempts on the part
of the Allies to effect a break through the German lines,
interrupted and delayed by the counter-stroke—with
gas—of the Germans at " Second Ypres."   Of the
purely British attacks, we have described Neuve
Chapelle and Aubers Ridge at some length, and these
will ever have a mournful interest for the 58th and
48th respectively.   Now, in September, a greater Allied
offensive was to take place, in which the task of the
British was to break the German line in the mining
district round Loos.   Four days' bombardment on a
scale hitherto unknown was to precede the attack, in
which six divisions of the New Armies were included.
It had been decided, too, to employ against the Germans
their own device, gas.   The XI Corps, in which was
the 24th Division, was in support.   The attack opened
at 6.30 a.m. on September 25th, and, in spite of heavy
losses and the strenuous resistance from redoubts and
slag-heaps, by noon the prospects of a break-through
were bright enough.   The essential thing was reserves.
No reserves, however, were available, and the XI Corps
was three miles from the original front line and had to
thread its way through an area congested with traffic
of every description.   Worse still, the Germans had
begun to counter-attack, so that when the XI Corps
began to arrive, the aspect of the battle had changed
distinctly for the worse.

The 24th Division had been making a forced march.

In one battalion, over 200 men fell out. The 7th Northamptonshires had the honour of having the lowest return of march casualties, and owing to its magnificent marching it was given the honour of leading the division into its first battle. By this time, considerable confusion had set in at the front, and the staff orders were merely, " Follow this man, and hurry up "—with a general indication of the direction. To the commanding officer's request for further instructions, all that could be vouchsafed was, " You know as much as I do, sir." Pushing on, the 7th formed a defensive flank to an exhausted brigade of Highlanders. At midnight, these were withdrawn, and it was not till dawn broke that the 7th could get even a rough idea of what was taking place. Several things were, however, plain. Shelling was persistent. Some score of our men had been hit. Snipers were annoying. The transport had been ordered away and could not be found. Rain had been falling, and the trenches were knee-deep in water.

The attacks and counter-attacks, the confusion and set-backs, the high hopes and disappointments of Loos would need a long chapter for themselves. During the morning after the arrival of the battalion in the front line, Lieutenant Morley greatly distinguished himself. The Germans came down and bombed " B " Company trenches. Another battalion had taken refuge here, and the order to retire was given it. Realizing that this was a fatal mistake, Lieutenant Morley, with a party of four bombers—but without bombs, for none had come up—waited. Two of the party were knocked out, but Lieutenant Morley with the remainder charged and killed five Germans with the bayonet. Then Lieutenant Morley collected the enemy bombs, ascertained how they worked, and with them repelled the next attack. The remainder of the company, which had fallen back, were now told of the mistake in the order, and " to a man they went straight across the open for some 600 yards and took up their original position." This was but one of many gallant actions performed by the 7th. Its work in the battle has been well summarized in a glowing narrative by Mr. Holloway, the editor of *The Northampton Independent*.   The battalion had been marching at night for a week, and had only three hours' rest on Friday, were in their packs all Saturday, and under fire from 1 p.m.   They went into battle without proper orders or any bombs.   Only two officers had ever been under fire.   They held an exposed flank, were attacked in front and rear, and without food, water, bombs or much ammunition—but held the position for three days.   They suffered casualties of 50 per cent. of their strength, including the commanding officer and every officer of experience.   In spite of all these disadvantages, and after being repeatedly attacked and continually shelled, they only gave ground to the extent of the advanced trenches by the village, in which they were taken in rear, and then held the next position until relieved by an old Regular division.   Lord French's words were well deserved when he declared, "No men could have fought with greater gallantry under adverse circumstances."

In 1916, the outstanding work on the Western Front, so far as the British were concerned, was the Battle—or rather the succession of battles—of the Somme.   In Chapter IX we have dealt with the part played in it by the two Regular battalions.   But the 5th, 6th and 7th also bore a noble share in that epic struggle.   It was not, however, the sole contribution of those battalions to the great work of the year.   In the spring, in the neighbourhood of Loos, the 5th were busy mining, crater fighting, and consolidating craters in the Hohenzollern Redoubt.   On two occasions, they repulsed counter-attacks.   For the work in this crater fighting they were mentioned in the commander-in-chief's despatches, and the commanding officer, Lieutenant-Colonel G. A. Trent, received a very complimentary letter from the divisional commander.   The casualties in the redoubt were over 130.   As for the 6th, it moved early in the year to the Somme area, and was called upon to repulse a very determined raid in the early hours of April 13th. In the 7th Battalion, Edgar Mobbs had risen to command of the battalion. The Ypres Salient, Messines and Locre were the scenes of its activities. In both the latter sectors, the shelling at times had been particularly severe, and in June alone the casualties were 113 of all ranks.

At the Somme, the 5th, 6th and 7th Battalions were present, and if to the latter two a greater share of fighting came, it was because the 5th had pioneer work to do as well. The 5th fought and worked round Albert, Ovillers and Thiepval, and in the winter it returned to the Somme near Longueval and Trones Wood, taking part in three attacks there. As for the 6th Battalion, the capture of Trones Wood by it and the 12th Middlesex on July 14th, 1916, ranks as one of the finest achievements of the war. Two divisions had been commanded to capture the enemy's second line. Just before dawn, it was discovered that Trones Wood, supposed to be in our hands, had been recaptured by the Germans except a small portion where the 7th Royal West Kents were holding out, and in danger of being surrounded. Hasty orders were sent to the Northamptonshires to go to the rescue. There was no time to explain the plan of attack when Major G. M. Clark soon after daybreak led the battalion to the attack. The way led across a thousand yards of open ground, swept by a heavy barrage of high explosive. The wood proved to be a positive wilderness of fallen trees, thick undergrowth, a maze of trenches and barbed wire, with snipers and machine guns everywhere. Enormous shells were bursting all the time, and trees flying bodily in every direction. Terrific hand-to-hand fighting took place. The Germans had received orders to hold the wood at all costs. They fought with stubborn bravery, but the Northamptonshires were not to be denied. Corporal Radley, after losing his rifle, fought four Germans with his fists. The din was terrific—the roar of shells, rattle of musketry, the crash of falling trees mingling with the shouts of the combatants and the cries of the wounded. For hours the struggle lasted, but by ten o'clock the wood was won. Many were the deeds of heroism performed, and the heavy losses among officers threw a great responsibility on the non-commissioned ranks, who proved equal to the emergency. Here Sergeant W. E. Boulter won the Victoria Cross. Although severely wounded in the shoulder, he seized a bag of bombs and rushed alone across the open. When within striking distance of an enemy machine gun, he threw his bombs with such accuracy as to put the gun out of action. In the words of the official record : " His gallantry not only saved many casualties, but was of great military value, as it materially expedited the operation of clearing the enemy out of the wood, thus covering the flank of the whole attacking force and enabling the Northamptonshire Regiment to capture and consolidate their position in the German stronghold which the enemy had proclaimed impregnable."

Many were the congratulatory messages showered on the 6th Battalion. But the victory was dearly bought. Within three hours, 15 officers had fallen. At the finish, Major Charrington and two young subalterns were all that were left. In other ranks, 32 were killed, 204 wounded, and 35 were missing. After a rest and reorganization, the battalion took part in the capture of Thiepval. Here again the fighting was very severe, and the casualties heavier even than at Trones Wood. The killed numbered 105 and in wounded and missing the casualties were 258. Five officers were killed or died of wounds, and 9 wounded, and amongst the former was Colonel Ripley, who succumbed after the amputation of his right arm. No officer could have held the affection and confidence of men in a higher degree. Thereafter, the 6th remained in trenches in the Albert area, constantly under heavy fire, and spending a dreary winter in snow and frost.

No less for the 7th Battalion was the Somme an

ordeal of fire.   On the night of August 17th, 1916, the battalion prepared for its memorable attack on Guillemont.   Just before zero hour, the commanding officer, Lieutenant-Colonel Mobbs, was severely wounded, and had to leave the field.   In the attack, the left flank of the battalion gained its objective, but the right was driven back owing to the failure of another battalion which had lost all its company commanders.   It was a critical moment for the 7th, but the battalion Lewis gunners kept the Germans at bay till relief arrived. The casualties were severe, 373 in all, of which 50 were killed.   Thereafter there was hard work in the line between Delville and High Wood, and this second spell on the Somme is described as " by far the worst in the history of the battalion."   And after that there was strenuous trench warfare at Souchez and Vimy Ridge and round Loos.

The Service battalions in France were engaged in 1917 as follows : The 5th worked and fought at Arras, and in this battle and round Monchy they won repeated praise.   The casualties were more serious than usual, amounting to over 220, of which 50 were killed. Towards the close of the year, the 5th were well to the fore at the Battle of Cambrai, especially in repelling the great German counter-attack.   Although the 5th Battalion was separated and split up, the various companies put up a splendid resistance.   As for the 6th Battalion, it was the right assaulting battalion on February 15th in the fight towards Miraumont and Grandcourt, carried out in weather conditions too terrible for words.   Later, the battalion moved back to the Thiepval area to take part in the pursuit of the retiring Germans to the Hindenburg Line, a pursuit which involved some heavy fighting, for the Germans were retiring voluntarily to a strong position, and put up very vigorous rear-guard opposition at times.   A change for the worse came in July, when the battalion was transferred to the water-logged Ypres Salient, which at that time was a positive hell upon earth.

As for the 7th, the early spring of 1917 saw the battalion back in the Souchez area, where it took part in the assault on Vimy Ridge on the left of the Canadians. In June, the battalion was in the great Battle of Messines, when nineteen huge mines, after two years of preparation, were exploded and blew the German position sky-high. The cataclysm was terrific. Months afterwards, some of the craters were big enough to hold All Saints' Church, Northampton, and contained sufficient stretches of water to float a tug. During this battle, Lieutenant-Colonel Mobbs was twice wounded by shell fire, but was able to rejoin on June 26th, to prepare for what was to be his last battle. This was in the attack on Shrewsbury Forest in the Ypres Salient on July 31st. The battalion was held up by a machine gun at a strong point known as Lower Star Post, and Lieutenant-Colonel Mobbs, with characteristic self-sacrifice and dash, made a frontal attack, armed with bombs, and accompanied but by his runner, while Captain Berridge and a few men worked round by a flank. The gallant effort of Colonel Mobbs cost him his life, and in this part of the Third Battle of Ypres the 7th Battalion had 4 officers killed and 8 wounded, as well as nearly 250 casualties in other ranks. The death of the commanding officer was a great blow to the battalion and to the town and county of Northampton; and a beautiful memorial was subsequently erected to his memory in Northampton Market Square. The new commander of the 7th was Major D. W. Powell, who was shortly afterwards succeeded by Lieutenant-Colonel S. S. Hayne.

As we enter the year 1918, the story overtakes the narrative of the 1st and 2nd Battalions. In France, the 5th, 6th and 7th Battalions were involved in the " Big Push " of the Germans in March. The men of the 5th were rushed up by motor-buses to Albert, and succeeded in holding up heavy attacks at a cost of 34 killed and 45 wounded. The 6th Battalion was at Morlincourt with the Fifth Army when the German onrush began.

The 6th Northamptonshires counter-attacked in fine style, and here Lieutenant A. C. Herring won his V.C. His post was cut off and surrounded, but he immediately counter-attacked, taking 20 prisoners and 6 machine guns.   Subsequently the 6th took part in a memorable and successful effort to save several batteries of French guns, and the gallant remnant of the 6th obtained the coveted distinction of a *citation* in French Army Orders. The 7th Battalion was at Jeancourt on the Somme, and had ten days of almost continuous fighting.   Again and again their flanks were in the air, but Colonel Hayne managed each time to extricate the battalion.

The curtain is now about to ring up for the last act of the great world-drama.   All the Northamptonshires' characters are in the wings ready to take their cue. But before the entrance of the 1st Battalion takes place, just a little prologue is necessary.

By the spring of 1918 Russia had made a separate peace, and although over a million American soldiers were now in France to help the Allies, they would not be fit to take an effective part till well on in the year. Germany decided, therefore, to make a desperate effort before it was too late, and accordingly in March, April, May and June the enemy delivered a series of smashing attacks against the Allied front near Amiens, in Flanders, on the Aisne, and in Champagne.   We have already had occasion to say something of these. By the end of June the Germans had created three great bulges in the allied line.   But their situation was precarious, for the bulges were salients and exposed to flank attacks.   The Allies adopted unity of command, placing all their forces on the Western Front, under General Foch.   He brought off a great counterstroke between the Aisne and the Marne on July 18th.   Then he assigned to the British Army the task of breaking the Hindenburg Line, that deeply fortified belt where the Germans proposed to sit tight and await a peace by negotiation.   On August 8th our Fourth Army made a splendid start by flattening out the Amiens bulge and taking an enormous number of prisoners and guns. Then towards the end of August there began the general advance of the French, British and Belgian Armies that was not to cease until the Armistice of November 11th.

The terrific punch delivered by Sir Henry Rawlinson was a staggering blow to German pride, and a deadly one to the declining *moral* of the German soldier. Ludendorff called August 8th the " Black Day " of the German Army. Five days later German military commanders and ministers met at Spa. It was there agreed that the game was up, and that peace would have to be negotiated at the first favourable opportunity. Such opportunity never came. The Allies saw to that. Foch threw in the Americans—there were one and a quarter millions of them in France—to reduce the St. Mihiel salient, near Verdun. On August 20th a French attack near Oise and Aisne forced back the German line. Still more serious for the Germans, on the following day, was the attack by the British Third Army, north of the Somme, on the line Bapaume— Péronne, which brought about another crisis. By the end of August the military situation had become sufficiently defined to enable the Allied leaders to look beyond merely driving back the Germans to a fortified position in rear. It was now a question of ultimate victory following a knock-out blow.

Of the Allies, the British Army had been made up approximately to its nominal fighting strength—a process rendered easier by the enormous contingent retained in the United Kingdom after the dubious Battle of Jutland and by utilizing "low category" men. The French Army had suffered the greatest losses, and France was almost bled white. The Americans were numerous and spoiling for a fight. The Belgians were relatively insignificant in numbers. Marshal Foch—he had been elevated to that rank on August 6th—therefore determined on two main offensives, to be carried out chiefly by the British and Americans. The British, supported on their right by the French, were to break the Hindenburg Line in the direction of Cambrai—St. Quentin. The Americans, after completing the reduction of the St. Mihiel salient, were to break through the German lines north of Verdun and to advance in the direction of Mézières. In other words, the German line, where it bulged forward in an immense salient, was to be pinched on each flank. In these circumstances Ludendorff's grandiose scheme of capturing the Channel ports definitely collapsed, and by the end of August the German High Command ordered the evacuation of the Lys salient.

The 48th did not share in the great Amiens offensive mentioned above, for, as already related, it was in the neighbourhood of Arras, but it was directly affected by the victory.

The success won by the allied forces had an excellent effect upon the *moral* of the 1st Northamptonshires. Officers and men alike realized that the long years of trench warfare and stalemate had ended; that the German defensive system, once seemingly impregnable, was beginning to shiver and crumble beneath the hammer-strokes of our armies. In many ways the 48th were exceptionally well fitted to take part in the final advance. Like all other units of the 1st Division, they had undergone a prolonged and intensive period of training for open warfare at Le Clipon. Since that date the battalion had seen something of the realities of war in the Ypres salient and at Givenchy, but had never suffered the disheartening effects of a serious defeat; nor had they sustained casualties of an exceptionally heavy nature. Hence the majority of the officers and men had served together for over twelve months, and had learnt to know and trust one another. Thus when the day of trial came all ranks of the 1st Northamptonshires felt confident in their ability worthily to uphold the great traditions of the old 48th.

The battalion arrived at Arras at 2 a.m. on the morning of September 1st. A day was spent in billets in the ruined cathedral city. The 1st Division had been brought to the Arras area to support the offensive which the Canadian Corps was about to undertake against the Drocourt—Quéant switch line. The Canadians were to attack on September 2nd, and on the preceding night the 48th marched to Wancourt, a village some five miles south-east of Arras, moving forward in artillery formation at 10.30 a.m. on September 2nd, the line of advance being parallel to the Arras—Cambrai road, and somewhat to the south of it. The 2nd Brigade was in divisional support, and only advanced about three miles. Meanwhile the Canadian Corps had broken through the Drocourt—Quéant switch. On the night of September 3rd, the 48th occupied a portion of the newly-captured line east of Eterpigny, a village about a mile and a half to the north of the Arras—Cambrai road. Here they remained four days reorganizing the defensive system. During this period 16 casualties were incurred from the enemy artillery fire.

On September 7th, the 48th were relieved by the 1st London Scottish, and next day motor-buses conveyed them back to Hermaville, a village some eight miles west of Arras. They took no further part in the operations in the Arras area, but moved by road and rail to the district south of the Somme. On September 11th the battalion arrived at Proyart. This village was very familiar to some of the officers and men, and it was only about two miles from Morcourt, where the battalion had spent a month in the spring of 1917. Since that time the district had been the scene of much hard fighting, and its appearance had changed considerably. The 48th did not remain long at Proyart. On the morning of September 13th motor-buses conveyed them to the eastern side of the Somme, not very far from Brie and Mons-en-Chaussée. After a night in bivouac north of Athies, the 48th began their march to the St. Quentin area, where General Rawlinson's Fourth Army was steadily pressing back the German troops.

On the evening of September 16th the battalion

arrived in the forward area. The night was spent in Caulaincourt Wood, just north of Vermand, a small town some ten miles east of Brie. The enemy soon showed evidence of his proximity, for during the night the wood was heavily bombarded with gas shells. In addition, German aeroplanes came over at about 3 a.m., dropping bombs among the Northamptonshires with deadly effect. Three men were killed and 22 wounded, while 5 horses were also killed. Meanwhile arrangements were being completed for an attack upon the German position north-west of St. Quentin. The line of advance allotted to the 2nd Brigade lay along the River L'Omignon, the 60th Rifles on the right working along the south bank, while the Royal Sussex, who were on the left, advanced along the north bank. The Northamptonshires were to act in support of the Royal Sussex, if necessary, and before daybreak on September 18th the 48th moved to their assembly position, about a mile and a half north-east of Vermand.

At 5.20 a.m. the attack began. The Royal Sussex, advancing under the protection of a heavy barrage, succeeded in gaining all their objectives; while the 4th Australian Division, on their immediate left, was equally fortunate. The Northamptonshires were therefore not called upon to advance, but a fair number of casualties were sustained from the shell fire of the enemy. Three men were killed and 28 were wounded during the day, while Second-Lieutenant R. O. King (attached from the Lincolnshire Regiment), Second-Lieutenant G. D. Adamson, and 22 other ranks were incapacitated by gas. Two days later the battalion was relieved, and went back to a wood a mile to the south-west of Vermand for a brief period of rest and reorganization. The 1st Division had been detailed to carry out a fresh operation of considerable importance, in which the 48th were to play a more prominent part than they had done in the action of September 18th.

Three and a half miles to the north-west of St. Quentin lies the village of Gricourt, while about a mile

U

and a half farther on in the same direction is Pontruet. Between them, running from north-east to south-west, is a spur of rising ground, the summit of which is about 500 feet above sea-level. It is crossed by two roads. One of these, which will hereafter be described as the sunken road, runs south-east from Pontruet, and passes within half a mile of Gricourt, which it leaves to the west of it. This sunken road crosses the spur at its highest point, whence an extensive view of the surrounding country can be obtained. The other road, which runs from Pontruet to Gricourt, parallel to the sunken road and somewhat to the west of it, crosses the spur at a rather lower level. It was thought that the continued possession by the Germans of the spur would be prejudicial to the success of the attack which the Fourth Army intended to make against the main Hindenburg Line north of Pontruet. The work of driving the enemy from this point was entrusted to the 1st Division.

The task was undoubtedly a difficult one. Not only did the enemy hold Pontruet and Gricourt in considerable strength, but he was also established in Fresnoy-le-Petit, a village standing on high ground about a mile west of Gricourt. North of the Fresnoy-le-Petit—Gricourt road, and roughly parallel with it, lay a valley. On the southern slope of the valley was Marronniers Wood, which bristled with machine guns; while in the valley itself were two small copses, also strongly held by German machine-gunners. Thus the right flank of a force advancing directly towards the spur from the west would be subjected to a deadly enfilade, while its left would be exposed to the fire of the Germans holding Pontruet.

The main object of the contemplated operations was to obtain possession of the sunken road that crossed the spur, and it was decided to attempt to do this by means of three distinct, but simultaneous, attacks, as follows: on the left, the 46th Division was to attack Pontruet from the north; in the centre, the 2nd Brigade was to advance directly towards the spur and occupy the sunken road; on the right, the 3rd Brigade was to attack Fresnoy-le-Petit and Marronniers Wood, in conjunction with the 6th Division on its right.

The various barrages were so timed that at the moment when the 2nd Brigade was passing Fresnoy-le-Petit and Marronniers Wood the activity of the Germans holding these positions would be neutralized by the fire of the British artillery. It was calculated that Pontruet would be captured by the 46th Division in so short a time that no enfilade fire would be directed against the left flank of the 2nd Brigade from that village. The 2nd Brigade attack was to be carried out by the 48th on the left, and the 2nd Royal Sussex on the right. The 60th Rifles were to deal with the copses in the valley, and afterwards to act as a reserve battalion if required. On September 23rd, the day before the attack, the battalion unfortunately lost the services of two very good officers, Captain B. C. Carey being killed and Lieutenant A. O. F. Winkler wounded, while they were going forward to reconnoitre the German position. Although both these officers were quite young, they had seen a great deal of service with the 48th. Captain Carey had commanded " B " Company for over eighteen months, while Lieutenant Winkler had been with the battalion ever since the early stages of the Somme battle of 1916, and was one of the few survivors of those engaged in the operations at Clark's Trench.

During the night of September 23rd/24th, the battalion left the wood near Vermand and moved up to its assembly position just south of the ruined village of Berthaucourt, and about 2,000 yards from the sunken road, which was its final objective. The leading company on the right next to the Royal Sussex was " D," under Lieutenant F. G. D. Willson, the left front company being " B," under Captain F. W. Twigg. " A " Company, under Capt. A. C. Pickering, supported " D "; " C " Company, under Lieutenant

U I

R. D. Martin, supported " B." Four tanks were to assist the battalion. This was the first time that the 48th had had the co-operation of these machines.

There was a certain amount of shelling while the battalion was forming up, but comparatively few casualties were sustained. At 5 a.m. the attack began, the leading companies pressing on to their objective behind the heavy barrage. On the right, the fire of the enemy was effectually neutralized by the barrage and by the success of the 3rd Brigade, who rapidly pushed through Fresnoy-le-Petit and into Marronniers Wood. But on the left the 46th Division failed to capture Pontruet, and " B " Company soon came under a deadly machine-gun fire from the southern edge of the village, which checked its advance. The tanks proved to be of little assistance : one missed its direction, and did not arrive at the assembly point, two were put out of action by shell fire before the advance began, while the remaining one missed its direction and disappeared from sight somewhere in the neighbourhood of Pontruet. Captain Twigg was killed quite early in the action, and his company was unable to reach its objective.

Meanwhile " D " had pushed on with the Sussex, and had occupied the sunken road. But the check received by " B " Company exposed the left flank of " D " to the enfilading fire of the Germans in Pontruet. Consequently " D " was obliged to withdraw to a trench parallel with and just east of the Pontruet—Gricourt road, known as Sampson Trench, where connection was established with " C " and a defensive flank formed on the left. Thus the situation remained during the greater part of the day, for the efforts of the 46th Division to capture the southern extremity of Pontruet continued to be of no avail, and while the German machine guns remained there it was impossible to occupy the left portion of the sunken road while daylight lasted.

Meanwhile the 3rd Brigade had made good progress

on the right, while down in the valley the 60th Rifles
had taken one of the copses and was attacking the
other. The 3rd Brigade later took over the work of
capturing the remaining copse, thus leaving the 60th
free to support the attack of the 2nd Brigade. The
60th Rifles were then ordered up to Sampson Trench,
whence, after dusk, they attacked the sunken road on
the crest of the spur. A short preliminary bombardment drove the Germans from the sunken road, and the
60th occupied the position without any casualties.

Thus after a hard day's fighting the 2nd Brigade
finally succeeded in reaching and holding its objective,
while Fresnoy-le-Petit, Gricourt and Marronniers Wood
had been taken by the 3rd Brigade. Quite apart
from the fact that the capture of the sunken road secured
the success of the subsequent operations undertaken by
the Fourth Army against the main Hindenburg Line,
over a thousand German prisoners and many machine
guns had been taken, while the total losses of the 1st
Division were under 600. The 48th had sustained over
200 casualties. Both the officers in command of the
leading companies, Captain Twigg and Lieutenant
Willson, were killed, as was also the medical officer,
Lieutenant M. J. O'Flynn. No less than 11 other
officers were wounded: Captain A. C. Pickering,
Lieutenants R. D. Martin, B. A. Hall, J. C. Gent,
W. Young, F. H. Tucker, E. A. P. Palmer, and
A. E. S. Bayley, Second-Lieutenants E. G. Eastwood
and W. Ellis (both attached from the Bedfordshire
Regiment), and H. P. Cockle. Lieutenant Bayley was
afterwards awarded the Military Cross for his services
in this action. The casualties among the non-commissioned officers and men were 250 in all.

During the night the captured position was consolidated. "D" Company again went forward, its right
joining the left of the 60th Rifles on the sunken road,
while its left met the right of "C" Company at
Sampson Trench. The only troops immediately available to support the three weary and depleted battalions

of the 2nd Brigade were the 1st Cameron Highlanders from the 1st Brigade, and the divisional commander wished the Camerons to have an opportunity of resting and refitting, in order that the 1st Division might have one brigade sufficiently fresh to take an active part in the impending operations against the Hindenburg Line. The situation was explained to the battalions of the 2nd Brigade, who at once volunteered to hold, without the support of the Cameron Highlanders, the position that they had won. Next morning the enemy, who fully realized the importance of the position on the spur, launched a counter-attack against the 60th Rifles. The Germans were driven back with considerable loss, the Lewis guns of "D" Company of the Northamptonshires rendering effective aid from the left flank. No further counter-attacks were attempted, and at night "A" Company relieved "D."

September 26th passed fairly quietly, though there was a certain amount of artillery activity. The next day Second-Lieutenant C. Smeathers, who was now in command of "D" Company, was unfortunately wounded by one of our own shells. Posts were pushed out farther in the direction of Pontruet by "B" Company, which now occupied the front line.

On September 28th the battalion was relieved by the 1st South Wales Borderers, and returned again to the wood near Vermand. This was the end of its activities in the St. Quentin area. It took no part in the great attack of September 29th, in which the 46th Division forced the passage of the St. Quentin Canal near Bellenglise. That splendid feat of arms has been made familiar to the nation by the vivid narratives and striking pictures which appeared in the public press at the time of its accomplishment. No one will begrudge the 46th Division that honour, which is its rightful due, but let it not be forgotten that the way was paved for the success of September 29th by the less spectacular but equally arduous exploits of the 1st Division during the preceding fortnight.

The battalion remained encamped in the wood near Vermand until October 10th. A reinforcement draft arrived to fill its depleted ranks, and the necessary work of reorganization was carried out. On October 10th the battalion left the wood and marched through Pontruet, now far behind the fighting line, to Bellenglise, where they crossed the canal, and thence to Magny-La-Fosse, a village some six miles north of St. Quentin. Here they remained for nearly a week, the companies bivouacking in some disused trenches, while battalion headquarters was among the ruins of the château.

On October 16th the battalion again moved north, halting at 2 p.m. just beyond Bohain, a small town about ten miles south-west of Le Cateau. The 1st Division was now about to take part in a general advance on a ten-mile front by the Fourth Army against the German troops holding the line of the Selle and the wooded country east of Bohain. Five or six miles to the east of the Selle position lay the Canal de la Sambre à L'Oise, which would in all probability be the next line upon which the enemy would attempt to make a stand. The attack was planned to commence at 5.20 a.m. on the morning of October 17th. The 1st and 2nd Brigades of the 1st Division were to assemble just to the west of the village of Vaux Andigny, which is about seven miles from the Sambre Canal. In front of the 1st Division was the 6th Division, which was to open the attack.

The direction of the line of advance was roughly from west to east. This part of the country is more broken up by hedges and enclosures than is usual in France, while the ground is very undulating. The 6th Division was to advance from Vaux Andigny for about a mile, halting just west of a village called La Vallée Mulâtre. The barrage which had preceded the attack was then to remain stationary for half an hour, while the 1st and 2nd Brigades advanced through the 6th Division. The forward movement was then to be continued by the 1st

Division, the 2nd Brigade being on the left or northern flank, and the 1st Brigade on its right. When a line to the east of La Vallée Mulâtre had been reached, there was to be a halt of three hours, while the artillery and machine guns moved forward. The advance was then to be continued in the direction of the canal.

During the night of October 16th/17th the 48th marched north to their assembly position. They were on the right of the 2nd Brigade, the left battalion being the 60th Rifles, while the 2nd Royal Sussex were in support. " A " Company of the Northamptonshires was on the right in the front line, with " C " on its left; " D " Company was in support and " B " in reserve. Four tanks were to accompany the battalion. " C " Company, which had the assistance of two machine guns, was to occupy the high ground north of La Vallée Mulâtre, while " A " Company was to capture the village itself. " A's " final objective after the three hours' halt included the village of Wassigny, near which the 48th had fought its first rearguard action in the great retreat of 1914.

In order to avoid the main road through Vaux Andigny, which was sure to be the target of German artillery as soon as the advance began, certain tracks running among the gardens and hedges that surrounded the village had been carefully reconnoitred beforehand. Unfortunately there was a dense fog from dawn until 10 a.m., which made it impossible to find these tracks, so the 2nd Brigade had to advance along the road under a heavy shell fire. Moreover, the fog prevented the 6th Division from discovering all the German machine-gun posts that lay in the line of advance, so that when the leading companies of the Northamptonshires emerged from the eastern outskirts of Vaux Andigny they were met by the machine-gun fire of an unseen enemy. In spite of these difficulties, and the fact that the advancing troops were compelled by the fog to rely solely upon compass observations to determine their direction, the battalions composing the 2nd Brigade arrived at their appointed positions west of La Vallée Mulâtre at the stipulated time.

Half an hour later the barrage again crept forward, and behind it the Northamptonshires advanced through the 6th Division towards their objective. Although the fog had not yet lifted, it was now somewhat more easy to keep direction, as the right of the battalion's line of advance was bounded by the railway. The first forward rush of " A " Company carried the whole of La Vallée Mulâtre, but later a counter-attack made by the enemy from a wood lying south-east of the village drove the Northamptonshires back to the centre of it. Here the struggle continued fiercely for some time.

At 10 a.m. the fog lifted. It is a remarkable fact that the 60th Rifles and the Northamptonshires, who had not seen anything of each other during their advance of nearly five hours in a fog over an undulating and enclosed tract of country, now found each other in the correct place on the inner flank. When all the attendant circumstances are taken into account, it will be realized that this was an achievement highly creditable to both battalions.

It was now decided that a farther advance could not be attempted until a fresh artillery preparation had been organized, as the stubborn opposition of the enemy had rendered it impossible for the attacking troops to keep up with the original barrage. Shortly after 5 p.m. the artillery bombardment began again, and under its protection the Northamptonshires once more cleared La Vallée Mulâtre of the enemy, and established themselves somewhat to the east of the village. " C " Company was already in possession of the high ground on the left. This was the situation at sunset. This attack resulted in the capture of 8 guns and between 20 and 30 machine guns.

Next morning, at 11.30, the 3rd Brigade passed through the 2nd Brigade and continued the advance, capturing Wassigny. The 48th were withdrawn in the evening to Bois St. Pierre, a hamlet situated between

Vaux Andigny and La Vallée Mulâtre. During the advance on the 17th they had lost 14 killed and 84 wounded or gassed. Two officers, Second-Lieutenants R. S. Strange and F. A. George, were amongst those killed, while the wounded included Lieutenant A. St. G. Coldwell, who had acted as battalion signalling officer for over two years, Second-Lieutenant R. Lewis (attached from the Welsh Regiment), and Second-Lieutenant A. Fullen. Second-Lieutenants J. T. Roberts and B. L. Keesham were gassed.

At 4.30 p.m. on October 19th the 48th left Bois St. Pierre, and marched north to relieve the 119th American Infantry Regiment at Mazinghien. This village, which is two and a half miles north of Wassigny and two miles west of the Sambre Canal, had been captured that morning by the American troops operating on the left flank of the 1st Division. Reconnoitring patrols sent out by the Scots Greys, a squadron of which regiment was then attached to the 1st Division, had ascertained the enemy were still present in some strength on the western side of the canal. Preparations were accordingly made for another attack by the 1st and 6th Divisions, the former operating on the right of the latter. This forward movement was to take place during the moonlight hours of the night of October 22nd/23rd.

The 1st Northamptonshire Regiment was the right attacking battalion of the left brigade, the Royal Sussex being on their left and the 3rd Brigade on their right. The left attacking company of the Northamptonshires was " D," now under Captain L. H. M. Mackenzie, an officer who had seen much service with the battalion. " D " Company was to advance and capture the high ground south-east of Catillon, a fair-sized village which lies on the western bank of the canal about two miles north-east of Mazinghien. " A " Company, under Lieutenant E. Farrell, was to advance on the right of " D," and occupy a position to the south of it, keeping in touch with the 2nd Welsh Regiment of the 3rd Brigade on the right. "C" Company, under Captain G. C. Totten, was to advance in support of "A," and deal with any of the enemy who might be left behind in woods or orchards. A weak company of the 60th Rifles—the support battalion of the 2nd Brigade—was also placed under the orders of Captain Totten. These men were to be used to protect the right flank of the Northamptonshires if the 3rd Brigade failed to make progress on the right. "B" Company, less one platoon, lent to Captain Mackenzie, remained under the control of battalion headquarters.

The attack began at 1.20 a.m. on the morning of October 23rd behind a creeping barrage, which advanced 100 yards every four minutes. The counter-bombardment of the enemy was fairly heavy, Lieutenant L. T. D. Stables, of "C" Company, being killed while waiting in the assembly position. Again the operations were impeded by a fog, and it is impossible to follow in detail all that took place during this night attack over enclosed country, but it can be said that both the leading companies succeeded in reaching their objectives without heavy loss. The rear platoons of "D" Company lost direction in the fog, but Capt. Mackenzie pushed on resolutely with about thirty men and two machine guns, and finally occupied the high ground which was his objective. For a time both his flanks were exposed, but he soon got in touch with the Royal Sussex on the left, while on the right he formed a defensive flank with some men sent up to him from "B" Company. During the day touch was established with "A" Company, whose left had halted about 400 yards to the right of "D" Company's right and somewhat in rear of it. At night the newly-occupied line was taken over by the 1st Black Watch, and the 48th returned to La Vallée Mulâtre. The casualties incurred during the operations near the canal had been 14 killed and some 50 wounded. Second-Lieutenant G. O. Timmins, of "B" Company, had lost his life during the advance, while Second-Lieutenant

C. H. Anscomb was among the wounded. After three days at La Vallée Mulâtre, the battalion once more moved up to the position north-east of Mazinghien, and relieved the 1st Black Watch. On October 27th the enemy shelled the area while the relief was in progress, " A " Company suffering 12 casualties.

The enemy were still on the western side of the canal south of Catillon, and the village itself remained in German hands. At this point the canal curves in an easterly direction, forming a species of re-entrant. The 48th were entrusted with the task of clearing this re-entrant south of Catillon of the enemy, and of establishing themselves along the line of the canal. This minor operation was intended to pave the way for a general attack at a later date on the defensive position held by the enemy east of the canal. Accordingly, on October 28th, the battalion began to work its way forward through the wooded country that fringed the canal. No barrage was employed. On the right " C " Company met with no opposition, and took up a position on the canal bank, but " B " Company, in the centre, was checked by the fire of the German snipers and machine-gunners, who lay ensconced in various points of vantage between them and their objective. " A " Company, on the left of " B," was also unable to make much progress. " D " Company remained behind in support.

It was determined to arrange for artillery support, and to make a regular attack on the following morning. At 8 a.m. on October 29th the advance began. The artillery bombardment neutralized the activity of the enemy in front of " B," while a machine-gun barrage swept the southern outskirts of Catillon, against which village " A " formed a defensive flank as the advance proceeded. " B " Company gained its objective in under half an hour, save on the right flank, where a party of Germans continued to hold out. Fifteen prisoners and a number of machine guns were captured. At 2.30 p.m. a second attack carried the strong point on the right flank.

The enemy made a determined counter-attack at about 5 p.m., and succeeded in driving a wedge between " B " and " A " Companies, which had joined hands near the canal bank. The situation remained unchanged during the night, but just before dawn the Germans again counter-attacked, one body of the enemy issuing from Catillon and the other crossing the canal on " B " Company's front by means of a bridge. Both these movements achieved some success, and fighting continued throughout the morning. At noon " B " and " A " Companies again attacked, this time behind a creeping barrage, but for the moment they were again checked by machine-gun fire from the same strong point which had caused trouble before. However, by 4.30 p.m. the enemy was once again driven back, and all three companies moved forward to the line of the canal, where they were relieved by the 1st Gloucester Regiment at 7 p.m. Considering the stubborn nature of the enemy's resistance, it cannot be said that the casualties sustained during the engagement were very heavy. Second-Lieutenant R. P. Bull and 15 men were killed, 34 men were wounded, and 13 were reported missing. The battalion marched back to Vaux Andigny, there to reorganize and prepare for the general advance against the line of the Sambre Canal, to which the actions of the last fortnight had been a necessary preliminary. And here, even at the cost of interrupting the narrative of the advance of the 48th to victory, we must break off to follow the doings of the other battalions.

After its terrible experience on the Aisne, the 2nd Battalion deserved a long rest, and this it was fortunate enough to secure. The 8th Division had, so to speak, a holiday by the seaside, on the strip of Picardy coast between St. Valery and Le Tréport. Although the inevitable training and reorganization played a large part, there was a good deal of holiday feeling and play. Actual fighting was a long way off. The weather was gloriously fine. There was excellent sea-bathing, boxing competitions and brigade and regimental sports.

Bands played, and the stay by the sea coast was a thoroughly enjoyable one. Advantage was taken of this period of rest to complete the rewelding of the personnel of all sorts who made up the new 58th, for we read in the battalion war diary that a draft on July 8th " paraded under the regimental sergeant-major for drill and explanation of regimental customs."

These halcyon days could not, of course, last for ever; least of all now that the war was entering upon a new phase. Four mighty thrusts had the Germans made since the opening of the fighting of 1918, but, although the Germans were known still to have large reserves on our Flanders front, the thrusts had been warded off, and the enemy had, for a time at least, shot his bolt. On the Allied side, more and more Americans were daily entering the theatre of war, and unity of command had been secured by the nomination of General Foch as Generalissimo of the Allied forces in France. On the 18th, he launched his first counter-stroke, and from that date onwards the initiative lay with the Allies. " From this time," as a German writer has put it, " the German Supreme Army Command was subject to the strategical dictation of the enemy."

In more prosaic language, henceforth the Allies were attacking and the Germans were on the defensive. It was clear that, in order to push the attack home, every available man would be required, and it was inevitable that the 8th Division would be called upon to play its part. On July 19th, the seaside holiday came to an end, and the division soon found itself in the Vimy sector. Here, during the night of July 22nd/23rd, the 2nd Battalion relieved the 5th Royal Scots Fusiliers in the front line. The sector proved to be a quiet one, and the Germans put in but a rare appearance at night in " No Man's Land." Advantage was taken of this state of affairs to send out nightly two patrols from the battalion, each of 1 officer and 2 sections, between the hours of 11 p.m. and 3 a.m., with instructions to reconnoitre the enemy's wire and trenches. Much useful information was obtained in this way. The battalion remained in the front line for just a week, and, although some hostile shelling took place towards the end of the tour, nothing of any serious importance resulted. On the 30th, the 1st Worcestershire Regiment relieved the 58th—by daylight, too. The 2nd Northamptonshires returned to Durham Camp, Mont St. Eloi, and the following afternoon listened to the divisional band playing. What with a quiet week in the trenches, an empty " No Man's Land," a daylight relief, and a band performance behind the line, the war had clearly entered upon a new phase.

The month of August, 1918, was marked by a series of great victories for the Allied side, in which the British armies played a memorable part. It so happened that the sector in which the 2nd Northamptonshire Regiment found itself was not one in which an offensive was carried out, and on the whole there is not much to chronicle during the month in the Vimy area. There was the normal routine of trench life, and the divisional war diary speaks of " comfortably colourless reports." It will be convenient, perhaps, to give very briefly an account of the offensives carried out elsewhere, and then to show how the 8th Division, and, incidentally, the 2nd Northamptonshire Regiment, contributed, even if indirectly, to the successes gained.

On August 8th, the Fourth Army began the great Battle of Amiens, and took nearly 22,000 prisoners and over 400 guns. This was followed on the 21st and succeeding days by a second thrust delivered by the Third Army north of the old Somme battlefield. A great success was here achieved, and the flank of the attack was pushed farther north. During this fighting between August 21st and September 3rd, the Third and First Armies took 470 guns and a further 53,000 prisoners. On August 26th was begun the Battle of the Scarpe, in which the Canadian Corps on the right of the First Army drove forward strongly and successfully in front of Arras, bringing the fighting to the vicinity where the 58th found itself.

Although the battalion did not actually share in the spectacular successes just enumerated, it must be borne in mind that, as every man and gun which could be spared was sent to these offensives, the troops holding the quieter sectors had to do double duty, and in this Vimy sector the holding of a relatively long line threw a great strain on the troops, especially as many of them were not fully trained. It was training which occupied the 58th for the first week, and then on August 7th it marched back to the Vimy area, relieving the 1st Sherwood Foresters as battalion in support of the 24th Brigade. Very shortly afterwards, it was found necessary, owing to the extension of the line, to have all three brigades in front, but, on the other hand, the sector was so quiet that it was possible to keep one battalion from each brigade out of the line for training. For a week, the 58th was engaged in work upon the trenches, and on relief it returned to Fraser Camp, Mont St. Eloi. It was back in the Oppy portion of the sector on the 17th, to find now that either side, in order to avoid stagnation, had taken to drenching the other with gas. The night of the 20th/21st was an exciting one, for a strong enemy force attempted a raid upon the right, bombing part of the line. The attack was met with great promptitude, and the enemy was prevented from penetrating the line, being compelled, indeed, to beat a hasty retreat. In this spirited little action, the 58th had three casualties, one being killed. So severe did the gas business become at the end of the month, that on the 23rd " A " Company had to be withdrawn from the front line to the railway embankment, owing to heavy gas shelling of the previous night which had caused 22 casualties. These were from mustard gas, and it was found that many of the cases of blister and irritation were caused by the liquid evaporating in the sunlight during the day following a night bombardment. Stringent orders were therefore issued that gassed areas must be immediately evacuated and not re-entered until reported " all clear " by the gas experts.   The battalion was relieved on the 25th, but had soon to return.   On the night of the 28th, a battalion of the brigade was driven out of Oppy Wood and a portion of Blandford Trench.   The lost ground was, however, regained on the following day by the 58th.

Further progress was also made by the two other brigades, but orders were received at the end of August that the 8th Division should consolidate its gains, but make no further forward movement for the present. Consequently the quiet of August ran on for the first half of September.   For the first week, the battalion was in the front line near Oppy, but during this period there is practically nothing worthy of remark, except the capture of a German deserter.   He proved to be from the 17th Regiment of the 15th Reserve Division, and much valuable information was thus obtained.   A week in reserve line followed, and on the 16th the battalion was back in the Oppy sector once more. During the night of the 20th/21st, a raid was made on the German trenches north of Oppy Wood by a party of twelve from " A " Company, under Second-Lieutenant Hunt.   Artillery fire was first opened on the objective, and when the raiders reached the trench it was found empty : the birds had flown.

The trench situation was now rather peculiar, for successive bounds by the 8th Division had brought it about that both sides were occupying part of the same trench system, namely, the old German third line of 1917.   There were obvious inconveniences in this state of affairs, and from September 21st the division began pushing farther on, the attempt, though successful on the whole, calling forth a smart counter-attack by the Germans.   The 58th did not actually take serious part in these attacks until the night of September 26th/27th, when an attack was launched at midnight by three battalions of the 8th Division—including the 2nd

V

Northamptonshires—and one of the 20th Division. All objectives were gained, a total of 28 prisoners and 10 light machine guns being captured. Five prisoners were taken by the 58th. The following day, the small garrison of a post at Crucifix Corner was bombed out of it by the Germans, but there is a contented note in the war diary for the last day of the month : " Exceptionally quiet. Fine weather."

Without going too deeply into the situation on the Western Front, it may briefly be said that between September 26th and 29th the British, French and Americans had made a still further advance, and it was to assist such advance that the fighting just related had taken place. In order to keep place in the line, so to speak, the 8th Division advanced again in October, the attack commencing at dawn on the 7th of that month. The 58th did not participate in the opening stage, being in rest camp until the 8th, on which date it returned to the front. The Germans were now retiring from this area; by the morning of October 9th, the division was well forward of the Rouvroy—Fresnes line all along its length. The operations were now indeed taking the form of open warfare, and it is almost curious to read of the battalion acting as " advanced guard to the brigade." Between the 8th and the 13th, the casualties of the 58th in this advance were Second-Lieutenant Ballard missing, Second-Lieutenant Allan wounded; 4 other ranks killed, and 44 wounded. An obstacle, in the shape of the Drocourt—Quéant line, faced the division, but the enemy evacuated it with but little fighting. The enemy was now frankly in retreat, and he was being hustled sometimes out of his positions before his preparations for excavation were complete. Meals left half-finished on the tables and valuable articles of a personal kind left behind, in addition to great quantities of stores, made it clear that the retirement had become a hurried and disorderly flight rather than a methodical retreat. The Germans, however, took care to render the pursuit by the 8th Division as inconvenient and dangerous as possible. Great care had to be exercised in moving along roads, entering dug-outs and houses, and in touching anything lying about. Booby-traps and mines were everywhere. Timber, embedded in roads and tracks and connected to a mine which exploded if the timber was either raised or depressed, was a favourite device.

These ingenious devices, though annoying, could not, of course, seriously check the pursuit. Douai was abandoned by the Germans, and the British still pushed on. On the 24th, it was found that the enemy were holding the village of Odomez, but a heavy artillery and machine-gun fire during the night was enough for the Germans, and on the morning of the 25th, " B " and " D " Companies of the 58th captured the village without much difficulty. On this day, Second-Lieutenant Murchison was wounded; Second-Lieutenant Smalley was wounded two days earlier.

In three weeks, the battalion had moved forward some thirty miles, and now found itself, at the end of October, within a few miles of Condé, which was the left of the British position at the Battle of Mons in 1914. The wheel was coming full circle, and the end was clearly near.

Meanwhile, the Service battalions had been worthily maintaining the reputation of the regiment.

The final fight of any importance of the 5th Battalion was at Epéhy in September, where it had 128 casualties. The 6th were fortunate enough to share in the glory of smashing through the Hindenburg Line. In August the battalion crossed the Ancre in a brilliantly-conducted operation, and, when relieved on September 4th, the battalion had the fine record of having captured 17 officers and 737 other ranks of Germans, besides achieving all its objectives. Then came the capture of Ronssoy on September 18th, where the battalion gained its third Victoria Cross. Lance-Corporal A. L. Lewis led a small section on the right of the attack, and was held up by two machine guns. Crawling forward alone, he bombed both teams successfully, and later used his rifle with such deadly effect that he caused the survivors to surrender. Our line was thereby able to advance. Three days later, this gallant young non-commissioned officer again showed great powers of command, but, having rushed his company through the enemy barrage, he was killed whilst getting his men under cover from heavy machine-gun fire. Yet another Victoria Cross was won in a big fight north of Le Cateau on October 24th, where the battalion, fighting side by side with American troops, was severely handled. In this engagement, Captain F. W. Hedges, with Sergeant F. Gibson, of " C " Company, went out to reconnoitre the strength of the enemy. They found sixteen machine-gun emplacements, and captured 14 prisoners and 6 guns. In putting the first gun out of action, Captain Hedges lost his rifle, but rushed on unarmed with the sergeant, who had a revolver, a few shots from which caused the enemy to throw up their hands. For this heroic exploit Captain Hedges was awarded the Victoria Cross and Sergeant Gibson the Distinguished Conduct Medal. Captain Hedges was wounded in the head and shoulder, but Sergeant Gibson came through unscathed, but was wounded a fortnight later.

The 7th Battalion started in the final push from " the now painfully familiar Loos area," and had some lively fighting, particularly at Haussy, where during a German attack upon the bridgehead the battalion had 3 officers killed and 85 casualties in other ranks. The good work of the battalion helped to pave the way for the capture of Cambrai and Maubeuge.

CHAPTER XV.

The End of the War.

Meanwhile, the wheel had come full circle, and Germany was to pay for the catastrophe she had brought upon the world. Bulgaria, Austria and Turkey had collapsed and fallen out of the ranks of the Central Powers. Germany, alone and impotent, was at her last gasp. Some fighting, however, was yet to ensue, and so far as the Northamptonshire Regiment is concerned this fell to the 1st Battalion, whose doings in the early days of November are here recorded.

The final great attack on the German positions behind the Sambre Canal was to begin on November 4th. Four armies were to take part in these operations : on the left was the British First Army; next the British Third Army; then the British Fourth Army; and on the right the French First Army. On the right wing of the Fourth Army was the 1st Division, which was to force the passage of the canal on a three-mile front south of Catillon. The task of capturing Catillon and of establishing a bridgehead beyond it was entrusted to the 3rd Brigade. The remainder of the 1st Division was to deliver its attack farther south, the 1st Brigade being on the left, and the 2nd Brigade on the right, next to the French. The two leading battalions of the 2nd Brigade were to be the 60th Rifles on the right and the 2nd Royal Sussex Regiment on the left. The 1st Northamptonshires were to be in support during the early stages of the attack.

It was planned to effect the crossing at a lock situated about a mile and a half south of Catillon. When the 2nd Brigade had forced the passage of the canal, and had formed a bridgehead on its eastern side, the Northamptonshires were to attack and capture Fesmy, a village which lay about two miles beyond the lock. During the night that preceded the battle, the 2nd Brigade quietly assembled in the positions that had been assigned to them, the Northamptonshires being drawn up about half a mile from the lock, in rear of the Royal Sussex.

The morning of November 4th was dull and misty. At 5.20 a.m., the British artillery opened fire, a heavy barrage was put down along the line of the canal, and the 2nd Brigade moved forward to the attack. The enemy's guns replied vigorously, shells falling thickly among the advancing troops. The front line of the Sussex was accompanied by men carrying light wooden bridges, with which the gap between the two abutments of the lock was to be spanned. For a moment, the advance was checked by a stream that ran parallel with the canal on its western side; this proved a more formidable obstacle than had been anticipated. In consequence, the barrage had lifted to a line well in rear of the canal before the bridges could be brought up to the lock. The officers and men whose duty it was to bridge the gap between the abutments were met by a heavy machine-gun fire from the houses that stood by the lock on the far side of the canal, and from the Bois de L'Abbaye on the left flank. The German artillery also put down a barrage on the western bank, causing many casualties. In spite of all this, the bridging parties, among whom was a contingent of the 48th under Second-Lieutenant Mansfield, stuck to their work with grim determination, and by 5.45 a.m. the space between the abutments was spanned. The leading platoons of the Royal Sussex at once raced across and stormed the lock-houses after a short but desperate fight. The successful bridging of the canal was largely due to the gallantry and skilful leadership of Lieutenant-Colonel D. G. Johnson, of the Royal Sussex, and Major de C. Findlay, of the 409th (Lowland) Field Company, R.E., both of whom were subsequently awarded the Victoria Cross.

Once the passage of the canal had been forced, the Royal Sussex and the 60th Rifles quickly crossed to the eastern side. The Northamptonshires followed them at about 6.15 a.m., " D " Company being the first to cross, with " A," " B " and " C " close behind in the order given. Two companies were at once pushed forward to support the Royal Sussex, who were advancing rapidly in order to get close up behind the barrage again. For the moment the resistance of the enemy had collapsed, and numerous prisoners were sent back as the advance continued. By 9 a.m., the 2nd Brigade were holding a line nearly a mile east of the lock. By 2 p.m., the way was clear for the attack on Fesmy, and " B " and " D " Companies of the 48th dashed forward to storm the village. Very little resistance was encountered on the western side, but in the eastern portion the enemy made a most determined stand, his machine-gun fire holding up the advance for over two hours. At length, some trench mortars were brought up to support the attack, and by 4.30 p.m. the whole village was in British hands.

It was now becoming dark, and as yet there was no liaison between the 2nd Brigade and the French troops on its right. A patrol of the 48th was sent out some distance east of Fesmy to the cross-roads at La Justice, at which it had been arranged that the English and French should join hands. No sign of any French patrol was to be found : it was subsequently discovered that the French troops had not yet advanced so far east as had the 1st Division. A defensive flank facing south was therefore formed by " B," " D " and " C " Companies, " A " Company remaining in support. Thus the situation remained through the night. The casualties sustained during the advance had not been heavy; among the officers, Second-Lieutenant L. J. Morten (attached from the Oxfordshire Regiment) had been mortally wounded, and Second-Lieutenant A. J. Jouguet had been wounded also.

Early on the morning of November 5th, another

patrol was sent out to the cross-roads at La Justice,
and by 5 a.m. connection had been established with the
French. The defensive flank was thereupon withdrawn,
" B," " C " and " D " Companies swinging round
and coming into support again.   It was now found
that the enemy had retired during the night. The task
of pursuing the retreating enemy was assigned to the
46th Division, whose infantry moved forward through
the 2nd Brigade, and joined hands with the French at
about 3 p.m.   An hour and a half later, the 1st
Northamptonshires closed their ranks and marched back
to Wassigny and La Vallée Mulâtre.

Thus ended the last engagement in which the 48th
took part.   Since September 18th, they had been
constantly in action.   Seven times they had attacked
the Germans, three times they had withstood a counter-
attack of the enemy.   They had captured over 600
prisoners, 9 pieces of artillery, and about 100 machine
guns.   It was a strange coincidence that the march
back from the last battle took the battalion through the
very village near which it first encountered the enemy in
1914.   Very few of those who marched through
Wassigny on the evening of November 5th, 1918, had
been with the 48th when the battalion first passed along
that road.   One of those few was Lieutenant-Colonel
G. St. G. Robinson, who in 1914 had been a subaltern
in command of No. 16 Platoon ; another was his adjutant, formerly Transport Sergeant A. G. McNaught.

After a night's rest at La Vallée Mulâtre, the
battalion continued its march to Fresnoy-le-Grand, three
or four miles south of Bohain.   Here the whole of the
1st Division was concentrated for a rest.   As yet it was
not certainly known whether the enemy was willing to
admit that he was beaten, and the probability of an
armistice being concluded within the next few days did
not cause any slackening of the training for future
offensive operations.   Lieutenant-Colonel Robinson
aptly voiced the prevailing sentiment in his speech to
the battalion on November 5th :

" We know that the enemy is near the end, and that we are the better men. When peace comes and how it comes are questions for those above us to decide; our job is to continue to knock him about as we have been doing."

But happily the 48th was not called upon once more to take its place in the line of battle. Since November 4th the 58th had been resting in the town of Marchiennes. During November 8th signs of a general German withdrawal on the Corps front were evident, and on the following day the 58th moved in pursuit to La Croisette, near St. Amand. Rumours that touch with the enemy had been lost, and that the end was near were in the air. The following morning the battalion crossed the Scheldt at Condé by a pontoon bridge. Everywhere it was met by excited Belgians offering brandy to the troops. One old lady even went so far as to attempt to place a garland of chrysanthemums round the C.O.'s neck. More than half-starved and bitterly oppressed for years, the Belgians welcomed the 58th as their deliverers. It is also pleasant to record that the men of the Regiment, at their own suggestion, willingly gave up a considerable part of their none-too-ample rations to save the children from starvation. Towards the evening of November 10th the 58th entered the squalid mining village of Bernissart on the Mons—Condé Canal, and dispersed to very bad billets, with orders to resume the march at 7 a.m. next morning. The march never took place. In the early hours of November 11th the news came that the long and weary struggle was over at last, that the cause of right had finally triumphed.

Meanwhile, Germany had been feverishly pressing for an armistice, and her envoys had been admitted through the French lines to listen to the terms imposed. So stringent were the terms laid down, and to such humiliation would Germany have to submit should she accept them, that it was thought that, even in her extremity, she must refuse. To such a state of collapse, however, had the foremost military Power in Europe been reduced, that the terms were accepted, and on the morning of November 11th, 1918, this telegram was received at the headquarters of the division :—

> " Following message from G.H.Q. begins AAA
> Hostilities will cease 1100 November 11th AAA
> Troops will stand fast on the line reached at that
> hour AAA Defensive precautions will be main-
> tained AAA There will be no intercourse with
> the enemy until receipt of instructions from G.H.Q.
> Further instructions follow AAA Ends."

The war was over. Europe was safe. The cause for which the Allies had poured forth their blood like water was attained.   True to her promise, England, having drawn her sword, had not sheathed it until the military domination of Prussia had been beaten to the dust.   The guns, which had not ceased fire for more than four years in France, were now silent, and, although a state of war was to exist for well on into the following year, of active hostilities there were no more.

The whole British Army on the Western Front felt, when the hour of the Armistice struck, as if an intolerable burden had been lifted from its shoulders. The news was almost stupefying in its tremendous signification and incredible in the gladness and relief which it conveyed.   But, on the whole, it was received with true British phlegm and not least by the war diarist of the 2nd Battalion, who made this nonchalant entry :

" November 11th.—Armistice with Germany com-menced at 1100, when all fighting ceased.   Weather : fairly heavy rain."

On November 15th the 8th Division moved back by road and bus to Tournai, where it came under the orders of the III Corps. Shortly afterwards the III Corps was transferred from the Second Army to the Fifth Army, so that the 2nd Battalion did not share with the 1st Battalion the honour of marching to the Rhine.

About a week before Christmas the 58th moved back

to the village of Silly, not far from the battlefield of
Waterloo. Here it remained until the end of February,
1919. The arrival of the Band from England did much
to relieve the monotony of life in a little Belgian village.
In January, King Albert expressed a wish to honour the
British Army by reviewing the III Corps in Brussels,
and the 58th were selected to represent the 24th Infantry
Brigade. The battalion arrived at Brussels on January
18th, and were welcomed as guests by the citizens of the
suburb of St. Gilles. The following morning the 58th,
eight abreast, with band playing and Colours flying,
marched past the man who perhaps more than any other
embodied the spirit in which the war had been fought
and won. In spite of the falling snow, the citizens of
Brussels crowded the pavements with shouts of " *Vive
les Anglais,*" and stood bareheaded as the Colours
went by.

Afterwards came the return of the battalion to Silly
and the anti-climax of demobilization. To the very
last the 58th maintained the high standard of discipline
which had kept its honour clean on many a battlefield.
Finally, in early April, the cadre of the battalion, consisting of seven officers and seventy-five other ranks,
arrived at Northampton, and was publicly welcomed by
the Mayor and Corporation.

Thus, so far as the 58th was concerned, the war
ended. Throughout four years of bitter fighting, in the
face of the machine guns of Neuve Chapelle and
Aubers Ridge, amidst the mud and horror of the
Somme and Passchendaele, in the days of March, 1918,
when all seemed lost, in the darkness of the terrible
night battle of Villers Bretonneux, and the grim early
dawn of May 27th on the Chemin des Dames, the 58th
remained true to its tradition of self-sacrifice, loyalty
and courage, and added fresh honour to its name.

The march to the Rhine is an event of such
outstanding importance in the history of the 48th
that it is worth while to reproduce several narratives in
full, so that from the total of information given a vivid

picture may be made up. The first narrative runs as follows :—

" On November 13th the battalion embussed at Fresnoy le Grand, and was taken to Favril, where we stayed for two days. On the 16th the march to the Rhine commenced, and that night found us billeted in Sars Potières. Two days later we marched to Strée. It was during this march that we met hundreds of prisoners of war, composed of all nations of the Allies, but chiefly French, Italian and our own. Needless to say, they were delighted to see us, but none more so than a man of the Battalion, who had been captured a few months before. On the 20th we marched to Pry, where we stayed two days. In Pry station we discovered many train-loads of war material left behind by the Germans. There was a complete train-load of medical stores. On investigation these stores were rather wonderful to a non-medical eye, but our doctor raved about some sets of instruments which he discovered. General Stickland appeared on the scene at this moment, and we quaked in our boots, but it is believed he had already cast his eye over a train-load of guns; but there were no dial sights left. On November 23rd we continued the march to Morialmé, and the following day arrived at Falaen. Up to this point the outstanding part of the march was our wariness in crossing bridges : nearly every bridge and many points on the road had been charged with delayed action mines. The railway, too, was mined at various intervals. On the first two or three days the blowing up of mines was fairly frequent. These mines were, I think, the cause of our having to stop for two days or more at a stretch, as it prevented the movement of trains and lorries bringing forward rations. Our quartermaster and transport officer had many hectic days, as the battalion transport on many occasions had to travel many miles farther than the troops owing to the route taken by the latter being impassable for transport. The Royal Engineers had a thankless and dangerous task preceding us and removing the mines. The battalion stayed six days at Falaen, ceremonial parades being the chief occupation during the period. On December 1st the march was continued, and we reached Sommière. On the following day we had a long march to Miranda Château via Dinant."

More lengthy and more detailed is the narrative which now follows :—

" After the Armistice the battalion prepared to settle down in Fresnoy. The prevalent idea was that we should be left alone for a fortnight or so to get fit and reorganize.

" On the night of November 12th-13th it was raining hard at the time, and headquarters were all asleep, when a runner appeared from brigade head-quarters with a message, which was brief and to the point : ' The battalion will commence the march to the Rhine to-morrow.' Battalion orders had to be written and companies warned in the middle of the night. Next morning in the dark the battalion embussed in lorries on the outskirts of Fresnoy and proceeded to Favril on the Rivièrette, passing through Catillon on the way, where the 1st Brigade had crossed the Sambre and Oise Canal on November 4th. At Favril the first delay action mine left by the Germans was seen. It consisted of a ladder, with a box of explosive on it, slung underneath a bridge over the River Rivièrette, and was rendered harmless by the Engineers. Favril was a pretty little village, and the first undevastated one we had seen for some months.

" The next night we stayed at Avesnes, where the Boche had wrecked several large houses with mines. From Avesnes we marched to Sars Potières, where the whole battalion was billeted in a large factory, a company on each floor, the easiest task the billeting officer had in the whole march. The next day's march was to Beaumont, a very pleasant march, as the day was gloriously fine, though frosty, an ideal day for route marching. At Beaumont the town was decorated with flags of the Allies (which had been sold to the inhabitants by the retreating Germans, so it was said), the townspeople gave the battalion an enthusiastic welcome, and the commanding officer rode into the town with two babies in his arms; in fact, the battalion was practically mobbed by the people, who threw flowers at the men.

" From Beaumont we went to Pry, where we halted for a few days. Pry was a very pretty village, with a stream running through it, where some of the men tried to fish. Battalion headquarters was in the Mayor's house on the banks of the stream. The Germans had pushed their bayonets through several valuable old pictures in this house, and had also stabbed the chairs and sofas. While at Pry the guard mounted at ' Retreat ' every evening and the drums beat ' Retreat.' Most of the villagers turned out to watch. Unfortunately, the water here was bad, and an epidemic ran through the battalion, and was only stopped by boiling all water.

" Near Pry a railway siding was found, which was full of German supply trains. There were truck-loads of ammunition and guns, and also a train of medical stores, over which a guard was placed. This medical train proved very valuable, and the medical officer spent a considerable time classifying and sorting its contents. The weather was now getting colder, and in the mornings the roads were covered with frost, which made it difficult for horses to keep their feet, even with frost nails.

" From Pry to Chevetogne I was away from the battalion. At Chevetogne Abbey a countess and the mayor dined with the battalion. The next march was to Sinsin—not a very good billet—a small village. The weather now began to break up, and several of the day marches were through pouring rain. At Malempre, a small village in the Ardennes, the inhabitants were rather hostile. They made billeting a difficulty, stating that every house was either infected with scarlet fever

or foot-and-mouth disease, and during the night they
cut up some of the transport harness.   The marches
through the Ardennes were rather trying.   The roads
were bad, often mere forest tracks; it rained very often,
and the transport had great difficulty in getting the
wagons up the hills.

" The battalion next marched from Beho, our last
billet in Belgium, across the frontier, through St. Vith,
and billeted at Neidingem.   The Colours were flown as
the battalion marched over the frontier.   They were
carried by Lieutenants Kinsley and Irons.   St. Vith
was the first German town the battalion marched
through, and the band played ' When we wound up
the watch on the Rhine.'   Its first night in Germany
the battalion was scattered in small villages; the
accommodation was very poor, and the weather rainy.

" For the next few days the march was continued
through Schonberg, Manderfield, Dahlem and Blanken-
heimerdorf.   All these were fairly small villages, but it
was noticeable how much cleaner and well-kept were
the German villages and towns than those of Belgium;
also the Germans were most respectful and helpful.
On a snowy evening the battalion marched into
Munstereifel, the prettiest town we passed through on
the march to the Rhine.   Munstereifel is in a valley,
with a river flowing through the town.   The buildings
were of old grey stone, with mullioned windows; in fact,
that night the town looked like a city out of Hans
Andersen's fairy tales.

" From Munstereifel the battalion marched through
Odendorf to Duisdorf.   Duisdorf was reached on
Christmas eve, December 24th, where the battalion was
finally billeted.   On arrival two lorries were sent off,
one to find vegetables and green stuff, as the men were
very much in need of them, and another to divisional
headquarters, where socks and underclothing were
drawn.   Billets at Duisdorf were very comfortable, and
the inhabitants seemed glad to see us.   They were very
short of food, except garden and dairy produce, and
soup was issued in the streets.

" A few days after arriving at Duisdorf, the battalion marched to Bonn, and on to the bridge over the Rhine, so that the men could actually see the Rhine. After its long march the battalion were very fit, since from November 11th it had marched through part of France, Belgium and Germany, and it had shared its rations with the inhabitants and with returning prisoners of war, all of whom had very little food. At Duisdorf the men were very well billeted, most of them having beds, and they soon made friendships with the local people, and also experienced great glee at meeting the demobilized Boche soldiers, who had fired trench mortars and *minenwerfers* at them at Ypres and La Bassée.

" During the march the transport had had a difficult time, owing to the steep gradients in the Ardennes; the wagons often had to make considerable detours. the weather also had often been bad, rain and sleet predominating, but no one seemed to have suffered any ill effects, though boots and clothing were in a bad state by the time we arrived at Duisdorf."

Another officer writes :—

" After the crossing of the Sambre—Oise Canal on November 4th, the 1st Division were at last relieved and marched back for rest. The battalion was billeted at Fresnoy le Grand, where they heard the news of the Armistice. I was not with the battalion during the first portion of the march into Germany.

" On December 2nd the 1st Division crossed the Meuse at Dinant, and the battalion billeted for the night at Miranda Château. On the following day the march was continued to Villers-sur-Lesse, where we stayed for a few days. This village—one of the many which had suffered from four years of foreign occupation—did all it could to make the stay of all ranks a happy one. We were received by a deputation headed by the Mayor, and aided by the village band, playing on instruments which had been carefully hidden away for four years. What they lacked in music they made up in enthusiasm. Near this place are the famous caves of Han-sur-Lesse

" On December 6th the adjutant, who had been sent home to get the Colours, rejoined. On December 7th we marched to Chevetogne Abbey, and on the 8th—Sunday—the colours were with due ceremony handed over once more to the care of the battalion. I have a note in my diary that the officers went for a boar hunt in the afternoon, but got none. From December 9th to the 16th the march was continued by easy stages each day or so. My chief recollection at this time is rain—torrents of rain every day. On December 17th came that proud and unforgettable moment when the 48th crossed the German frontier at 10 a.m. The 1st Division went past the divisional commander by brigades, the 2nd being specially commended by Sir Peter Strickland for their smart appearance. We had made special efforts, in spite of the rain, to smarten up men, horses and vehicles, and the difference in appearance between our men and those of the retreating German Army, I am told, made a marked impression on the German population. At the frontier a Union Jack had been mounted, and beneath it Sir Peter Strickland stood and saw his division marching at last towards the Rhine. When that day ended we were all billeted in Germany, the battalion some ten miles beyond the frontier at Neidingen.

" From December 18th to the 23rd the march continued without incident; the weather was still bad. Supplies, however, never failed, and it must be remembered that the Army of Occupation had left their railheads behind, and were entirely dependent on lorry convoy for the many administrative details necessary. The rate of advance was, therefore, governed both by the ability to supply and the rate of the German retreat.

" On December 24th we reached our final billets at Duisdorf, about four miles west of Bonn, where we were to remain until March 5th. We were naturally unable to hold Christmas festivities to any great extent on the following day, but we made up for it shortly

W

afterwards, and the battalion had a real Christmas dinner. We found Duisdorf a comfortable billet. We were lucky in having two large halls, where the men had their meals. The inhabitants, I must say, proved friendly and helpful, and never gave or caused trouble, nor was there any harshness or unjustice displayed on our side. We found the lack of playing fields very trying, as every available piece of land was under cultivation. We, however, managed to organize games and recreational training. We played football throughout our stay, and the officers played comic polo on the transport animals, and thoroughly enjoyed themselves, especially when the second-in-command or quartermaster became unseated, or a specially hard-mouthed animal refused to take his hoof off the polo ball. Inter-unit competitions were started, and the battalion won the 2nd Brigade Football Cup, which they still hold. They were beaten, after two re-plays, by the Divisional Royal Engineers in the divisional competition. We also provided the winners of the brigade tug-of-war. Bonn and Cologne provided places of interest to visit, and what with our usual hours for training and route marching, etc., the time quickly passed without special incident. Early during our stay the opportunity was taken to march the battalion and colours down to the banks of the Rhine, a fact which should prove of historical interest when these colours are finally laid by."

We may now supplement these interesting and vivid narratives with a couple of accounts dealing with the stay of the 48th in the Rhineland and the return of the cadre to England to reorganize and re-form. Here is the first account :—

" IN GERMANY.

" The battalion soon settled down in Duisdorf. The Christmas dinner took place on New Year's Day. When we first arrived one company was employed on outlying picquet and one on the inlying. Curfew was instituted, and the first few nights the officer of the inlying picquet found himself in charge of several Germans who were found out after hours. The men were apathetic, and took the curfew as a matter of course, but the German women were indignant, and the guard had an exciting time dealing with a roomful of angry and gesticulating fraus. Eventually the local people got accustomed to being indoors after dark, and all was well.

" Games were organized, and there was a keen rivalry between platoons at soccer, usually played in the snow.

" The regimental team played the Royal Sussex at hockey, also in the snow, and won easily. Several cross-country races were held, and also paper-chases. The officers, among whom shot guns had mysteriously appeared from England, went shooting buck and hares until this was stopped by an Army order. We also used to go to Cologne and see the opera.

" The battalion competed in the 1st Division sports held at Bonn. The division also held a race meeting, at which the padre distinguished himself, his pony being the only one to finish the course in a steeplechase after refusing every jump at least twice.

" During January demobilization started, and the strength of the battalion gradually decreased; also education was commenced, and was not very popular. Some of the men started to learn German from the women in their billets, but the amount they picked up was about the same as the soldier learns in India of Urdu, and in each case the soldier's complete confidence in his ability to ' sling the bat ' is evident, if amusing.

" While we were at Duisdorf, the bandmaster (Mr. Cresswell) arrived with the band. He was met on his arrival by several of the officers, and his appearance, after five or more days in a cattle truck, dirty and scruffy, with his temper rather frayed, evoked peals of laughter, which only increased when he expressed his opinion of the rolling stock of the British Expeditionary Force. After this the band used to play in the evenings

W I

in the square at Duisdorf, and was much appreciated both by the Germans and ourselves. There was a large hall at Duisdorf, which was used for concerts and also for one or two dances There was also a dinner at Bonn to celebrate the V.C.'s won in the last advance. It was a most excitable and enjoyable evening."

The other narrative deals chiefly with demobilization and the return of the cadre of the battalion to England :

" Early in the New Year demobilization began in accordance with the prepared scheme, whereby certain officers and other ranks termed ' pivotal ' were given priority of release to enable the various industries at home to make a start on their normal occupations once again. This was a sad time for the regular soldier, who saw a fine and trusted battalion gradually disappear. At the end of our stay at Duisdorf we were required to send 300 officers and other ranks to help the formation of a Young Soldiers' Battalion.

" On March 5th we were relieved in Duisdorf by the 52nd Welch Regiment, a Young Soldiers' Battalion, and to them we handed over the whole of our transport and horses. This was another sad day for the battalion, especially for the transport personnel. They had had—many of them—animals under their care for years. We had gradually collected together a fine type of light and heavy draught horses, of which we were all proud. We had won many prizes for ' turn-outs ' during transport competitions in the war, and the men were really fond of the animals in their charge.

" On relief the remnants of the battalion marched to Lengsdorf, a village a few kilometres away, and there demobilization proceeded very rapidly, until finally we were reduced to a mere skeleton. Reduced by demobilization, and transfers, only a pitifully small remnant of the battalion returned to Northampton. Of the seventy officers and other ranks who were welcomed back to the town, only two had set forth with the battalion nearly five years before. These were Captain and Adjutant McNaught and Lance-Corporal Moss.

The old 48th had added thick clusters of laurel to its older symbols of victory, but the price paid for the fame thus won was a terrible one. Over 1,000 had been killed in action, and over 600 more had died of wounds or sickness. More than 3,000 had been wounded, and with prisoners of war the total of casualties had reached the figure of 5,091, of which 166 were officers. Such was the toll demanded of the 48th in the Great War.''

CHAPTER XVI

THE 4TH BATTALION THE NORTHAMPTONSHIRE REGIMENT.

ON July 26th, 1914, the 4th (Territorial) Battalion of the regiment went to its annual training camp at Ashridge Park, Berkhampstead, under the command of Lieutenant-Colonel S. L. Barry, D.S.O. During the first week the ordinary work of the camp went on, rumours of events which were happening on the Continent providing plenty of material for discussion in the spare time. On the Sunday before Bank Holiday a telegram summoned the Colonel to join Sir John French's staff, and that evening, naturally, talk centred round the war that had already started. No one knew whether the country would become involved or not, but a well-known politician who was a guest that night, speaking as a supporter of the Government, said that we should not take part.

August Bank Holiday saw the battalion leaving camp for its day's work on the training area. When a few miles away a message was received, the battalion returned to camp, packed its kit, and entrained, and everyone returned to their homes. The following day brought orders to mobilize, the Battalion reassembled at Northampton, and, within a week, left for Romford, where the division to which it belonged—the 54th—concentrated. Lieutenant-Colonel E. G. Curtis, of the Bedfordshire Regiment, was appointed to command in place of Lieutenant-Colonel Barry.

After completing its mobilization stores the battalion marched by easy stages to Bury St. Edmunds, where training was continued, interrupted by frequent alarms. Men who were too old or too young for service abroad were taken to form the nucleus of a second line battalion, while drafts of recruits brought the 1st/4th, as it was now called, up to strength. In November a move was made to Thetford, where the adjutant, Captain S. H. J. Thunder, left to join the 1st Battalion in France, Captain J. Brown being appointed to succeed him.

At Easter, 1915, the division was moved to the East Coast for defence purposes, the battalion being stationed at Norwich; on the withdrawal of the division in May the battalion proceeded to St. Albans to fit out for overseas service; to everyone's disgust webbing equipment was withdrawn and replaced with the stiff leather pattern. In the middle of July khaki drill and pith helmets arrived, which pointed to the fact that the battalion was destined for service in the East.

On July 29th it entrained, and, on the following day, sailed from Devonport in the *Royal George*.

The following officers embarked with the battalion :—

Lieutenant-Colonel E. G. Curtis.
Major G. Fuller.
Major A. C. Henson.
Captain and Adjutant J. Brown.
Captain L. P. Dorman.
Captain H. M. Wilson.
Captain H. L. Wright.
Captain R. D. Pendered.
Captain F. A. Wright.
Captain W. S. Fisher.
Captain C. G. Guy.
Lieutenant A. J. Wright.
Lieutenant G. P. Crampton.
Lieutenant G. P. Lankester.
Lieutenant F. H. Preston.
Lieutenant P. L. Murray.
Lieutenant A. G. A. Hodges.
Lieutenant S. J. Marlow.
Lieutenant C. J. Crockett.
Lieutenant J. G. C. Heywood.

Second-Lieutenant M. E. Hancock.
Second-Lieutenant St. J. Rands, who went with the
    Transport (probably in another ship).
Second-Lieutenant H. Burditt.
Second-Lieutenant G. G. Leadbitter.
Second-Lieutenant F. H. Cronshay.
Second-Lieutenant A. Howard.
Second-Lieutenant J. R. Dawbarn.
Second-Lieutenant J. White.
Second-Lieutenant R. W. Fay.
Lieutenant C. F. Searle, R.A.M.C. (T.), Medical
    Officer.
Major and Quartermaster R. Goacher.

The voyage was uneventful, and after calling at
Malta the ship reached Lemnos on August 13th, being
more fortunate than her sister ship, the *Royal Edward,*
which was torpedoed after leaving Malta.

In the early hours of August 15th two destroyers,
H.M.S. *Foxhound* and H.M.S. *Scourge,* came along-
side and the battalion was transferred to them, 28
officers and 913 other ranks strong.   On reaching Suvla
Bay, on the Gallipoli Peninsula, the troops were transferred to lighters and to the ship's small craft, and were
towed or rowed ashore, receiving their baptism of fire
from a few shells which fell near them as they landed.

Fighting had been in progress at Suvla for several
days, but the battalion, which had collected behind
Ghazi Baba after landing, was told that it would
not yet be wanted and that the men could bathe.
Accordingly, about half of them took to the water,
to the accompaniment of the sounds of rifle fire on
the one hand and the bombardment of the guns of
our ships on the other.   At about 5 p.m. orders were
given for the battalion to move up to a position in
support of other units of the brigade—the 162nd—
which had been engaged throughout the day; the
men were hurriedly collected from the sea and the
battalion moved up, passing on its way many
wounded from other units. It did not escape

unscathed, for the brigade diary records that Captain H. L. Wright was wounded.

On August 17th the battalion had its first experience of trench work, for it was brought into the line to fill a gap between its own division—the 54th—and the 53rd. During its tour here it had the misfortune to lose Major A. C. Henson, the second-in-command, and Regimental Sergeant-Major A. W. Hatton, who were killed by the same shell on August 22nd. Lieutenant J. G. C. Heywood was killed a week later.

Although the battalion had only taken part in normal trench warfare it had not escaped unscathed, for up to the end of August three officers and seven other ranks had been killed, three officers and 53 other ranks wounded, and one man was missing.

At the beginning of September the battalion was transferred to the 163rd Brigade of the same division, and remained with it until the end of the Gallipoli operations. This brigade held the portion of the line about Hill 60, and the 4th Battalion spent its time between this place and South Wales Borderers Valley, the ordinary trench routine when in the line being varied with patrolling and raids; as No Man's Land was only some 15 to 50 yards wide at Hill 60 there was plenty of scope for bombing, which was done with home-made jam tin bombs. Shortage of water and food, the lack of exercise, the tropical heat of August followed by the biting cold of November, all told on the health of the battalion, and many fell sick of dysentery and jaundice, while enemy action took a regular, if small, toll. Between September 3rd and November 30th the battalion's casualties were 35 killed and 129 wounded, and the diary records that on the latter date only four officers and 200 men who had mobilized with it in August, 1914 were still serving.

On November 27th the 4th Battalion were due to embark for a month's rest at Mudros, but that very day brought a heavy south-westerly gale, a thunderstorm, and torrential rain which filled the trenches with water and turned the roads into running rivers, rendering movement impossible; so the promised rest did not materialize. The weather then changed; the wind swung round to the north, the water froze, and the peninsula was covered with snow. Conditions were appalling and there were numerous cases of frostbite, but the battalion, though it had a bad time, fared better than others, for Hill 60, which it was occupying, lay slightly above the surrounding terrain and was the first to drain after the frost broke.

It was not until December 8th that the battalion saw the last of Anzac. Proceeding to Mudros, it stayed there for a week and then embarked, 18 officers and 427 other ranks strong, for Alexandria, where it landed on December 18th and went into camp at Sidi Bishr. It was not to remain there long undisturbed, for on December 30th it moved by march and rail to Hosh Isa, in the Western Desert, where it was in support of the raid of the cavalry and armoured cars, led by the Duke of Westminster, against the Senussi, but did not come into action.

For their services on Gallipoli Lieutenant-Colonel Curtis was awarded the C.M.G., and Second-Lieutenant Hancock the M.C.

Returning to Sidi Bishr Camp on January 19th, 1916, the battalion stayed there until the end of the month, when it moved to Mena Camp, near Cairo, where the whole division was concentrated. During the two months which were spent here the battalion was made up to strength—by the middle of March it was over 900 strong again—the drafts including a number of men from the Royal Warwick and Leicestershire Regiments, who had already seen service in France. The steady training which was carried out, combined with the healthy conditions in the camp, soon made all traces of the hard times of Gallipoli disappear, and once more the 4th were ready for action.

In April the period of rest finished and the division moved to the Suez Canal to relieve the 42nd Division, which was under orders for France. On arrival at Shallufa the 4th marched into the desert and took over the posts of Darb el Haj, Halfway House, and Kubri Railhead, which formed part of the Canal defences. For the remainder of the year the battalion remained in this area, various posts being occupied in turn. Most of the time was spent in work on improving the defences, while periodically they were called upon to form part of the columns which moved into the hills through the Mitla and Raha passes on the road to Nekhyl; on occasions brushes with enemy posts took place, the conditions of fighting being similar to those on the Indian frontier. During the hot weather conditions were trying, as may be judged from the fact that the diary records that on two successive days in May the temperature reached 117° in the shade and 122° in the tents, though the record seems to have been 123° in the shade on June 4th. In spite of this the health of the battalion was good, and this was probably partly due to the fact that during the summer large parties of two to three hundred men went in turn for a week's rest at Alexandria. The battalion was unlucky, however, to lose the officer who had commanded it ever since it left England, Lieutenant-Colonel Curtis being evacuated to hospital on May 14th. Major John Brown was appointed to command in his place.

In the autumn the battalion, together with the rest of its brigade and some other troops, was withdrawn to Suez with a view to joining Lawrence and the Arabs near Mecca. Some of the troops actually embarked, but the plan did not materialize and the force returned to the Canal.

On January 9th, 1917, the 4th marched into camp at Suez, where it spent the remainder of the month training. At this time a depot battalion for the division was formed at Romani, the advanced base, and Captain H. St. J. Browne was appointed to command it.

On January 30th the battalion entrained for Kantara, and arrived there 35 officers and 849 strong, with another officer and 60 men at Romani. Two days later the march across the Sinai Peninsula, prelude to the advance into Palestine, began. There was no fighting. The cavalry were ahead protecting the advance, and all that the infantry had to do was to keep on marching, at first along roads made of wire netting laid on top of the sand, but later over the desert. A day-to-day narrative of the march would be of little interest; it is sufficient to say that twelve days of actual marching brought the 4th through Romani to El Arish. After a rest there, another four days' marching saw them reach Bela, south-west of Gaza. The 4th seem to have ably maintained the regimental reputation for good marching; for the first two days their diary proudly records the fact that no men fell out; after that, the diarist seems to have got tired of recording the same fact daily, and merely states that the total number of men admitted to hospital for the six days after leaving Romani was three.

On March 26th an advance on Gaza took place. The 4th were given the task of occupying and entrenching a position on the Gaza road in order to cover the operations of the mounted division. The position was duly occupied; fighting around Gaza could be heard in the distance, and the mounted troops went through and disappeared. Night fell, and the battalion received no orders until, at about midnight, they were informed that the fight at Gaza had been broken off, that they were in danger of being cut off by Turkish troops and that they were to withdraw at once. This was easier said than done, for they were separated from the rest of our troops by a stretch of country intersected by deep wadis and without roads or landmarks. However, all ended well, and after a trying march they managed to rejoin their brigade. For the following three weeks the 4th were in the line, and things were quiet until the next advance against Gaza took place.

On April 17th, the first day of the attack, the battalion was in support of the 5th Bedfordshire and 11th London

Regiments, whose advance reached the edge of Sheikh Abbas Ridge, a range of hills some fifty feet high rising out of the plain in the shape of a crescent. On the next day there was no further movement, but late in the evening orders were issued for the attack to be resumed on the 19th. Accordingly, at daybreak, the 4th advanced through the Bedfordshires on a front of 3,500 yards, with three companies forward and one in reserve.

The country towards the Beersheba road, which was the first objective, was undulating and covered with barley about nine inches high, but devoid of trees or cover of any description. Everything favoured the Turks, who were strongly entrenched with many machine guns and good artillery support. The attack managed to reach the trenches, but could not enter them, and at 4.30 in the afternoon Captain Church reported that 80 per cent. of the battalion and of the 11th London Regiment were casualties, and that they were still under heavy fire and that as he had no reserves they could not advance without further support. In this message he omitted, however, to state that he himself had already been severely wounded twice.

Any further attempt to advance was obviously impossible, and at dusk the survivors withdrew behind a line which had been dug about a thousand yards in rear by other troops.

The losses in this attack were heavy, amounting to 20 officers out of 21 who took part in the attack, and 366 other ranks killed, wounded and missing. Although unsuccessful, the 4th had done all that was possible under the circumstances; when the position was taken in November many of the dead were found lying on the Turkish parapet.

After the battle the divisional commander, Major-General S. W. Hare, C.B., issued the following message to the troops who had taken part :—

" All ranks, those who fell and those who survived, acted up to the very highest traditions of the British

Army. Actual success was an impossibility, and I do
not believe that any troops in the world could have done
more or shown greater gallantry or better discipline."

For their gallantry in this action Captain D. R.
Church was awarded the D.S.O., Lieutenant H. Burditt
(attached Machine Gun Corps) and Second-Lieutenant
S. R. Bower the M.C., Company Sergeant-Major
Hardy and Sergeant T. C. Briody the D.C.M., and
Lance-Corporal A. Watts and Pte. C. H. Norton the
M.M. At about this time Captain A. J. Wright
received the M.C. and was later awarded the D.S.O.
for services while on the Staff.

After this attack the strength of the Battalion was only
11 officers and some 400 other ranks, so it was fortunate
that a comparatively quiet period ensued, during which
it could be built up again. The positions of the
opposing forces became stationary, trench warfare being
enlivened by occasional raids. Meanwhile preparations were made for another attempt to capture Gaza,
which became more and more heavily entrenched as
time went by. In May, Corporal W. Jones and Lance-
Corporal L. West were awarded the M.M. for their
work on patrol and sniping duties.

By the end of October preparations were complete
and the 4th were once more up to strength. On
November 2nd the attack was launched from Beersheba
to the sea.

The main push was to take place to the east of Gaza,
the attack on the sea flank being designed to prevent
Turkish troops being withdrawn to oppose our main
effort.

The 54th Division was in the sector next to the sea.
The plan was for the main attack by the 161st and 163rd
Infantry Brigades to capture the Gaza defences,
including the village of Sheikh Hasan. As soon as this
had been done, "A" Company of the 4th, under
Captain Marriott, assisted by tanks, was to go through
and capture some further enemy posts known as
" Lion," " Tiger " and " Dog," north-west of Gaza,

clear all wire entanglements off the beach in order to allow of the passage of cavalry, and, finally, to occupy a defensive line to cover the latter should they be forced to withdraw.

By 6.30 a.m. on November 2nd the first part of the attack had succeeded and "A" Company went forward. "Lion," about fifteen hundred yards beyond Sheikh Hasan, was captured in an hour, although the supporting tanks broke down and the covering machine-gun fire was ineffective owing to the mist which prevented observation. The wire on the beach was soon cleared away, but the company was unable to take the other enemy posts.

At eight o'clock the Turks counter-attacked in strength, threatening to surround the company: since they were so far in advance of the rest of our troops little artillery support was available to help them and Captain Marriott was forced to withdraw to Sheikh Hasan, though not without having to leave behind some of the seriously wounded. Further attempts at the same operation later in the day were also unsuccessful and were defeated by Turkish counter-attacks.

The casualties suffered by the 4th were heavy. Five officers (Lieutenant Elliott, Second-Lieutenants Mastin, Pickering, Bell and Bown) were killed, and Captain Marriott, Captain Law and Second-Lieutenant Chaplin wounded. Of other ranks there were 45 killed, 129 wounded and 33 missing.

As a result of the success obtained on the Beersheba flank of attack the Turks broke and commenced a withdrawal all along the line, closely followed by our troops, and by November 25th the 4th had reached the outskirts of Jaffa.

Here the brigade took over from the cavalry, the 4th being allotted the sector Mezerieh—Yehudieh. The position to be occupied was about two miles in extent, lying in a hollow between two ridges and looking up the plain of Sharon. It was held by three companies, "C" (Lieutenant Mudford) at Mezerieh, "B"

(Captain Church) in front of Wilhelma, and "A" (Lieutenant Haptie) at Yehudieh, with battalion head-quarters at Wilhelma and " D " Company (Lieutenant Fay) in reserve behind it. Wilhelma, as the name indicates, was a German colony, and it was strange for the troops to see the children wearing German caps and to hear the German language.

On November 26th considerable enemy movement was seen on the range of hills to the east, arousing suspicion of the Turks' intentions. An officer's patrol was sent out before daylight on the following day and discovered many new shallow trenches and digging in progress in the neighbourhood of Rantieh.

When day broke on November 27th further signs of enemy activity were observed, and at 6.15 a.m. a heavy bombardment opened on Wilhelma; two hours later the enemy were seen to be advancing, but made no attempt to press home an attack, contenting themselves with digging in about a mile from our trenches.

At 11.40 a.m. there was more heavy shelling, in the course of which battalion headquarters sustained a direct hit which destroyed communications for some time. The bombardment gradually increased in intensity and was followed by an advance of some two or three thousand of the enemy; this was stopped by our rifle and machine-gun fire, the Turks suffering heavy casualties.

When this attack had ceased to make headway the enemy's artillery fire, which had lifted on to the rear of the village, reopened on our foremost trenches and shortly after 4 p.m. a second attack was launched. This, however, quickly died away, though the Turks continued to strengthen their firing line and to push forward snipers and machine guns wherever the ground admitted of it.

Then, for a third time, the artillery fire on our front line grew intense, and at 5 p.m. a third attack developed; this was pushed forward resolutely, being partially covered by the fire of the advanced troops of the previous attacks, and, in spite of the casualties incurred, the Turks managed to reach the wadi about four hundred yards in front of Wilhelma.

Lieutenant-Colonel Brown now realized that the position would soon become untenable, as the left flank of the battalion was in the air; he therefore ordered two platoons of the left company and two platoons of the reserve company to counter-attack the enemy flanks, an operation for which he had already made preliminary arrangements. The attack was made without hesitation and undoubtedly saved the situation, for the Turks were forced to withdraw towards Rantieh, and though further attacks were made against other parts of the line during the succeeding days these made no progress.

Later information showed that the object of the Turkish attacks was to cut the Jaffa—Jerusalem road, which was the main artery for the supply of the British forces operating against Jerusalem. The success of this plan would have been a serious matter; its failure was in no small degree due to the prompt action of the 4th.

In the course of the action the battalion lost 20 killed and 69 wounded, a much heavier toll being taken from the Turks.

A week later the battalion was relieved, its next action being on December 22nd, when it took part in an advance towards Ras-el-Ain, in the course of which little opposition was encountered and all objectives were gained.

The rest of the winter was spent in the neighbourhood of Mulebbis, active operations coming to a standstill owing to the heavy rain which rendered the supply of the forces a difficult matter.

The following were awarded decorations in December, 1917, and February, 1918, for their actions in the operations in which the 4th had recently taken part:—

D.S.O.: Lieutenant-Colonel J. Brown.

M.C.: Captain R. A. Marriott, Second-Lieutenant

x

338 The Northamptonshire Regiment

H. A. Chaplin, Second-Lieutenant S. F. Dorrington, Captain Searle, R.A.M.C., Rev. F. J. Walkey, C.F., and Regimental Sergeant-Major W. D. Marsden.

Four D.C.Ms., one M.S.M. and nineteen M.Ms. were also awarded and Second-Lieutenant H. E. Hardy and Company Sergeant-Major A. Pratt were mentioned in despatches. Most of these decorations were presented to the recipients by H.R.H. the Duke of Connaught in March. On this occasion Sergeant A. E. Bennett received the D.C.M. and bar.

The next forward movement was carried out on March 12th, an operation in the course of which the British line was advanced in the neighbourhood of Mejdel Yarba, a town in the western portion of the hills running down to the Jordan. Little opposition was encountered and the 4th only had two men wounded from one shell at rear battalion headquarters.

On the following day the 4th suffered a severe loss when Lieutenant-Colonel Brown was evacuated sick to hospital. One of the few officers remaining of those who had gone out with the battalion in 1914, he had led it through most of the major actions in which it had taken part, but he was not to rejoin it until he reassumed command after its return to England; but that, as Kipling says, is another story.

Major T. Ryan, of the Yorkshire Regiment, who had been with the 4th for some time, took over command until Lieutenant-Colonel J. F. S. Winnington, D.S.O., of the Worcestershire Regiment, was appointed in May.

The early summer was spent in trench warfare and strenuous preparations were made for an offensive at a later date. There was a brief interlude, however, for in June the 54th Division was detailed to proceed to France. The 4th marched to Ludd and went on by train to Kantara, where they encamped. The orders for France were then cancelled, and on July 7th the division returned to Ludd, remaining as the only complete white one in the Palestine force.

The attack which was virtually to finish the campaign started on the morning of September 19th. The 4th left their bivouac at 5.30 a.m. and moved northwards with their brigade—the 162nd—following in rear of another brigade which attacked and captured Kefr Kassin. As soon as this had been done the 162nd Brigade turned east and continued the advance, the 4th leading with " C " (Captain Mudford) and " D " (Major H. St. J. Browne) Companies forward, supported by " A " (Lieutenant Rands) and " B " (Lieutenant Haptie).

This stage of the attack started at 9.40 a.m. and immediately met with considerable machine-gun and shell fire. Soon after midday the Commanding Officer, Lieutenant-Colonel Winnington, was mortally wounded, Major Ryan assuming command in his place, and Second-Lieutenant C. S. Anthony, the scout officer, was killed. The weather was intensely hot and water very scarce, consequently the troops became extremely exhausted; they continued to push on, however, and, after a short rest during the hours of darkness, reached their objective at 6.45 on the morning of September 20th.

In the course of this running fight the battalion had covered some fourteen miles of country and had captured a number of prisoners, including a German officer and 15 German men with their three machine guns, in addition to large quantities of booty. Their total casualties were 75 killed and wounded.

After this battle Major H. St. J. Browne and Lieutenant G. E. Haptie (Prince of Wales's Volunteers, attached) were awarded the M.C., and Company Sergeant-Major W. Jacobs, Sergeant W. S. Turner, Lance-Sergeant A. Judge, Privates T. B. Warburton, D. R. Hornsby, H. Stanford and W. Salisbury the M.M.

As a result of the operations of September 19th/20th the Turks broke into retreat and the cavalry took up the pursuit; as far as the infantry were concerned, fighting was over.

X I

The 4th marched northwards with their brigade, reaching Haifa on October 1st; then on through Acre and Ras el Ain to Beirut. On the day of their arrival there the armistice with Turkey was signed and they marched past the corps commander, General Bulfin.

Another few days' marching brought them to Nahr Ibrahim, where they remained until the beginning of December. Embarking at Beirut on December 4th, they went by sea to Kantara and thence by rail to Helmieh, outside Cairo. The New Year brought trouble in Egypt, and the 4th took part in suppressing the riots, which reached serious proportions in various localities during February and March. Major H. St. J. Browne was awarded the Order of the Nile for his services as President of a Military Court which dealt with the offenders in these riots. Lieutenant Pattison and Second-Lieutenant Dransfield received the M.C. for previous services.

When order had been restored demobilization commenced, small parties of men being sent home at intervals until there remained only a cadre consisting of Captain R. A. Marriott, M.C., and six other ranks. These eventually reached Northampton on November 4th, 1919. On arrival there they were met by the Mayor, Councillor J. J. Martin, J.P., and given a civic welcome, being subsequently entertained at Althorp by Earl Spencer, K.G., the Lord Lieutenant of the county and Honorary Colonel of the battalion.

So ends the narrative of the doings of the 1st/4th. Before closing the chapter reference must be made to the service of the other Territorial battalions of the regiment, who, though not chosen for service overseas, carried on with the work at home. During 1915 the 2nd/4th, which had been at Elmswell, Wellingborough, Peterborough and Newmarket, moved to Darlington, Harrogate, Stockton-on-Tees and Worksop, and became a home service unit, being disbanded at the end of 1917, while the 3rd/4th was raised in Windsor and became the training and draft-finding unit for the

1st/4th. Remaining at Windsor until 1918, it moved to Crowborough and thence to Hastings, where it was disbanded after the Armistice.

In 1915 a Reserve Battalion was formed from the 2nd/4th and 2nd/1st Cambridgeshire Regiment, and, at first known as the 62nd Provisional Battalion, was subsequently renamed the 9th Battalion The Northamptonshire Regiment. It served on the Norfolk coast and was disbanded early in 1919.

APPENDICES

BATTLE HONOURS GAINED BY THE NORTHAMPTONSHIRE REGIMENT IN THE GREAT WAR.

*" Mons."

" Retreat from Mons."

*" Marne, 1914."

*" Aisne, 1914, '18."

*" Ypres, 1914, '17."

" Langemarck, 1914, '17."

" Gheluvelt."

" Nonne Bosschen."

" Givenchy, 1914."

*" Neuve Chapelle."

" Aubers."

*" Loos."

*" Somme, 1916, '18."

" Albert, 1916, '18."

" Bazentin."

" Delville Wood."

" Pozières."

" Flers Courcelette."

" Morval."

" Thiepval."

" Le Transloy."

" Ancre Heights."

" Ancre, 1916, '18."

" Bapaume, 1917, '18."

*" Arras, 1917, '18."

" Vimy, 1917."

" Scarpe, 1917, '18."

" Arleux."

" Messines, 1917."

" Pilckem."

" Passchendaele."

" Cambrai, 1917, '18."

" St. Quentin."

" Rosières "

" Avre."

" Villers Bretonneux."

" Amiens."

" Drocourt-Quéant "

" Hindenburg Line."

*" Epéhy."

" St. Quentin Canal."

" Selle."

" Sambre."

" France and Flanders, 1914-18."

" Suvla."

" Landing at Suvla."

" Scimitar Hill."

" Gallipoli, 1915."

" Egypt, 1915-17."

*" Gaza."

" El Mughar."

" Nebi Samwil."

" Jerusalem."

" Jaffa."

" Tell 'Asur."

" Megiddo."

" Sharon."

" Palestine, 1917-18."

Those marked * are emblazoned on the King's Colour.

HONOURS AND AWARDS LESS PROMOTIONS AND FOREIGN DECORATIONS.

(Decorations of Past Officers of the Regiment are not included in these Lists.)

*V.C.

BOULTER, W. E., No. 14603 Sergeant, 6th Battalion Northamptonshire Regiment. For most conspicuous bravery. When one company and part of another were held up in the attack on Trônes Wood, on July 14th, 1916, by a hostile machine gun, which was causing heavy casualties, Sergeant Boulter, with utter contempt of danger, and in spite of being wounded in the shoulder, advanced alone over the open under very heavy fire in front of the gun, and bombed the gun team from their position. This very gallant act not only saved many casualties, but was of great military value, as it materially expedited the operation of clearing the enemy out of the wood, and thus covering the flank of the whole attacking force.—*London Gazette*, Oct. 26th, 1916.

COLYER-FERGUSSON, T. R., 2nd-Lieutenant (Acting Captain), 2nd Battalion Northamptonshire Regiment. For most conspicuous bravery, skilful leading and determination in attack. The tactical situation having developed contrary to expectation, it was not possible for his company to adhere to the original plan of deployment, and owing to the difficulties of the ground and to enemy wire, Captain Colyer-Fergusson found himself with a Sergeant and five men only. He carried out the attack, nevertheless, and succeeded in capturing the enemy trench and disposing of the garrison. His party was then threatened by a heavy counter-attack from the left front, but this attack he successfully resisted. During this operation, assisted by his orderly only, he attacked and captured one enemy machine gun and turned it upon his assailants, many of whom were killed and a large number were driven into the hands of an adjoining British unit. Later, assisted only by his Sergeant, he again attacked and captured a second enemy machine gun, by which time he had been joined by other portions of his company, and was enabled to consolidate his position. The conduct of this officer throughout forms an amazing record of dash, gallantry and skill, for which no reward can be too great having regard to the position won. This gallant officer was shortly afterwards killed by a sniper.—*London Gazette*, Sept. 6th, 1917.

HERRING, A. C., 2nd-Lieutenant, 6th Battalion Northamptonshire Regiment. For most conspicuous bravery, initiative and devotion to duty on January 22nd, 1918, when, after severe fighting, the enemy gained a position on the south bank of the canal. His post was cut off from the troops on both flanks and surrounded. 2nd-Lieutenant Herring, however, immediately counter-attacked, and recaptured the position, together with twenty prisoners and six machine guns. During the night the post was continually attacked, but all attacks were beaten off. This was largely due to the splendid heroism displayed by 2nd-Lieutenant Herring, who continually visited his men and cheered them up. It was entirely due to the bravery and initiative of this officer that the enemy advance was held up for eleven hours at an exceedingly critical period. His magnificent heroism, coupled with the skilful handling of his troops, were most important factors, leading to success.—*London Gazette*, June 7th, 1918.

LEWIS, A. L., 6th Battalion Northamptonshire Regiment. For most conspicuous bravery at Ronssoy on September 18th, 1918, when in command of a section on the right of an attacking line which was held up by intense machine gun fire. Lance-Corporal Lewis, seeing that two enemy machine guns were enfilading the line, crawled forward, single handed and successfully bombed the guns, and by rifle fire later caused the whole team to surrender, thereby enabling the whole line to advance. On September 21st, 1918, he again displayed great powers of command, and having rushed his company through the enemy barrage, was killed while getting his men under cover from heavy machine-gun fire. Throughout he showed a splendid disregard of danger, and his leadership at a critical period was beyond praise.— *London Gazette*, Jan 31st, 1919.

READ, A. M., Captain, 1st Battalion Northamptonshire Regiment. For most conspicuous bravery during the first attack near Hulloch on the morning of September 25th, 1915. Although partially gassed, Captain Read went out several times in order to rally parties of different units which were disorganized and retiring. He led them back into the firing line, and utterly regardless of danger, moved freely about, encouraging them under a withering fire. He was mortally wounded while carrying out this gallant work. Captain Read had previously shown conspicuous bravery during digging operations on August 29th, 30th and 31st, 1915, and on the night of July 29th-30th he carried out of action an officer who was mortally wounded, under a hot fire of rifles and grenades.—*London Gazette*, Nov. 18th, 1915.

* Lieut. F. W. Hedges, Bedfordshire Regiment, was also awarded the Victoria Cross, while serving with the 6th Battalion Northamptonshire Regiment.

C.B.

Bt. Colonel (Tem. Brig.-General) H. H. S. Knox, D.S.O.

C.M.G.

Lieut.-Colonel S. L. Barry, D.S.O., M.V.O.
Lieut.-Colonel C. W. Barton, D.S.O.
Lieut.-Colonel E. G. Curtis.
Lieut.-Colonel G. S. H. Pearson.
Lieut.-Colonel (Tem. Brig.-General) P. C. B. Skinner, D.S.O.
Lieut.-Colonel E. O. Smith.
Lieut.-Colonel S. H. J. Thunder, D.S.O., M.C.
Lieut.-Colonel G. A. Trent.

C.B.E.

Bt. Colonel S. L. Barry, C.M.G., D.S.O., M.V.O.
Lieut.-Colonel G. H. Champion de Crespigny.

D.S.O.

Berridge, F. R., Captain.
Bostock, L., Captain.
Brown, J., Lieut.-Colonel.
Buckle, C. G., Lieut.-Colonel.
Church, D. R., Captain.
Cobb, E. C., Captain.
Dobbin, L. G. W., Lieut.-Colonel.
Drew, H. R. H., Major.
Fawkes, R. B., Captain.
Haldane, L. A., Captain.
Hayne, S. S., Lieut.-Colonel.
Hughes, E. L., Major.
Knox, H. H. S., Bt. Lieut.-Colonel.
Lake, R. D., Captain.
Latham, S. G., Captain.
Lister, C., Lieut.-Colonel.
Lloyd, H., Major.
Marriott, J. C. O., Captain.
Metcalfe, H. C., Lieut.-Colonel.
Mobbs, E. R., Lieut.-Colonel.
Mowatt, C. R. J., Major.
Parker, G. A., Captain.
Podmore, H., Captain.
Ratcliffe, W. C., Captain.
Robinson, G. St. G., Lieut.-Colonel.
Royston-Pigott, G. A., Major.
Skinner, P. C. B., Lieut.-Colonel.
Swell, A. E., Lieutenant.
Thunder, S. H. J., Lieut.-Colonel.
Trent, G. A., Lieut.-Colonel.
Williams-Freeman, F. C. P., Captain.
Wright, A. J., Captain.

Bar to D.S.O.

Barton, C. W., Lieut.-Colonel.
Metcalfe, H. C., Lieut.-Colonel.
Ratcliffe, W. C., Captain.

O.B.E.

Beacham, R. W., Major.
Coldwell, R. C., Major.
Grant, W. F. N., Lieut.-Colonel.
Hughes, E. L., Colonel.
Little, J., Lieut.-Colonel.
Wright, H. L., Major.

M.B.E.

Alston, R. A., Captain.
Higgins, A. H., Captain.
Hofman, A., Captain.

M.C.

Argles, E. R. C., 2nd-Lieut.
Aylett, C. A. C., 2nd-Lieut.
Bailey, J. M., 2nd-Lieut.
Bates, A., 2nd-Lieut.
Bayley, A. E. S., 2nd-Lieut.
Beasley, J. M., Lieut.
Beattie, S. H., Major.
Beckingham, H., Capt.
Beech, R. F., 2nd-Lieut.
Berridge, F. R., 2nd-Lieut.
Blake, C. E., Capt.
Bland, R., 2nd-Lieut.
Bostock, E. N., 2nd-Lieut.
Bourne, J. F., Capt.
Bower, S. R., 2nd-Lieut.
Brewin, J. V., Capt.
Browne, H. St. J., Capt.
Bryant, T. H., 2nd-Lieut.
Buckle, C. G., Capt.
Burditt, H., Lieut.
Butler, F. W., Capt.
Carey, B. C., Capt.
Carrick, W. E., 2nd-Lieut.
Carritt, H. W., Capt.
Carter, W., 3549 R.S.M.
Cathcart, M., Capt.
Chaplain, H. A., 2nd-Lieut.
Chapman, L. W., 3/10660, C.S.M.
Chisholm, D. C., Capt.
Clark, J., Capt.
Cuthbert, O., 3/10252, C.S.M.
Darling, N. J., Capt.
Dobson, W., 2nd-Lieut.
Dorrington, S. F., 2nd-Lieut.
Eldridge, H. M., Capt.
Essame, H., Capt.
Evans, W. H., Capt.
Farbon, S. E., 2nd-Lieut.
Fawkes, R. B., Capt.
Frost, A. J., Capt.
Frost, J. W., 2nd-Lieut.
Fulcher, F., 3/11054, R.S.M.
Fullen, A., 2nd-Lieut.
Fulton, T. C., 2nd-Lieut.
Furminger, W. C., 2nd-Lieut.
Gadsden, G. H., Capt.
Gillott, B. C., Lieut.
Goldson, J. W., Capt.
Gotch, D. I., 2nd-Lieut.
Hadley, P. S., Lieut.
Hancock, M. E., 2nd-Lieut.
Harding, G. P., 2nd-Lieut.
Hardy, C. J., 2nd-Lieut.
Heaton, A. W., Capt.
Higham, P. H., 2nd-Lieut.
Hill, C. C., Lieut.
Holmes, H., 5224, R.S.M.

Hunter, E. L., Capt.
Hunting, N. R., Lieut.
Irons, F., 2nd-Lieut.
Jacks, C. C. R., Capt.
Jarvis, J. E., Lieut.
Jervois, W. J., Capt.
Keep, H. S., 2nd-Lieut.
Keeshan, B. L., 2nd-Lieut.
King, H. B., Capt.
Kinsley, A. W., Capt.
Knight, H., 2nd-Lieut.
Lambert, A., Lieut.
Lane, H., 2nd-Lieut.
Latham, S. G., Capt.
Law, A. N., Capt.
Lee, G., 5875, R.S.M.
Le Rougetel, J. H., Lieut.
Lingham, J., 2nd-Lieut.
Lloyd, H. I., 2nd-Lieut.
Lovell, J. G., Lieut.
MacGregor, F. M., 2nd-Lieut.
Marlow, E., 2nd-Lieut.
Marriott, J. C. O., Capt.
Marriott, R. A., Capt.
Marsden, W. D., 200268, R.S.M.
Martin, B., 2nd-Lieut.
Martin, F. G. S., Capt.
Martin, R. D., Lieut.
Martyn, C. H., Lieut.
Matheson, R., Lieut.
Matthews, F. T., Lieut.
McNaught, A. G., Capt.
O'Brien, H. D. S., Capt.
Oldfield, J. B., 2nd-Lieut.
Osborne, H. C., 2nd-Lieut.
Palmer, O. B., Capt.
Papworth, F. S., Capt.
Parker, G. A., Capt.
Parker, O. K., Lieut.
Passmore, E. G., Capt.
Paterson, W., Lieut.
Pearson, R., 2nd-Lieut.
Perkins, B. W., Lieut.
Phipps, H. R., 2nd-Lieut.
Pickering, A. C., Capt.
Pierson, J. E. M., Capt.
Piper, J. H., Capt.
Pitcher, H. F., Lieut.
Pittman, J., 7130, C.S.M.
Prevel, J. A., 2nd-Lieut.
Price, F. R., Capt.
Roberts, C. E., Capt.
Robinson, Sir F. V. L., Capt.
Robinson, G. St. G., Capt.
Rolph, G. S., 2nd-Lieut.
Roughton, H., 7324, C.S.M.
Samm, C. A., 2nd-Lieut.

M.C.—continued.

Schreiner, O. D., Capt.
Shepherd, S. F., Capt.
Smeathers, C., 2nd-Lieut.
Smith, F. M., 2nd-Lieut.
Smith, G., 7806, C.S.M.
Smith, H. S., Lieut.
Smith, K. P., Capt.
Spence, G. B., 2nd-Lieut.
Stanbury, P. S., Lieut.
Taylor, W. J. N., 2nd-Lieut.
Tetley, H. C., Capt.
Tetley, J., 2nd-Lieut.

Thunder, S. H. J., Capt.
Tipler, M. W., Lieut.
Tippett, R. B., 2nd-Lieut.
Totton, G. C., Capt.
Townsend, W. H., 2nd Lieut.
Vickers, F. C., 2nd-Lieut.
Walker, F. D. S., 2nd-Lieut.
Williams, A., 2nd-Lieut.
Williamson, G. A., 2nd-Lieut.
Wright, A. J., Capt.
Wright, B., 2nd-Lieut.
Wyatt, J. D., Capt.

Bar to M.C.

Berridge, F. R., 2nd-Lieut.
Farbon, S. E., 2nd-Lieut.
Frost, A. J., Capt.
Jacks, C. C. R., Capt.
Latham, S. G., Capt.

O'Brien, H. D. S., Capt.
Oldfield, J. B., 2nd-Lieut.
Pickering, A. C., Capt.
Piper, J. H., Capt.
Shepherd, S. F., Capt.

2nd Bar to M.C.

Berridge, F. R., Capt.

D.F.C.

Lewis, G. H., Captain.

Morkam, J. P., Lieut.

D.C.M.

9055 Adams, R., C.S.M.
20048 Afford, W. H., C.S.M.
15770 Allibone, A. E., Cpl.
8937 Amour, J., C.S.M.
20095 Asbrey, F. E., Cpl.
4953 Asplin, C., C.S.M.
3/11182 Austin, C., Pte.
20202 Bailey, W. F., Pte.
7751 Bandy, F., C.S.M.
41598 Barnsdale, F. H., Sergt.
201318 Bateup, J. A., C.S.M.
7980 Batley, P., Pte.
3/10059 Bellamy, W. H., Pte.
200142 Bennett, A. E., Sergt.
16844 Billingham, H. F., Cpl.
18335 Blyth, C. V., C.S.M.
7929 Boulding, W. G., C.Q.M.S.
20803 Boyce, E., Sergt.
9300 Branker, W. J., L./Cpl.
200004 Briody, T. C., Sergt.
8561 Brightman, F., Sergt.
12839 Brown, J. G., Cpl.

3/10607 Budworth, W., Pte.
17027 Bull, S. O. J., L./Cpl.
9115 Bull, T., Pte.
8867 Burley, C. E., Pte.
9804 Butler, F. R., Pte.
9781 Butts, J. R., Cpl.
43051 Chalk, L., L./Sergt.
8651 Clements, S., Sergt.
9359 Climpson, S. C., Pte.
10068 Cockerell, W., Pte.
3/10812 Colton, V. M., L./Cpl.
58395 Cook, H. C., Pte.
16153 Cox, A., Sergt.
3/10265 Darnell, S., Pte.
18544 Davison, F., Sergt.
8613 Drage, W., Cpl.
206027 Drew, A. E., Sergt.
8366 Driver, E., Sergt.
17308 Drury, F., Pte.
8487 Dunmore, W., Cpl.
49640 Dye, A. H., Pte.
7756 Ellis, B., Pte.

D.C.M.—continued.

7725 Eustace, W., C.S.M.	28370 Osborn, F. L., Pte.
41831 Evans, W., L./Cpl.	3/10420 Owen, C., Sergt.
13070 Farrar, F., Pte.	20056 Owen, E. H., Pte.
6034 Fisher, C. J., C.S.M.	43550 Palmer, W. L., Sergt.
14775 Flanaghan, S., Pte.	7897 Parker, T., Sergt.
9536 Forrester, A., Sergt.	20507 Parkinson, F. E., Pte.
9207 Foster, C., Sergt.	13475 Partridge, J. W., Sergt.
13974 Gibson, F., Sergt.	3/9321 Pearson, T. R., Sergt.
8718 Goodman, A. L., Pte.	16734 Peet, H., C.S.M.
18170 Grand, W. G., Sergt.	8407 Pennyfather, J., C.S.M.
3/10867 Gray, W. T., C.S.M.	9468 Phillipson, T., L./Cpl.
18965 Green, H. W., L./Cpl.	8636 Pickard, F., Pte.
9370 Gudgeon, C. W., Pte.	13953 Plowman, W., Pte.
200044 Hardy, H., C.S.M.	201045 Pope, G. H., Sergt.
9653 Hawkins, B. W., L./Cpl.	8788 Preedy, W., Cpl.
8590 Henson, T., Cpl.	13537 Pullen, E. C., Sergt.
19321 Herbert, O. W., Pte.	13937 Quartermaine, G., Sergt.
8693 Hoare, H., C.S.M.	20013 Robinson, W. T. V., Sergt.
59215 Holmes, H., Pte.	200923 Roughton, A., Pte.
9620 Hubbard, G. H., L./Cpl.	7324 Roughton, H., Sergt.
27549 Hurst, E. E., L./Cpl.	15840 Russell, F. J., Pte.
28252 Jackson, R., C.S.M.	8285 Scrivener, H., Sergt.
8395 Jelly, J. A., Sergt.	7863 Sharpe, T., Cpl.
3/11043 Jordan, E., C.Q.M.S.	13183 Sismey, G. W., C.S.M.
43723 Kitchener, H. G., Sergt.	200780 Smith, F. H., L./Cpl.
13987 Knight, A. J., Pte.	43237 Smith, F. L., Pte.
14195 Koch, G. H., Sergt.	3/10516 Spollen, G. J., Sergt.
7909 Laddington, E., Pte.	28383 Stedman, C. S., L./Sergt.
5006 Land, F. W., C.S.M.	13104 Tack, E. W., C.S.M.
8711 Lapham, W. J., Pte.	15507 Toseland, G. H., Pte.
5875 Lee, G., R.S.M.	27154 Turner, F. G., Cpl.
201197 Letts, J. F., Sergt.	6141 Underwood, C. H., C.S.M.
200055 Line, W., Sergt.	13668 Varnham, W., L./Cpl.
6389 Linnell, F., C.S.M.	16948 Webb, W. J., Pte.
7978 Lodge, S., C.S.M.	4947 Willett, G. T., Sergt.
27223 Mansfield, A., Sergt.	14282 Wilson, W., Sergt.
41343 Mead, E., Pte.	7474 Winters, F., Sergt.
8439 Norman, R., Cpl.	7875 Woolsey, A., C.S.M.
17968 Norris, J. F., L./Cpl.	7751 Wright, J. T., C.S.M.

Bar to D.C.M.

200142 Bennett, A. E., Sergt.	13070 Farrar, F., Sergt.

M.S.M.

27694 Ambidge, S. R., L./Cpl.	14602 Bridgement,P.W.,L./Sergt.
10018 Attewell, H. C., Sergt.	5504 Buck, W. M., R.Q.M.S.
20048 Bailey, A. H., C.Q.M.S.	5028 Bull, J., R.Q.M.S.
49381 Beasley, H., Pte.	8422 Burford, W., Sergt.
9146 Belcher, C. H., C.Q.M.S.	17392 Bush, G., Sergt.
5184 Blake, J., R.S.M.	13166 Carter, R. J., C.Q.M.S.
3/11156 Boddington, F. C., Sergt.	3/11010 Colver, G. W., C.S.M.
10123 Bonfield, R., C.Q.M.S.	18421 Crow, A. C., Sergt.
200816 Bream, G., L./Cpl.	201586 Day, H. A., R.S.M.

M.S.M.—continued.

7903 Downs, C. E., C.S.M.
9966 Dunkley, F., Sergt.
32261 Edgeworth, E. J., Q.M.S.
5867 Fiddy, A., Q.M.S.
4959 Fisk, A., C.S.M.
8771 Foster, A., Sergt.
202209 Harvey, A. J., Sergt.
15677 Hayward, P. G., Sergt.
6397 Hillman, E. E., R.S.M.
8402 Hislop, D. J., C.Q.M.S.
16025 Hitch, F. A. D., Q.M.S.
6449 Ingram, A. G., Sergt.
6571 Johnson, H., L./Cpl.
9636 Keeling, K. E., Sergt.
225270 King, R. F., Sergt.
17438 Lickorish, B., Cpl.

16735 Lowe, W., Pte.
3/11141 McCarthy, T., R.S.M.
4326 Miles, C., R.S.M.
3/10864 Mulvaney, A. J., C.Q.M.S.
9075 Pulley, A., Pte.
9542 Rogers, G., Sergt.
7787 Searle, G., C.Q.M.S.
3/10320 Wadeson, E., Q.M.S.
9980 Walker, G. A., Sergt.
23165 Walker, G. C., Pte.
17116 Ward, L., Cpl.
15348 Watts, F., Pte.
9949 Wilson, E. W., Sergt.
50775 Worrall, A. J., Sergt.
21564 Worwood, G. W., R.S.M.

M.M.

9156 Abbott, P., Sergt.
14856 Adams, G., Pte.
9055 Adams, R., Sergt.
15772 Adkin, F. E., Sergt.
9926 Adson, F., Pte.
15086 Aldham, B., Sergt.
9386 Allen, G. W., Pte.
31037 Allen, W., Pte.
3/10591 Allen, W. T., Sergt.
12766 Alleway, E., Cpl.
32847 Allton, J., L./Cpl.
10086 Althorpe, F., Pte.
8757 Anderson, E., Cpl.
9876 Anderson, J., Pte.
39798 Andrews, J. A., Pte.
36227 Ansell, A., Pte.
10232 Arnoup, A., L./Cpl.
12539 Ashby, B. G., Sergt.
43003 Ashby, H., Pte.
31039 Ashdown, H. J., Pte.
27190 Ashton, P., Sergt.
60714 Austin, R., Sergt.
13570 Bailey, E. C., Pte.
1336 Bailey, S., L./Cpl.
17301 Bacher, P., L./Cpl.
9977 Ball, A. J., L./Cpl.
200181 Banks, H. E., Cpl.
17263 Barby, K. E., Pte.
25103 Barker, C., Pte.
19249 Barnett, G. H., Pte.
12342 Barnett, H. C., Sergt.
41598 Barnsdale, F. H., Sergt.
8004 Bartlett, C., L./Cpl.
41811 Bartlett, F. J., Pte.
8070 Battison, T., Sergt.
9879 Beasley, W., Pte.
43404 Beckett, P., Pte.

17891 Beeby, H. S., Cpl.
9616 Bellamy, F. J., Cpl.
14690 Benjamin, P., Pte.
3/9892 Bennett, G., Pte.
8995 Bennett, S., L./Sergt.
225061 Bettles, W., Sergt.
13015 Betts, P., Pte.
49528 Bigg, A. W., Pte.
17754 Bird, J., Pte.
18611 Bird, W. B., Sergt.
19113 Bishop, J., Pte.
201351 Bishop, W. H., Pte.
28257 Blackwell, G. A., Pte.
10055 Blake, A., Pte.
20223 Blake, J., Pte.
6097 Bland, A. S., Sergt.
13834 Blandell, A., Cpl.
59323 Bleese, J., L./Cpl.
19315 Blenkinsopp, T., Pte.
3/10888 Blunt, H., Pte.
31172 Boddington, E., L./Cpl.
8519 Boddington, P., L./Cpl.
16046 Boreham, V., Pte.
45512 Bowyer, E. E., L./Cpl.
14455 Bradbury, G., Sergt.
7731 Bradley, A., Sergt.
19468 Bradwell, E., Pte.
8561 Brightman, F., C.S.M.
47822 Brodrick, H., Pte.
16138 Brown, H. A., Pte.
3/9036 Brown, P. C., Pte.
202455 Brunt, W. H., Pte.
14035 Bryan, T. H., Pte.
14903 Bunyan, E. E., Cpl.
43612 Burcham, J. W., Cpl.
9486 Burgess, C., Sergt.
40763 Burns, M., L./Cpl.

M.M.—continued.

12570 Burton, F., Pte.	17109 Drage, W. R., L./Cpl.
14310 Bury, A. G., Sergt.	41307 Dyer, D., Pte.
15872 Butlin, J. L., Sergt.	17477 Eassom, W., Pte.
16438 Buttress, A. E., Pte.	20488 Ellaway, A., Pte.
14309 Byrne, G. W., Pte.	17543 Elliott, E. J., Pte.
40795 Callaghan, T., Pte.	12217 Elliott, J., L./Cpl.
10112 Cannon, J., Pte.	12936 Ellis, F. B., Cpl.
15731 Carr, E., Pte.	13131 Elson, F. J., Cpl.
13376 Carrington, F. R., Sergt.	3/10481 Ette, F. M., Pte.
22827 Carvell, A. C., Sergt.	14681 Evans, J., L./Sergt.
3/10210 Catling, R. D., Pte.	8527 Everitt, W., Pte.
15092 Cave, R., Pte.	17360 Ewenmecklin, F., Pte.
14531 Chantrell, C., Pte.	27504 Facer, W., Pte.
16308 Chapman, A., Pte.	28274 Fairey, G. E. C., Pte.
17059 Chapman, C. R., L./Cpl.	27692 Farden, T., Pte.
10067 Chapman, F. G., Pte.	3/9741 Felce, H., Pte.
14686 Chapman, M., Cpl.	12785 Filkins, C. H., Cpl.
43629 Chapman, S. W., L./Cpl.	58293 Filsell, A., Pte.
22616 Charles, J. H. B., L./Cpl.	15697 Fitch, C. B., L./Cpl.
14375 Chester, E., Cpl.	17036 Fitzhugh, W., Cpl.
12956 Childs, S., Pte.	14775 Flanagan, S., Sergt.
43595 Chivers, C. J., Sergt.	22313 Fletcher, A., Pte.
6551 Church, B., Sergt.	12553 Fletcher, A. J., Pte.
10083 Clements, R., Pte.	8480 Fletcher, W., Sergt.
14036 Coe, W. G., Pte.	25145 Flintham, J. W., L./Cpl.
8241 Cokram, S., L./Sergt.	15522 Ford, J. A., Sergt.
16805 Coley, J. G., L./Cpl.	9207 Foster, C., Pte.
15273 Collar, T., L./Cpl.	17537 Freeman, A. J., Pte.
16011 Compton, F., Pte.	13968 Freeman, J., Sergt.
9307 Connell, R. C., Sergt.	17836 Freestone, W., L./Cpl.
40035 Cooke, W. F., Cpl.	43082 Fritz, W. R., Sergt.
17421 Cooper, W. J., L./Cpl.	22971 Frost, F., L./Cpl.
9624 Cope, B., Sergt.	8952 Frost, W., Pte.
7438 Coppoch, J., Sergt.	12090 Fuller, G. F., Pte.
25470 Costa, G. T., Pte.	9549 Gammon, P. F., L./Cpl.
15720 Cotton, W. A., L./Cpl.	12523 Gammons, C. C., Cpl.
17268 Cowley, A. L., L./Sergt.	17539 Gandy, L., Pte.
16153 Cox, A., Sergt.	13115 Gardner, A., Sergt.
43058 Cox, H. H., Pte.	16972 Gates, F., Sergt.
27218 Croft, J., Pte.	12087 Gentry, W. G., Sergt.
12857 Cross, A. G., Pte.	13331 George, G., Pte.
40316 Darling, A., Pte.	12986 Gibbons, A., Pte.
202672 Davies, C., Pte.	13239 Gilbert, A., Sergt.
24389 Day, F. I., L./Cpl.	10095 Gilbert, G. J., Pte.
16930 Day, S. E., Pte.	202912 Gladding, R. T., Pte.
41638 Dean, C. F., Pte.	19256 Godfrey, A., Pte.
18339 Delamare, P. J., Pte.	12904 Godfrey, C., Sergt.
43715 Dentith, A., Pte.	14510 Golbey, G., Sergt.
20943 Denton, F., Pte.	13908 Golding, G., Pte.
17534 Denton, H., Sergt.	200371 Goode, T., Sergt.
9961 Denton, W., Pte.	200358 Goosey, W. H., Sergt.
17324 Dickens, G., Pte.	25525 Gowers, G. T., Pte.
26811 Dickinson, B. W., Cpl.	43092 Grace, H. J., Pte.
16914 Dicks, F. W., Pte.	204866 Graham, A. E. W., Pte.
12341 Dion, J., Pte.	18170 Grand, W. G., Sergt.
17618 Door, F., Pte.	43670 Granger, H., L./Cpl.
25149 Drage, C. M., Pte.	8612 Green, J. C., Cpl.

Y

M.M.—continued.

22890 Green, W., Pte.
20483 Green, W. H., Cpl.
13439 Gregory, J., Cpl.
18092 Hackney, E., Pte.
3/10147 Halbard, R., Pte.
14030 Hales, S. M., Sergt.
48672 Hall, A. E., Pte.
7472 Hall, H., Sergt.
15806 Hall, J., L./Cpl.
15673 Hammond, W. H., Cpl.
20054 Harlock, T. H., Pte.
9539 Hart, C. R., L./Cpl.
30295 Hawes, J., Pte.
16232 Haynes, C., Pte.
49036 Haynes, L., Pte.
9777 Hearn, P., Cpl.
19321 Herbert, O., Pte.
205896 Hill, A., Sergt.
14631 Hill, A. F., L./Cpl.
3/11090 Hillam, L., Pte.
23150 Hirons, W. F., L./Cpl.
31209 Holden, H., L./Cpl.
13821 Hole, W., L./Cpl.
24580 Holgate, C. H., Pte.
58203 Hooker, E., Pte.
47089 Hornaby, D. R., Pte.
16399 Horne, W. G., Pte.
9132 Horner, R. E., Cpl.
12681 Houlden, A., Sergt.
40900 Howard, E. W., Pte.
12490 Howard, H., L./Cpl.
20290 Howard, W., Pte.
9031 Howlett, A., Pte.
13848 Howlett, J. E., Pte.
13180 Hoyles, F., Pte.
40872 Huddison, A. E., Pte.
40430 Hulatt, E., Pte.
200378 Hull, H., Cpl.
12877 Hussey, P., L./Cpl.
3/10540 Ireson, F., Sergt.
9120 Irons, W., Sergt.
15256 Jackson, G., Pte.
13592 Jackson, J. T., L./Cpl.
200778 Jacobs, W., Sergt.
13194 Jakes, P., Cpl.
18429 Jarvis, E., Pte.
15255 Jinks, C., L./Cpl.
50006 Johnson, B. H., Pte.
8370 Johnson, R., Sergt.
20551 Jones, A., Pte.
7723 Jones, F., Cpl.
12080 Jones, F., Pte.
8446 Jones, H., Sergt.
14160 Jones, H. R., Sergt.
17423 Jones, T. W., L./Sergt.
201407 Jones, W., Cpl.
7340 Jouquet, A. J., Sergt.

19498 Joynes, W., Pte.
200383 Judge, A., A./Sergt.
7145 Justice, W., Sergt.
59447 Keech, A. C., Pte.
43603 Kemp, G. W., Pte.
9077 Kent, E. J., Pte.
16472 Kirkland, R., Pte.
43577 Kittle, J. P., L./Cpl.
9566 Knowles, F., L./Cpl.
3/9734 Lack, J., Pte.
27338 Langdale, G. C., L./Cpl.
225713 Langley, T. W., Pte.
20462 Lattimore, J. W., Pte.
200288 Laundon, E. R., L./Cpl.
10012 Lawrence, A. H., Cpl.
25151 Laxton, B. F., Pte.
14625 Leatherland, F. R., Sergt.
13524 Lee, A., L./Cpl.
15905 Littlemore, J., Pte.
48918 Lloyd, H. G., Pte.
13151 Love, E., L./Cpl.
9250 Lovell, J. W., L./Cpl.
9303 Lovell, O., Cpl.
15644 Luck, A., Pte.
17879 Luck, W. A., Pte.
24888 Mack, A., L./Cpl.
12144 Mackay, R. T., Pte.
200187 Malsher, L., Sergt.
8798 Malyon, G. T., C.Q.M.S.
31237 Mandley, A., Pte.
18868 Manger, A. G., Pte.
40063 Mangham, L., L./Cpl.
27223 Mansfield, A., Sergt.
17608 Markham, R., Pte.
6996 Markham, T., Pte.
43179 Marriott, I. P., Pte.
31252 Martin, F., Sergt.
40033 Martin, G. H., C.S.M.
7890 Mason, O. E. W., Pte.
8865 Maycock, F., Sergt.
43333 Mayes, R. W., Cpl.
15910 Mayes, S., Pte.
205909 McGrath, A. J., Sergt.
27468 McMorran, H., Pte.
9890 Meadows, A., L./Cpl.
18425 Meads, F., Pte.
16873 Miles, G. W., Pte.
17416 Miles, W. L., Sergt.
9019 Mimms, G., L./Cpl.
23985 Mitchell, J., Pte.
46046 Moore, F. R., L./Cpl.
14041 Moore, G., L./Cpl.
16772 Moore, H. W., Pte.
18042 Moore, P., Cpl.
201234 Moring, S. T., Pte.
14044 Morris, G., L./Cpl.
8283 Moss, W., Cpl.

M.M.—continued.

6094 Mouatt, H., Pte.	15216 Redley, W., L./Sergt.
43408 Mummery, A. E., Pte.	3/10655 Reeve, T. G., L./Cpl.
31345 Munton, J. K., Pte.	6414 Reynolds, M., Pte.
18394 Mutton, A. H., L./Cpl.	24375 Richardson, A., L./Cpl.
13857 Needle, T. J., Pte.	8667 Richardson, W., Pte.
17963 Neville, A., Pte.	13920 Richardson, W., Pte.
17857 Newell, B., Pte.	15592 Roberts, L. J., L./Cpl.
204851 Newell, H., Pte.	17985 Robinson, C., Sergt.
43757 Newman, J. G., L./Cpl.	16144 Robinson, F., Pte.
43613 Nice, P. R., Pte.	200116 Robinson, H. C., Sergt.
42945 Nichols, G. W., Pte.	200806 Robinson, J. F., Sergt.
18171 Nicholls, J. T., Pte.	18239 Rochester, R., L./Sergt.
14009 Nicholls, W., Pte.	200926 Rogers, H. T., L./Cpl.
3/8995 Nix, A., Pte.	50461 Roper, W. H., Pte.
8127 Nobes, W. L., Cpl.	7985 Rowland, S. T., C.S.M.
8439 Norman, R., Cpl.	7364 Roy, A., L./Cpl.
17968 Norris, J. F., Pte.	15585 Rushton, A. M., Sergt.
200504 Norton, C., Pte.	23745 Russell, T. G., Pte.
41444 Orme, W., Pte.	226050 Ryder, R., Pte.
15360 Orpwood, S. W., Cpl.	200882 Salisbury, W., Pte.
49787 Osgood, F., Pte.	13945 Sanders, G. H., Pte.
3/10420 Owen, C., L./Cpl.	20019 Saunders, F. G., Pte.
14944 Palmer, A. H., Pte.	15068 Scott, L., Cpl.
15837 Palmer, F. W., Sergt.	12864 Scott, W., Sergt.
43550 Palmer, W. L., Pte.	14584 Scriven, W. T., Sergt.
14462 Panter, J. C., L./Cpl.	25409 Sewell, W., Pte.
15916 Parris, A., Pte.	12235 Seymour, W. J. H., Sergt.
24136 Parrott, F., Pte.	7636 Sharman, H. C., Pte.
6004 Parsons, E., Sergt.	3/10190 Sharpe, A., Pte.
24794 Partner, W., Pte.	12710 Sharp, F., Sergt.
200399 Pascoe, E. J., Sergt.	27920 Sharp, F. E., Pte.
3/10818 Patrick, E. J., Sergt.	12019 Shaw, E. J., Pte.
17398 Patrick, J. O., Pte.	52124 Sherrington, W., L./Cpl.
52370 Payne, J., Sergt.	17105 Sherwood, J., Pte.
43200 Payne, R. W., Pte.	12180 Shine, N., Pte.
9578 Pears, C. W., Cpl.	13451 Shipton, F., L./Cpl.
15607 Pebody, H., Sergt.	13830 Shrive, C., Pte.
12404 Pedley, W., Pte.	3/10914 Simmons, A. F., Cpl.
30627 Pell, A., Cpl.	6504 Sims, G. A., Cpl.
8407 Pennyfather, J., R.S.M.	22254 Sixsmith, B., Pte.
8977 Pepper, H., Pte.	12931 Skelton, W., Pte.
9348 Perkins, J. D., Sergt.	7415 Sleet, A. M., Sergt.
10051 Phillips, C., Cpl.	7557 Smallwood, B., C.Q.M.S.
8636 Pickhard, F., L./Cpl.	43609 Smart, W. J., L./Cpl.
16441 Pitcher, F. J., Pte.	12061 Smith, C. J., Pte.
200965 Plant, J. W., Sergt.	16152 Smith, G. F., Pte.
10157 Plowright, T., Pte.	15818 Smith, H., Pte.
8090 Plume, J. A., C.S.M.	52132 Smith, J., Pte.
9582 Poole, G. A., Cpl.	8682 Smith, J., Cpl.
15918 Pratt, W. E., Pte.	12218 Smith, J. G., L./Cpl.
9097 Pridmore, J. T., L./Cpl.	20537 Smith, L., Pte.
10006 Puttnam, A. G., Pte.	200867 Smith, W., Pte.
13378 Quartermaine, E., L./Cpl.	17504 Snapes, C., Pte.
13937 Quartermaine, G., L./Cpl.	17937 Snelling, S. C., Pte.
14495 Radley, L., Cpl.	8577 Southgate, J. G., Sergt.
24365 Read, F. J., Pte	8483 Spencer, F., L./Cpl.
18099 Read, J., Pte.	14975 Spencer, J. H., Pte.

M.M.—continued.

12734 Spencer, R., Pte.	41586 Tytherleigh, E. A., Cpl.
12110 Spooner, J., Cpl.	6141 Underwood, C. H., Sergt.
19383 Spowage, W., L./Cpl.	18262 Underwood, H., Pte.
17292 Sprigett, G., Pte.	7748 Underwood, W. F., Sergt.
200408 Squires, H. I., Sergt.	13319 Upstone, J., Pte.
48403 Stafford, H. F. H., Pte.	13696 Vede, E., Sergt.
40810 Stanfield, G., Pte.	8052 Vickery, G., L./Cpl.
8535 Stanley, F., Sergt.	203362 Wake, A., L./Cpl.
52120 Stansby, G. B., L./Cpl.	30990 Walden, F. W., Cpl.
8239 Stapleton, M., Cpl.	19344 Walker, A. P., Pte.
25580 Stayton, E., Pte.	13138 Walker, W. H., Pte.
28383 Stedman, C. S., L./Sergt.	16599 Walpole, C. H., Sergt.
13396 Stevens, F., Pte.	22119 Walsh, J., Pte.
6503 Stevens, H., Pte.	8780 Walton, F. G., Sergt.
45625 Stevens, J., Pte.	18264 Waples, A. G., Pte.
10161 Stevens, J. H., Pte.	201411 Warburton, T. P., Pte.
19535 Stevenson, W., L./Cpl.	7906 Ward, A. J., Sergt.
7188 Stewart, A., C.Q.M.S.	15504 Ward, G., Pte.
9569 Stimpson, B. C., L./Cpl.	16461 Ward, W., Pte.
14579 Stimson, W. H., Pte.	200796 Warren, G. A., Pte.
47068 Stock, G. P., Sergt.	39294 Waters, E., Pte.
9652 Stockwell, P., Pte.	8486 Watford, W., Sergt.
9597 Stringer, E., L./Cpl.	16946 Watson, R., Pte.
8277 Sullivan, W., Sergt.	200177 Watts, A., Sergt.
13178 Sumpter, H., Pte.	43281 Weaton, H., Pte.
8410 Swallow, E., L./Cpl.	24369 Webb, A. W., Pte.
13104 Tack, E. W., Sergt.	203453 West, L., Pte.
8927 Talbot, H., Sergt.	14737 West, W., Pte.
49429 Taylor, W. T., Pte.	58937 Whiddett, A., Cpl.
28096 Tear, S. A., Cpl.	8194 White, A., L./Cpl.
18463 Thompson, J. B., Sergt.	18910 White, A. E., L./Cpl.
20321 Thompson, S., Pte.	204877 Whitlock, J., Pte.
15087 Thompson, T., L./Cpl.	3/10297 Whyman, F., Pte.
16936 Thompson, W. R., Cpl.	31012 Wiles, R., Pte.
39289 Thorpe, E., Pte.	12540 Wilkinson, C. H., Pte.
10242 Thrower, W., Pte.	41135 Willett, C. J., Pte.
43255 Tibbett, A., Pte.	52155 Williamson, J. Pte.
18445 Tilley, G., L./Cpl.	15423 Wills, A. E., Pte.
200938 Tipler, W., Sergt.	8322 Wilton, C. G., Pte.
12784 Tite, J., Cpl.	18780 Worley, F., Pte.
43254 Toe, W. D., Sergt.	15242 Worrall, W., Sergt.
13998 Travell, W., L./Cpl.	13528 Wreford, W. H. A., L./Cpl.
14183 Trickey, A., Pte.	3/10475 Wright, A., Pte.
3/8827 Tunnicliffe, G., Pte.	43529 Wright, G., Pte.
14800 Turner, F., Pte.	28357 Wright, W. C., Pte.
8810 Turrell, G., Sergt.	40736 Younger, A., Pte.
12679 Twentyman, R., Cpl.	49271 Ziggles, H. L., Pte.
52149 Twyford, B., Pte.	

Bar to M.M.

9926 Adson, F., L./Cpl.	16308 Chapman, A., Pte.
10086 Althorpe, F., Pte.	43595 Chivers, C. J., Sergt.
31039 Ashdown, H. J., Pte.	14681 Evans, J., L./Sergt.
8519 Boddington, P., L./Cpl.	12523 Gammons, C. C., Sergt.
40763 Burns, M., Cpl.	13115 Gardner, A. Sergt.

Bar to M.M.—*continued.*

204866	Graham, A. E. W., Pte.	24375	Richardson, A., Sergt.
20290	Howard, W., Sergt.	25409	Sewell, W., Pte.
43603	Kemp, G. W., Pte.	12180	Shine, N., Pte.
15644	Luck, A., Sergt.	43609	Smart, W. J., L./Cpl.
205909	McGrath, A. J., C.S.M.	40810	Stanfield, G., Pte.
6996	Markham, T., Pte.	13396	Stevens, F., Pte.
17857	Newell, B., Pte.	18445	Tilley, G., Cpl.
17968	Norris, J. F., Pte.	12784	Tite, J., Sergt.
3/10420	Owen, C., Cpl.	12679	Twentyman, R., Sergt.
43550	Palmer, W. L., L./Sergt.	203362	Wake, A., L./Cpl.
52370	Payne, J., Sergt.	13138	Walker, W. H., L./Cpl.
9348	Perkins, J. D., Sergt.	22119	Walsh, J., Pte.
13378	Quartermaine, E., Cpl.	16946	Watson, R., L./Cpl.
14495	Radley, L., C.S.M.	3/10297	Whyman, F., Pte.

2nd Bar to M.M.

13378 Quartermaine, E., Sergt.

INDEX

EUROPE
Scale 1:1,000,000

0° (Greenwich)   E   a   s   2

52°

Newport
Thaxted
Sible Hedingham
Halstead
Bishop's Stortford
Gr. Dunmow
Braintree
Coggeshall
Hatfield Broad Oak
Harlow
Witham
Tolleshunt

Chelmsford
Epping
Chipping Ongar
Ingatestone
Maldon
Brentwood
Billericay
Romford
Rayleigh
Ilford
Barking
Canvey I.
Woolwich
Greenwich
Grays
THAMES
Dartford
Tilbury
Port Victoria
Gravesend
Bromley
Strood
Chatham
Rochester
Sittingbourne
Wrotham
NORTH
Sevenoaks
Maidstone
Westerham
DOWNS
Leenham
Edenbridge
Tonbridge
Headcorn
Ashford
Tunbridge Wells
Goudhurst
Cranbrook
Tenterden
Crowborough
Hawkhurst
Oxney I.
51°
Uckfield
Salehurst
Rye
Hailsham
Battle
Winchelsea
Lewes
Hastings
Bexhill
St. Leonards
South Downs
Seaford
Newhaven
Eastbourne
Beachy Head

ENGLAND
LONDON
Essex
Hertfordshire
Kent
Surrey
Sussex

CHANNEL

LINCOLNSHIRE
LINCOLN
KESTEVEN
HOLLAND
RUTLAND
The Wash
King's Lynn
Marshland
50°
St. Valery-en-Caux
Cany-Barville
Fécamp
Valmont

(A) (B) (C) (D) (E)

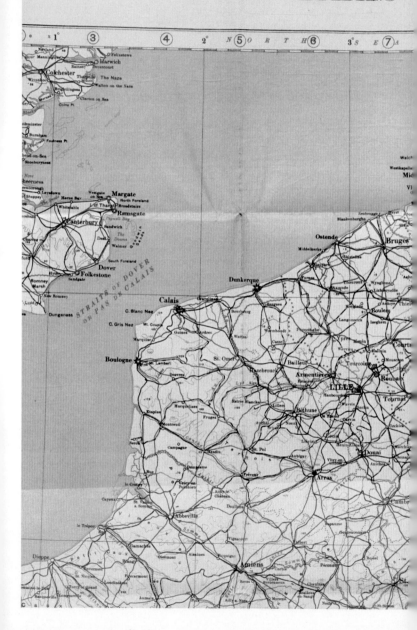

PARIS

MAP 2

PROVISIONAL EDITION

(NORTH M 31)

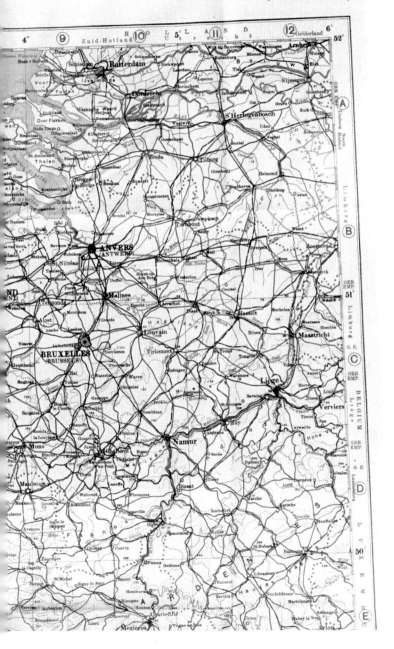

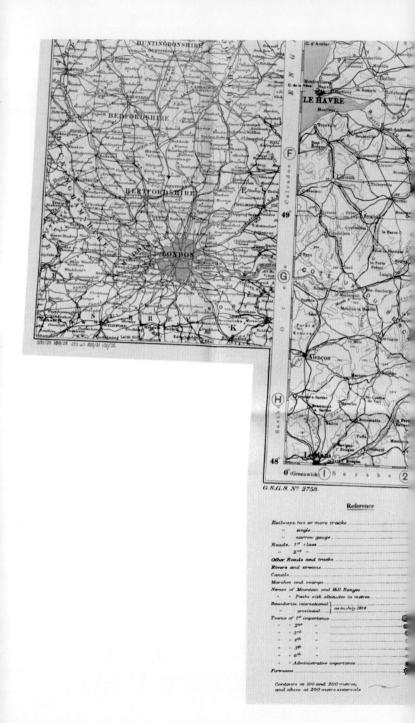

G.S.G.S. Nº 2758.

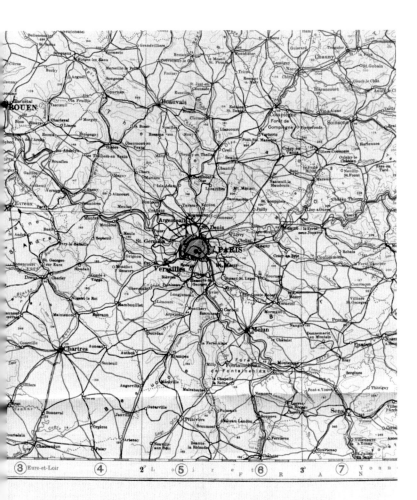

Authorities

Carte internationale du Monde au 1000,000° Sheet Nord M.31 Pa
Carte de France dressée au Dépôt des Fortifications 1:500,000
Ordnance Survey of Great Britain and Ireland 1:1000,000, 1905
Topographische Atlas van het Koningrijk der Nederlanden 1:200,00
Carte de la Belgique Inst. Cart.Milit. 1:160,000
Übersichtskarte von Mitteleuropa 1:300,000 (Germany)
Carte des Chemins de Fer français 1:800,000, 1912.
Carte des Chemins de Fer ... de la Belgique 1:320,000, 1911

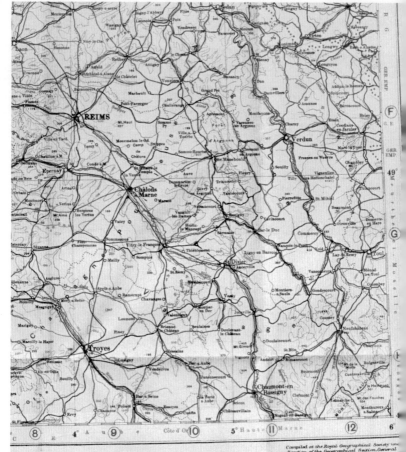

Compiled at the Royal Geographical Society under the
direction of the Geographical Section, General Staff.
Drawn and printed by the Ordnance Survey 1911

Pronunciation Glossary

Dutch	English equivalent
a (short)	o short in "hot"
ae	a long
eu	ö (German)
ie or ieu	e long (nearly)
ij	y long (vowel)
oe	oo short in "hood"
ou	o long
ui	eü (German) nearly
ch	ch (German)
d (final)	t
g (initial)	h
gg	ch (German)
rg (terminal or after 'l' and 'r')	r-h (nearly)
sch (otherwise)	s-h (nearly)
v (initial)	f (nearly)
v (medial)	between V and "w"
w	v

The Walloon (S. Belgian) "w" is the English "w"

INDEX TO BOUNDARIES

Abbreviations

L.	Loir-et-Cher
Se.	Seine
Z.H.	Zuid-Holland
Z.	Zeeland
U.	Utrecht
F.Oc.	Flandre Occidentale
F.Or.	Orientale
N.	Northbrabant
S.	Surrey
Lo.	London
C.	Côte d'Or
G.E.	GERMAN EMPIRE